Autism

To my mentors:
Beate Hermelin
Neil O'Connor
John Morton
Margaret Dewey

Autism

Explaining the Enigma

Second Edition

Uta Frith

BLACKWELL PUBLISHING

350 Main Street, Malden, MA 02148-5020, USA
9600 Garsington Road, Oxford OX4 2DQ, UK
550 Swanston Street, Carlton, Victoria 3053, Australia

First edition published 1989
First published in paperback 1989
First published in paperback in the USA 1992
Second edition published 2003

7   2007

Library of Congress Cataloging-in-Publication Data

Frith, Uta.
    Autism: explaining the enigma / Uta Frith.—2nd ed.
        p. cm.
    Includes bibliographical references and index.
    ISBN 978-0-631-22900-1 (hbk) — ISBN 978-0-631-22901-8 (pbk)
    1. Autism in children. I. Title.
RJ506.A9 F695   2003
618.92'8982—dc21

                                                2002012932

A catalogue record for this title is available from the British Library.

Set in 10 on 12½ pt Baskerville
by Graphicraft Ltd, Hong Kong
Printed and bound in India
by Replika Press Pvt. Ltd

The publisher's policy is to use permanent paper from mills that operate a sustainable forestry policy, and which has been manufactured from pulp processed using acid-free and elementary chlorine-free practices. Furthermore, the publisher ensures that the text paper and cover board used have met acceptable environmental accreditation standards.

For further information on
Blackwell Publishing, visit our website:
www.blackwellpublishing.com

Contents

Preface to the Second Edition

Just like the original version of this book, which was written more than 12 years ago, this updated book tells the story of the scientific endeavor to understand autism. This story includes romantic ideas and reveals surprisingly strong emotional reactions that I have long accepted as part of my fascination with the study of autism. It also includes some new hard-edged facts from cognitive neuroscience. I believe that combining two opposites, hard science and romantic ideas, objectivity and passion, is not impossible, and the enigma of autism has given me opportunities to test this claim.

This book is an update. I have added new facts where these have made a difference, and removed old facts that have been overtaken by more recent research. In particular I have not gone into detail about the presumed genetic causes of autism and how they are currently being investigated, but have focused on cognitive theories and their neurological basis. I have discussed challenges that the original theories and ideas have encountered. The evidence for a "theory of mind" deficit in autism has been greatly enlarged, as has the evidence for "weak central coherence." Newer studies on executive dysfunction in autism have also been included. In the final chapter I have attempted a new synthesis of the three major theories of autism that currently dominate the field. As before, my reviews are selective rather than comprehensive, and I have not reported facts that can easily be accessed elsewhere. The Web now provides a convenient way to obtain answers to questions and evidence can be seen at first hand in scientific papers. It will be obvious to anybody that I have given most space to studies and theories that I have been involved with myself, and have given only brief accounts of studies that are much better related by the authors themselves. This is, after all, not a neutral survey, but in many ways a personal account. The references I have given in notes to chapters are highly selective, and reviews or other secondary references have been used by preference. This inevitably led to omitting references to original and important contributions of people whose work I greatly admire.

What has changed most in the last 12 years? There are new diagnostic criteria, which I discuss in chapter 1, and their use in population studies is reviewed in chapter 4. There are now data on brain structure and brain function that have come out only in the last few years due to the use of neuroimaging techniques. With the generous help of Chris Frith I have summarized these still fragile results in chapter 11. This chapter is different from all the others, as it is much more like a review in a scientific journal. This was necessary because primary research articles describing novel techniques and as yet unreplicated results needed to be referenced.

Not surprisingly, the least changed chapters are those dealing with legendary and historical material (chapters 2 and 3), although I have been able to add some new examples of unscientific myths. I have added the story of the Romanian orphans who showed a number of quasi-autistic symptoms, and their recovery in their adopted families. This story bears a remarkable resemblance to the case of Kaspar Hauser. I have also added brief descriptions of the case of John Howard and the case of Hugh Blair as eighteenth-century examples of Asperger syndrome and autism respectively. Despite my strong historical interests, however, most of the references in this book date from the last five years.

In chapters 5, 6, and 7 I have set out the many implications of a deficit in theory of mind in autism. I have taken pains to take account of further empirical studies from the last 10 years to clarify the basis of this still often misunderstood hypothesis. I believe that this work is still one of the best examples of how a cognitive theory can explain the core symptoms of a disorder, regardless of the amazing variability of symptoms in individuals who are affected by the disorder. Much of chapter 11 is dedicated to showing the fruitfulness of this endeavor in neuroimaging studies. I believe that we can now take for granted that there is such a thing as "mentalizing," and that the probably innate physiological basis of this ability is at fault in autism. The neural network that supports mentalizing can already be seen through a scanner.

In chapters 8, 9, and 10, I have reorganized my earlier ideas and theories that were intended to explain some of the cognitive deficits, and also the talents, in autism. Two major theories have now emerged, one about central coherence, which I introduced in 1989, and one more recent one, based on neuropsychological work, which is about executive functions. As far as I can see, these theories and their variants are both needed to account for the signs and symptoms of autism that do not relate to social communication.

Autism is now firmly established as a disorder of the developing mind and brain. What a relief to be able to state this without ifs and buts. Long ago, this was not sure at all, and while writing the first edition I struggled to remove lingering uncertainties. This has all changed. Then I argued that, even though no specific brain pathology had been found, it would be nonsense to think that autism is not a disorder of the brain. Now it is possible to discuss with confidence questions about the likely genetic abnormality, the likely anatomical fault, and the likely physiological dysfunction that gives rise to autism. Of course, these questions are still open, and autism is still full of mystery. New scientific endeavors are needed, and eventually these will make the present endeavor simply part of history.

But it is not history yet. My approach to autism has remained the same. In a sense this is pleasing. It means that the ideas discussed then were robust enough to withstand the challenges of empirical tests. In another sense it is disappointing because no breakthroughs have happened that might have allowed a radically new light to be thrown on autism. The light that was shed by the early cognitive and increasingly neurocognitive studies of autism is only a dim one, but still it illuminates. The consolidation and spread of knowledge from research to the general public is a slow process. We can point to gradually improved understanding and greater awareness of autism in its many different guises.

Updates give the opportunity to take critical stock of the past and look toward the future. The most positive change since 1989 is the huge increase in awareness of the disorder and the consequent attempts at educational and management programs. Greater awareness has led to increased diagnosis. A major change in diagnostic practice is the use of much looser criteria so as to include individuals of very different degrees of handicap and different levels of general ability. An important development has been the increasing interest in Asperger syndrome.

Twelve years ago I anticipated dramatic progress in genetic research. I was hoping for the identification of susceptibility genes. I was hoping that some biological marker would become available to allow the objective diagnosis of autistic disorder, independent of the variable behavioral signs and symptoms. All this has proved immensely difficult and is still to be achieved.

On the scale of progress in science, 12 years are very little. New techniques need to be applied to make a difference, and I am confident that such new techniques are already being developed. One example is functional brain imaging, which has just started to be applied to autism. What motivated me in writing this update was the wish to see if the accumulation of old and new knowledge has led to a better explanation of brain and mind in autism.

Certainly there is now better agreement between different researchers than ever before. This is what underpins the hope for an even better understanding in the future, and the search for the best treatment and care for the person with autism and a proper assessment of the potential side effects. For instance, the effort involved in compensatory learning is easily underestimated.

Most people have accepted that autism is a lifelong condition and that it is inappropriate to expect a cure, as if it were an illness like flu that could be shaken off. It is rather like blindness, which is also a lifelong condition with extensive effects on the family and the community of the sufferer. While the label "blind child" is acceptable to most people, this is not the case with the label "autistic child." Of course I realize that the label "child with autism" rightly emphasizes that first and foremost there is a child. A handicap should not be mistaken for a person's identity. But specialists writing about the condition need to be able to identify it without confusing their readers. This is why I have used the adjective "autistic" if this increased the clarity of the writing. I regret that this is at the cost of being politically incorrect. But how could one forget that autistic individuals, just as blind individuals, each have their distinct and unique personalities and their own way of managing their life?

Uta Frith
June 12, 2002

Acknowledgements

It is my privilege and pleasure to thank many people who have encouraged me to write this update, who have read the manuscript, and who have made helpful comments. However, most of all I am indebted to Margaret Dewey. She acted as my mentor, tireless critic, and conscience in the first edition of this book and did so again for the second. She has generously shared her own experience and knowledge of autism and has made sure that what I wrote is clear. This is thanks to her ability to see which parts of my manuscript were obfuscating or repetitive, and which could be cut or salvaged through her own deft pen. I am deeply grateful to her for this labor of love, which I know will benefit all readers, and especially parents.

Chris Frith, Francesca Happé, Lauren Stewart, and Elisabeth Hill have read all the chapters and made many insightful comments and suggestions. Sarah Blakemore read several versions of each chapter and gave invaluable feedback. Lorna Wing, James Blair, Simon Baron-Cohen, Mike Anderson, Heide Grieve, Martin Frith, and Alex Frith have commented on specific chapters. Sakina Adam-Saib has provided invaluable secretarial assistance. I am deeply grateful to all of them.

chapter 1

What is Autism?

"She was so pretty – hazel eyes with long curling eyelashes and finely tapered eyebrows, flaxen colored curls and such a sweet, far-away expression; I hoped against hope that all would eventually go well, and that she was just a slow starter." This extract from a mother's letter shows us the first of many puzzles of the disorder called autism. The typical image of the child with autism is surprising. Those familiar with images of children who suffer from other serious developmental disorders know that these children usually *look* handicapped. In contrast, more often than not, the young child with autism strikes the observer with a haunting and somehow otherworldly beauty. It is hard to imagine that behind the doll-like image lies a subtle yet devastating neurological abnormality.

What is this abnormality? How can one explain its many paradoxical features? These are questions that I shall try to answer in the course of this book. I will start with removing some obstinately persisting misunderstandings. The first of these is the idea that autism is a disorder of childhood. You hear a great deal about children with autism, far less about adults. In fact, autism starts to be noticed in childhood, but it is not a disorder of childhood. Instead it is a disorder of *development.*

Autism has to be seen not just as a snapshot. Since it is a disorder that affects all of mental development, symptoms will necessarily look different at different ages. Certain features do not become apparent until later; others disappear with time. In fact the changes can be dramatic. Autism affects development, and in turn, development affects autism. To illustrate this, I will sketch a picture of the life of an individual with autism. Peter is a fictitious case. I have put together unembellished facts from different cases to highlight common observations.[1] The story of Peter is chosen to fall right into the middle of what has become known as the autism spectrum.

Peter

Peter is the much-loved son of a well-adjusted family in London. In the first year of life Peter did not seem different from any other baby. He cried when he was hungry and laughed when he was tickled. In photographs he looks a handsome, healthy, and happy baby. There were subtle signs of problems, but nobody paid any attention to them. He did not look up when his name was called. He did not point at things nor look at objects that others tried to point out to him. He did not take much interest in people speaking to him. Instead, he could be totally absorbed in minute examination of a building block. When his mother came to pick him up he never stretched out his arms. "Look how disdainful he is," his parents said jokingly, when he turned away his head at their embrace.

Nobody at first considered that Peter was anything but a self-sufficient and strong-willed child who was late in talking. Was Peter deaf? Perhaps deafness would explain why he seemed to be so much in a world of his own and took so little part in the world of others. However, it became apparent that Peter was not deaf at all, and was in fact unusually sensitive to certain sounds. He never failed to rush to the window when he heard the familiar engine noise of a bus.

Peter's older sister was quite different. From when she was 18 months, she had delighted in playing "going to the shops," "having tea," "putting dolly to bed." Peter never did anything of the kind. He had a large collection of toy cars, but he was interested only in placing them in long straight lines in a particular pattern and in closely observing the spinning of the wheels. He hardly reacted to other children when they tried to play with him. In so many respects Peter seemed to be left behind by other children his age, and yet he showed many signs of precocious interests. He loved music and endlessly listened to Vivaldi's "Four Seasons," which he could hum perfectly. His bathtime and bedtime routine had to be in a particular order, or else the procedure had to start all over again.

Peter started to speak late. But language did not open the doors to communication, as everyone had hoped. Strangely, he often echoed what other people said and he repeated the same phrase over and over again. Often the family felt as if there were an invisible wall preventing them from making proper contact with Peter. However much they tried, he never joined in play with other children. Most of the time it seemed as if he was looking through people, not at them. He was often seen flapping his hands and looking at them from the corner of his eyes. Sometimes, on the street or in a shop, he made a high-pitched noise and jumped wildly up and down for no account-able reason. Peter was self-absorbed, obstinate, and intransigent to others' wishes. The family called him their little tyrant. They tolerated what could not be changed, but teaching Peter the mundane living skills such as dressing, eating, and washing was a long and tiring struggle.

When Peter was three years old autism was diagnosed. On psychological tests involving language Peter performed poorly for his age, but on a test where he had to fit geometric shapes together he performed very well indeed. Peter could do jigsaw puzzles even picture-side down. His mother could not help thinking that he was perhaps an unusually gifted child, who was simply not interested in the trivial things of daily life.

Peter became much easier to manage after he entered a special school. He readily learned words and numbers, and was eager to name all the shades of colors. He knew what a dodecahedron was, but he did not seem to know the meaning of such common words as "think" or "guess." He could not play a simple game of hide and seek: he always gave away his hiding place.

As he got older, Peter made excellent progress at his school. He learned to swim and enjoyed doing crafts. He continued to listen to classical and popular music. Peter's sister was the first to realize that he had memorized all London bus routes by number and destination. Nobody quite knew how he had managed to do this or why. He began to collect buses – much to the delight of relatives searching for presents for him. His room was soon full of miniature models and posters. Strangely, a visit to a transport museum left him indifferent, and soon after he abandoned his interest in buses altogether.

Friends and neighbors now often commented on how "sociable" Peter had become. He was not at all shy and often approached visitors to the house or the school, asking their names and addresses. "Dulwich," he would say, "that is number 12." Next time they came, the same interchange would take place. Although he was often rather too talkative, in a repetitive sort of way ("Today is Monday, yesterday was Sunday, tomorrow is Tuesday and we are going to visit Grandma"), it was often strangely difficult to get important information from him. For instance, when he was quite badly injured after a fall, he never told anyone about it, and his mother was horrified when she discovered blood on his clothes as she put them in the washing machine.

Peter's understanding was extremely literal. Once, when his mother remarked that his sister had been crying her eyes out, he anxiously looked on the floor to see if the eyes were there. However, he studiously learned the meaning of such "silly phrases," and was keen to use them himself, even when not entirely appropriate. Peter did not appreciate teasing. It just made him cross. Once, he considered a girl at a supermarket checkout his friend because she smiled as he passed by her. He clearly had no proper understanding of what a friend was, even though every effort was made to explain. Sometimes he had severe bouts of frustration and unhappiness that were difficult to deal with.

Having left school, Peter helped his mother in her office. He was given the opportunity to join a social skills group at the clinic and became a stalwart attender. He got to know people who were in many ways similar to him, and he found this comforting. He liked to watch television, and was glad to sit in front of the set with others for company. When there was slapstick comedy, he joined in the laughter. As for soap operas, which his mother watched with him, he could not fathom the plots. Yet he knew all the characters' names and the actors who portrayed them.

Peter is now middle-aged and leads a simple life. He spends many hours on his computer, playing games and reproducing faithfully the text from the music catalogs he reads. He helps with the gardening and with household chores. He likes his routine. Every day he goes to the local swimming pool, and afterwards he paces round the lawn. Peter is still totally naive and does not understand the ways of the world. He is baffled when he comes across examples of lying or cheating. His voice remains loud and peculiar, and his gait is stiff and ungainly.

Peter's family are aware that there are other individuals with autism who have few practical skills, who are difficult to cope with, and who have remained mute forever. They can see that Peter has come a long way from the days when he looked "through people" and would not speak at all. The realization that Peter would always be different from others and would always be autistic came only gradually to the parents, but they came to terms with it. Since their retirement from work, they appreciate Peter's steady companionship. With like-minded friends in a similar position they often laugh at the funny side of life with autism. They share jokes and memories of dreaded situations over which they used to fret. They marvel at how rich and interesting an experience autism can be for the family. With occasional help from sympathetic professionals they have found a way to cope with the inevitable troubles and tribulations. A friend of the family once remarked that she found herself envying Peter's autism: he was simply himself, never concerned with what others thought of him.

Peter's parents are understandably worried about what will happen when they can no longer look after him. They fear that in an indifferent environment he could fall into neglect or become prey to exploitation. They are therefore working together with local authorities and other parents to build a suitable group home where qualified professional workers will provide supervision. The future is uncertain but, fortunately, Peter does not worry about it.

How Autism was First Recognized

What is this puzzling disorder that is at once so subtle and so vicious in its effects: allowing so much developmental progress and yet cruelly preventing full integration into the community? From the very beginning of awareness of such strange developmental patterns, people have attempted to answer this question.

Any treatment of the topic of childhood autism must start with the pioneers Leo Kanner and Hans Asperger who, independently of each other, first published accounts of this disorder. These publications, Kanner's in 1943[2] and Asperger's in 1944,[3] contained detailed case descriptions and also offered the first theoretical attempts to explain the disorder. Both authorities believed that a fundamental biological disturbance was present from birth, which gave rise to highly characteristic problems.

It seems a remarkable coincidence that both chose the word "autistic" in order to characterize the nature of the underlying disturbance. Actually, it is not a coincidence. The label had already been introduced by the eminent psychiatrist Eugen Bleuler near the beginning of the twentieth century and was well known in psychiatry.[4] It originally referred to a particularly striking disturbance in schizophrenia (another term coined by Bleuler), namely the narrowing of relationships to people and to the outside world, a narrowing so extreme that it seemed to exclude everything except the person's own self. This narrowing could be described as a withdrawal from the fabric of social life into the self. Hence the words "autistic" and "autism," from the Greek word *autos* meaning "self." Today they are applied almost exclusively to the developmental disorder that we now call autism. The labels favored at one time, "early infantile autism" or "childhood autism," have fallen out of use, as they imply some contrast to "adult autism," wrongly suggesting that one can grow out of it.

Both Kanner, working in Baltimore, and Asperger, working in Vienna, saw cases of strange children who had in common some fascinating features. Above all the children seemed to be unable to establish normal relationships with their peers. In contrast to Bleuler's schizophrenia the disturbance appeared to have been there from the beginning. Furthermore, in contrast to schizophrenia the disturbance was not accompanied by progressive deterioration. If anything, behavioral improvements could be expected to occur with development and learning.

How Kanner and Asperger described autism

Kanner started his paper entitled "Autistic disturbances of affective contact" as follows: "Since 1938, there have come to our attention a number of children whose condition differs so markedly and uniquely from anything reported so far, that each case merits – and, I hope, will eventually receive – a detailed consideration of its fascinating peculiarities."[5] He then proceeded to present vivid pictures of the 11 children, nine boys and two girls, he considered to be suffering from this condition. The paper ends with a concise discussion and comments section. Some quotes from this part of the paper can illustrate the incisiveness of Kanner's observations. They will also serve as a reference point for the most important features of classic autism. These features, autistic aloneness, desire for sameness, and islets of ability, are still considered to hold in all true cases, despite variation in detail and despite the existence of additional problems.

Regarding "autistic aloneness":

> The outstanding, "pathognomonic," fundamental disorder is the children's inability to relate themselves in the ordinary way to people and situations from the beginning of life.[6]

> There is from the start an extreme autistic aloneness that, whenever possible, disregards, ignores, shuts out anything that comes to the child from the outside.[7]

> He has a good relation to objects; he is interested in them, can play with them happily for hours . . . the child's relation to people is altogether different . . . Profound aloneness dominates all behavior.[8]

Regarding "desire for sameness":

> The child's noises and motions and all his performances are as monotonously repetitious as are his verbal utterances. There is a marked limitation in the variety of his spontaneous activities. The child's behavior is governed by an anxiously obsessive desire for the maintenance of sameness . . .[9]

Regarding "islets of ability":

The astounding vocabulary of the speaking children, the excellent memory for events of several years before, the phenomenal rote memory for poems and names, and the precise recollection of complex patterns and sequences, bespeak good intelligence.[10]

Kanner's main conclusion is in the form of a bold statement:

We must, then, assume that these children have come into the world with innate inability to form the usual biologically provided affective contact with people, just as other children come into the world with innate physical or intellectual handicaps. If this assumption is correct, a further study of our children may help to furnish concrete criteria regarding the still diffuse notions about the constitutional components of emotional reactivity. For here we seem to have pure-culture examples of *inborn autistic disturbances of affective contact.* [italics in original][11]

Ironically, Kanner himself and a number of his followers later seemed to overlook this conclusion. Rather, they proposed that interpersonal psychodynamic factors resulted in autism, and thus for a while deflected attention away from the biological causes.

Asperger, who was not given to concise formulation, does not offer as many opportunities for sound bites. His strength lies in detailed and sympathetic descriptions. His attempts to relate autistic behavior to normal variations of personality and intelligence demonstrate a unique approach to the understanding of autism. This is how he introduced his case studies:

In what follows I will describe a type of child which is of interest in a number of ways: the children have in common a fundamental disturbance which manifests itself characteristically in all behavioural and expressive phenomena. This disturbance results in considerable and typical difficulties of social integration. In many cases, the failure to be integrated in a social group is the most conspicuous feature, but in other cases this failure is compensated for by particular originality of thought and experience, which may well lead to exceptional achievements in later life.[12]

The behavioral and expressive phenomena that Asperger referred to are captured in the following observations relating to the case of Fritz V when aged six years:

His gaze was strikingly odd . . . When somebody was talking to him he did not enter into the sort of eye contact which would normally be fundamental to conversation. He darted short "peripheral" looks and glanced at both people and objects only fleetingly. It was as if he wasn't there.[13]

The normal speech melody, the natural flow of speech, was missing. . . . his speech was often sing-song. . . . The content of his speech too was completely different from what one would expect of a normal child.[14]

Most conspicuous . . . were his stereotypic movements: he would suddenly start to beat rhythmically on his thighs, bang loudly on the table, hit the wall . . .[15]

From very early on he had shown an interest in numbers and calculations. He had learnt to count to over 100 and was able to calculate within that number-space with great fluency. This was without anybody ever having tried to teach him – apart from answering occasional questions he asked.[16]

The boy's emotions were hard to comprehend. . . . While demonstrations of love, affection and flattery are pleasing to normal children . . . such approaches only succeeded in irritating Fritz.[17]

Like Kanner, Asperger suggested that a "disturbance of contact" existed at some deep level of affect and/or instinct. Both stressed the peculiarities of communication and the difficulties in social adaptation of children with autism. Both paid particular attention to movement stereotypies and to the puzzling, patchy pattern of intellectual achievements. Both were impressed by occasional feats of intellectual prowess in narrow areas.

How are these odd and diverse features to be explained and how are they related? In the course of this book I shall consider the theories that try to make sense of the diverse symptoms as well as of the fact that these symptoms occur together.

Diagnostic Criteria Today

In international collaboration, experts have agreed to use certain behavioral criteria for the diagnosis of autism. These have been made explicit in published reference works, which are continuously updated. The main change over time has been a widening of the criteria.

The most detailed and most recent scheme is the one described in the *Diagnostic and Statistical Manual* (DSM) of the American Psychiatric Association.[18] A similar diagnostic scheme is available in the *International Classification of Diseases* (ICD) issued by the World Health Organization.[19] Currently, the following criteria are applied for the diagnosis of autistic disorder. All of these must be present, not merely one or two out of three, and all must have been present from early childhood.

1. There must be a qualitative impairment in reciprocal social interaction, relative to developmental level. Behavioral signs include poor use of eye gaze and of gestures; lack of personal relationships.
2. There must be a qualitative impairment in verbal and nonverbal communication, relative to developmental level. Behavioral signs include delay in the acquisition of language, or lack of speech; lack of varied, spontaneous make-believe play.
3. There must be a markedly restricted repertoire of activities and interests, appropriate to developmental level. Behavioral signs include repetitive or stereotyped movements, such as hand flapping; interests that are abnormally intense or abnormally narrow.

The first of the three criteria of autism is impairment of reciprocal social interaction. How can this be determined over the early years? Much of social interaction at early ages is through physical interaction, and even though some parents report a lack of interest in social games and only a passive tolerance or even dislike of physical contact in their children, this is by no means universal. Evidence for social impairment becomes much easier to obtain in the second and third year of life. Lack of normally expected social responses toward other children is often the key observation. Visits to pre-school playgroups may expose the difficulties for the first time. Sometimes it is the lack of appropriate response toward a newborn sibling that sets alarm bells ringing, but this may be explained away by jealousy. The normally developing child tends to be intensely interested in other children, and is not prevented by jealousy from expressing this interest. In contrast, the child with autism tends to be intensely interested in the world of objects.

The second criterion concerns impairments of communication. Language and communication are separate things. If a child does not speak or does not understand speech by the age of three years, then that is clearly worrying. Many children with autism do not speak until late, and some do not speak at all. In these cases, gestures and facial expressions are not used in the place of speech, and communication is severely limited. This is different from hearing-impaired children, who find ways to communicate their desires and emotions even without speech. In fact, even when speech develops, communication is impaired. The child who echoes words and phrases but does not spontaneously generate them should give rise to worry just as much as the child who does not produce any words.

The third criterion refers to a restricted repertoire of activities and behaviors. The repetitive phenomena of autism include simple motor stereotypies, such as scratching, hand flicking, and rocking. These behaviors may not have any significance in young babies, but they are strongly associated with autism if they persist in childhood. Such persistence is a sign of delay or disturbance in brain development. In older children who are not intellectually handicapped, elaborate routines and rituals can be observed. They often include insistence on sameness and obsessive tendencies. Peculiar preoccupations and oddly narrow interests are common in older and brighter children. When Eisenberg and Kanner specified the first diagnostic criteria in 1956,[20] "insistence on sameness," together with "autistic aloneness," were considered the cardinal features of autism.

A question mark hangs over the sensory phenomena, which are often reported but not currently required for the diagnosis. These are hypersensitivity and hyposensitivity to certain stimuli, experienced by sound, sight, smell, taste, or touch. One example is distress at feeling the texture of certain materials on skin, or of certain foods in the mouth. Asperger, but not Kanner, reported such features and mentioned their paradoxical nature. Thus, the same person who covers their ears in agony at the noise of a telephone ring may ignore the sound of a fire alarm bell. Hypersensitivity can lead to unexpected outbursts of fear or rage. It can also contribute to a severely restricted behavioral repertoire, for instance wearing only certain clothes, and eating certain foods. Hyposensitivity can result in unusual tolerance of cold or pain, and can be a problem if combined with an inability to communicate. These sensory peculiarities often persist and can be found at all ages.

Unlike the social features of autism, the nonsocial features form a ragbag of observations. They are not necessarily associated with behavior problems and may even contribute to outstanding skills. After all, autism is compatible with high talent.

Asperger Syndrome

Kanner's paper became the most quoted in the whole literature on autism; Asperger's paper, written in German, and published during World War II, was at first ignored. The belief was that Asperger described quite a different type of child, not to be confused with the one Kanner described. Gradually, the similarities have become apparent; however, Asperger's definition of autism was far wider than Kanner's. Asperger included cases that showed the consequences of undoubted brain damage in their poor intellectual abilities, and those with high intelligence, whose symptoms were so subtle that they shaded into normality.

The still controversial label "Asperger syndrome" has proved to be clinically useful in helping to identify cases that might otherwise be considered too "mild" to be diagnosed as having autism. This is not what Asperger intended, but having this special category was a way of recognizing his contribution in identifying autism in near normal cases.[21] The label "Kanner syndrome" has curiously not become popular. Yet it might be useful when referring to a person such as Peter.

The recognition of Asperger syndrome has been one of the biggest changes in diagnostic practice in recent years. People with Asperger syndrome are at the same time different from, and similar to, people with autism. The difference that is currently held key for the definition is that they show no language delay as children, nor delays in other aspects of their intellectual development. Yet at older ages they are not very different in their social impairments and obsessions from many of those who had such delays but were considered to have "high-functioning" autism.[22]

The diagnosis of Asperger syndrome tends to be much later than for autism, in late childhood, adolescence, or even in adulthood. This implies that the condition is milder and can be overlooked early in development. However, the effects of the condition are not necessarily mild and become more obvious with increasing age. In fact the difficulties experienced by Asperger individuals can be intolerable.[23] Their social communication impairments are especially evident in interaction with peers, and increase when expectations and demands increase with age. Their preoccupations and unusually focused interests become more visible outside the home. Parents may not seek help for many years if the child shows signs of precocious intelligence. Parents later report that their "little professor" was indifferent to other children, and related only to adults with whom he or she conversed in a rather unchildlike vocabulary. These observations suggest that neither language acquisition nor social development had been proceeding along normal lines.

Experts are divided as to whether Asperger syndrome and autism should be seen as different diagnostic categories.[24] However, the consensus tends to favor the idea that both are variants of the same underlying developmental disorder, with autism being a more severe form, detectable at an earlier age. In practice, many clinicians use the label for individuals who speak fluently and are socially odd rather than aloof. In this category individuals with a wide range of intelligence can be found. In some cases of superior intelligence a brilliant academic career is possible. This is confusing. It needs to be remembered that the presence of high intelligence makes an enormous difference to the manifestation of a disorder and can camouflage problems. On the other hand, the presence of low intelligence, or mental retardation, restricts the potential for compensation.

How Difficult is it to Diagnose Autistic Disorders?

In both autism and Asperger syndrome the earliest signs may go unnoticed although, with hindsight, they can often be recalled. One needs to know where to look. It is often hard to know what starts the first suspicion of autism in families. Usually, worries become pressing only after an accumulation of small observations, each by itself apparently insignificant. For instance, a baby not looking where another person is looking or pointing, a baby not turning round when called by name, a baby not responding to teasing. Home videos have recorded children later identified as autistic, and careful analysis has shown that, with hindsight, subtle signs are often evident at the end of the first year of life.[25]

In the well-documented cases of Elly Park and Ted Hart the parents reported that the first flickers of anxiety were not experienced until some time in the second year. Ann Lovell, the mother of Simon, says, "It is to my mind one of the most exquisitely cruel aspects of Early Childhood Autism that it only becomes apparent to parents very slowly that there is anything wrong with their child."[26]

Parents often have horror stories to tell about how long it took for their child to be diagnosed after they have sought professional help. They might have had to get several referrals until they came to the right specialist who asked the right questions. As awareness of the condition grows, the time to diagnosis is getting shorter, and the age at diagnosis is getting younger. However, any assessment based on behavioral criteria can never be quick. Behavioral observation and psychological tests take time if carefully done. Reliable and systematic interview and observation schedules have made a great difference to the ability to diagnose autism in clinics worldwide.[27] These instruments help in defining clinical symptoms at different ages. They reveal which signs and symptoms are typical of autism and form a constellation that is not seen in other disorders.

Parents also need time to get acquainted with the assessment procedure, why it is done, what the results mean for their particular case, and what can be done now and in the future. Parents will continue to need help and advice after the diagnosis has been made. This is when new people and agencies are likely to get involved, such as schools and local authority services, but also support groups and autism associations. In the best case, support is available immediately; in the worst case, the family has to fight the authorities for their child's rights.

Some people claim that autism is so diverse that it cannot be properly defined. However, diagnosticians are in good agreement, at least for core cases of autism. Of course, problems arise when it comes to borderline cases. Such borderline cases might be children with a low level of general ability, which makes it difficult to judge whether the limitations in social communication are mental age-appropriate or out of line with other achievements. Other cases might be children with high ability who might have learned a great deal about social communication and therefore are likely to pass the laboratory tests despite having difficulties in real life. Yet other cases might be children with additional problems that can overshadow the autistic features, for instance, severe attention deficit and hyperactivity. For all these reasons skeptics can say that a child may be labeled autistic at one center and something else at another. Lay people may sometimes jump to the conclusion that it is impossible to diagnose autism reliably.

This conclusion is unwarranted. In fact, the consensus among experienced clinicians is excellent, and this is due in large measure to the use of standardized interview schedules and standardized psychological tests. "Standardized" means that the instrument has been tried out first on a representative section of the whole population that the test is aimed at. Hence, the average test score expected at a certain age is known; and furthermore, the reliability, or the error margins, of an individual test score are known.

How can diagnosis be improved?

Why can autism not be recognized from birth? The answer is because we do not as yet have biological markers that could act as a test for autism regardless of age. If suspicions of autism arise very early, they can turn out to be false alarms. Some children have a slower pace of development with no adverse consequences in the long run.

One of the more surprising findings in the attempt to diagnose autism early is that signs of social indifference in young infants are not necessarily signs of autism. Likewise, signs of smoothly proceeding development do not rule out the hidden presence of autism. Autism can emerge after a period of apparently normal development. How is this possible? Is the answer in the lack of trained observational skills? Can professionals do better than parents at spotting the earliest stages of development?

An instructive example is shown in an early clinical study by the pediatricians Hilda Knobloch and Benjamin Pasamanick.[28] This study was based on a sample of 1,900 babies referred to a large general pediatric service in North America. The majority of the children were under two years old, and they were seen because their development was not proceeding normally. The authors identified 50 children showing a persistent "failure to regard people as persons." In theory such a sample should include at least some children who would later be diagnosed as autistic. These children were compared to another 50 children on the file who had also shown signs of abnormal development, but behaved sociably as best they could. The children in both groups showed a variety of neurological signs, including convulsions and excessively repetitive movements, and in many cases there had been complications of pregnancy, birth, and in the neonatal period.

The children were followed up three to ten years later. In the intervening time, none of the children had followed any particular treatment program, but all the parents had been told to expect delayed development. Indeed, in all cases, mental retardation was present. However, that potential harbinger of autism, namely "the failure to regard people as persons" had disappeared in all those children who had been seen before they had reached the age of 12 months. Not so their mental retardation. With hindsight none of them could be considered as suffering from autism. This strongly suggests that the symptom was useless as an early indicator. On the other hand, 6 out of 22 children who were first seen in their second year, and had then shown social impairment, were definitely diagnosed as having autistic disorder later on. This was also the case for five out of six children who had first been seen in their third year or after. In other words, the older the child, the more secure the diagnosis. Such is the nature of this developmental disorder.

This study draws our attention to two facts. First, a behavioral diagnosis of autism is unreliable when the behavior repertoire is limited, as it is in young babies. There are at least some babies who at first seem quite indifferent to social contact, but develop social responsiveness later. There are also those who at first seem socially responsive, but later show severe impairments in social interaction. The second fact is that our current notions of social responsivity in infancy are still very crude. In the future more refined behavioral indicators might become available. For instance, it may be possible to develop measures of reflexive orienting to social stimuli, such as human voices and faces, and it is conceivable that such measures can discriminate young babies who are at risk for autism.

This brings us to the subgroup of children whose parents report regression after a normal period of development, before the onset of autistic symptoms in the second year of life. The regression most often reported is loss of spoken words and social interest and does not progress further. This picture is different from some rare but devastating diseases of the brain that lead to progressive deterioration of mental and physical functions. Given that it is difficult to spot signs of autism in the first year of life, and without appropriate behavioral or physiological measures, there has to be an element of doubt about just how normal the development of this subgroup was at first. However, we can ask whether the subgroup differs in the further course of development from that of other children with autistic disorder whose parents did not report such regression. Apparently they do not.[29] The phenomenon of regression remains a puzzle. Perhaps it is no more and no less than a demonstration of the complex interplay of development and autistic disorder: the impact of development is such that it reveals the disorder only gradually.

Some disorders have obvious physical signs, and a diagnosis can be made even before the disorder unfolds and without understanding the nature of the disorder. Autism has no such signs, and we do need to understand its nature to make a diagnosis as early as possible and as accurately as possible. A theoretically guided approach to screening children for signs of autism at 18 months is now feasible.[30] This is not a diagnosis, but a filter that picks out children for subsequent assessment. In this way false alarms can be recognized for what they are. This approach depended on the development of a cognitive theory that attempted to explain at least some of the underlying and enduring features of autism: the mind-blindness hypothesis. This theory, which will be discussed in detail in later chapters of this book, proposes that the intuitive ability to understand that other people have minds is missing in autism. This ability has a basis in the brain. Of course the nonsocial features of autism also have a basis in the brain. What if we knew the physical signs of autism, in the genes or in the brain, and if we had the appropriate techniques to identify them in individual children? Would behavioral tests then become redundant? I do not think so. The physical signs are unlikely to inform us about the severity and the developmental course of the condition. We need sensitive tests to measure the variable behavioral manifestations of the underlying cognitive problems, at different ages and under different treatments. Such theoretically guided tests can now be developed.

What Happens in Adulthood?

The engaging film *Rainman* has made a major contribution to the public awareness that adults too can be autistic. The enigma of the condition is well portrayed in this fictional, yet truthful, account: Rainman can remember the exact sequence of playing cards, but he is totally unaware that his skill is being used to win money at gambling. He is willingly led to do things that are not in his best interest, but he stubbornly insists on having his own way in what he wears and how he travels. Being quite impervious to emotional manipulation, he ultimately changes his scheming brother by his very lack of social guile.

Kanner and Asperger made the point that autism is not a progressive disease. Asperger emphasized that, contrary to the process of deterioration, which is frequently seen in adult psychoses, his patients showed increases in adaptation and compensation. So convinced was he of this that he presented overall a quite optimistic picture of outcome. Many parents have pointed out that this does not reflect their own experience, and that even in cases of high academic excellence, their grown-up children had jobs that were below their potential. Asperger's optimistic view must be seen in the light of his belief in the powers of education and the possibilities of compensation for problems that he himself acknowledged as persistent. The autism does not go away. However, Asperger's belief that many able individuals with autism can live successful lives has been proved right.

What about individuals with autism who are also intellectually impaired? The general conclusion must be that like autism, intellectual disability does not go away, despite improvements in adaptation and positive changes in behavior. Nevertheless, people with autism can, and often do, compensate for their handicap to a remarkable degree. They may be guided to a niche in society where their assets are put to good use. Processes of learning and adaptation are active throughout life and are continuously ready to lead to change.

We now have the benefit of a number of startlingly candid autobiographical accounts written by individuals with exceptional writing talent and a desire to tell what it is like to be autistic. As adults these authors reminisce about their childhood and almost invariably note that as they got older their understanding increased and their interactions with others improved. Many tell about unhappy experiences that they no longer suffer from as adults. Such accounts give tantalizing glimpses of a different inner world.[31]

Finally, when considering what will happen when an autistic child grows up, one must remember that to predict the future of an individual child with autism is just as uncertain as it is in the case of any child.

chapter 2

The Enchantment of Autism

Sleeping Beauty

The classic fairy tales "Snow White" and "The Sleeping Beauty," popularized by Disney films in the twentieth century, but dating back to the brothers Grimm in the early years of the nineteenth century, and Charles Perrault at the end of the seventeenth century respectively, contain a number of different themes. One of these is the theme of death-like sleep or, rather, lifelike death. This strangely paradoxical image conveys a quality of experience that is familiar to those who are closely involved with certain cases of autistic disorder: the beautiful child is tantalizingly near, yet so far; physically present, yet remote. The hedge of thorns or the glass coffin are perfect for representing the impossibility of reaching the child. In the case of autism, however much the child's appearance seems to indicate that it is normal and healthy ("awake"), the child's social isolation shows after all that it is not ("asleep").

In the two stories two different causes of the death/sleep are proposed: in "Snow White" it is a simple physical one – a poisoned apple; in "Sleeping Beauty" it is a curse. Although differing in their explanation, in either case the cure is simple and related to the cause: remove the piece of poisoned apple, or remove the curse. When considering causes of autism, we come across precisely these extremes of biological and psychogenic explanations. The fairy tales remind us that neither precludes the possibility of cure, and both offer equal odds as regards the probability of finding it ("the prince"). Of course, one should not be taken in by the happy ending. This is, after all, only a thematic device of fairy tales for the purpose of stressing the moral argument.

People in the past must have encountered autism and must have attempted to come to terms with it. The chilling and fascinating combination of

Figure 2.1   Portrait of St Francis

From the thirteenth-century picture at Christ Church, Oxford

childhood innocence and disturbance cries out for symbolic elaboration. No
wonder a variety of stories and myths evoke images of autism. It is my contention that these myths have not come out of the blue. They partially owe
their existence and their survival to the real experience of autism. As Wilhelm
Grimm said in his introduction to the fairy-tale collection that he published
with Jakob Grimm in 1812, "the states of life portrayed here are so basic that
many people will have found them in their own lives. But, because they are
true, they remain new and moving."

The phenomenon of autism with its many puzzles has deep significance for individuals who experience it at first hand. But over and above this, it has a wider cultural significance. For instance, legends and ecclesiastical records from the Middle Ages suggest that autism has played a role in shaping models of religious and political conduct. It is no exaggeration to say that through understanding autism we can gain a better understanding of ourselves. It will be evident that this process was begun long ago.

Brother Juniper

The Little Flowers of St Francis is a collection of legends told from the time of St Francis, who lived in twelfth-century Italy, and written down in the thirteenth century. These legends have historical value since they repres-ent oral traditions of the first or second generation of Franciscans. But apart from this, they are one of the treasures of world literature. A whole section with some 14 legends in this collection contains the most charming and curious stories of one Brother Juniper. These stories seem not so curious, and indeed make complete sense, if one assumes that they were in fact based on the life of an individual with autism among the early followers of St Francis.

It is worth quoting from the first of the legends, in the nineteenth-century English translation.

How Brother Juniper cut off the foot of a pig to give it to a sick brother
One of the first companions of St Francis was Brother Juniper, a man of profound humility. Once when he was visiting a sick brother at St Mary of the Angels, he said to him, "Can I do thee any service?" And the sick man answered: "Thou wouldst give me great consolation if thou couldst get me a pig's foot to eat." Brother Juniper took a knife from the kitchen, and went into the forest, where many swine were feeding. Having caught one, he cut off one of its feet and ran off with it, leaving the swine with its foot cut off; and coming back to the convent, he carefully washed the foot, and diligently prepared and cooked it. Then he brought it to the sick man, who ate it with avidity.

Meanwhile, the swineherd, who had seen the brother cut off the foot, went to his lord, who, being informed of the fact, came to the convent and abused the friars, calling them hypocrites, deceivers, robbers, and evil men. "Why," said he, "have you cut off the foot of my swine?" At the noise which he made, St Francis and all the friars came together, and with all humility made excuses for their brother. But the angry man was not to be appeased. He refused to accept any excuse or promise of repayment; and so departed in great wrath. And as all the other friars wondered, St Francis sent for Brother Juniper and asked him privately: "Hast thou cut off the foot of a swine in the forest?" To which Brother Juniper answered quite joyfully, not as one who had committed a fault, but believing he had done a great act of charity: "It is true, sweet father, that I did cut off that swine's foot. I will tell thee the reason. I went out of charity to visit the brother who is sick." And so he related the matter. St Francis, in great zeal for justice, and in much bitterness of heart, made answer: "O Brother Juniper, wherefore hast thou given this great scandal? Not without reason doth this man complain, and thus rage against us; perhaps even now he is going about the city spreading this evil report of us, and with good cause. Therefore I command thee by holy obedience, that thou go after him until thou find him, and cast thyself prostrate before him, confessing thy fault, and promising to make such full satisfaction that he shall have no more reason to complain of us, for this is indeed a most grievous offence."

At these words Brother Juniper was much amazed, wondering that any one should have been angered at so charitable an action. And so he went his way, and coming to the man, who was still chafing and past all patience, he told him for what reason he had cut off the pig's foot, and all with such fervour, exultation and joy, as if he were telling him of some great benefit he had done him which deserved to be highly rewarded. The man grew more and more furious at his discourse, and loaded him with much abuse, calling him a fantastical fool and a wicked thief. Brother Juniper, who delighted in insults, cared nothing for all this abuse, and repeated the story all over again with so much charity, simplicity, and humility, that the man's heart was changed within him. He threw himself at Brother Juniper's feet, acknowledging with many tears the injuries which by word and deed he had done to him and his brethren. Then he went and killed the swine and having cut it up, he brought it to St Mary of the Angels. Then St Francis, considering the simplicity and patience under adversity of this good Brother Juniper, said to his companions and those who stood by: "Would to God, my brethren, that I had a forest of such Junipers!"[1]

If Brother Juniper was a person with autistic disorder, he also had an admirable personality. He is so different from Peter, the boy from chapter 1, that it might be hard to believe that there could be any connection. And yet we can pick out a common thread. Peter with his good language showed perfectly literal understanding and so did Brother Juniper. Neither of them showed in their actions that they were aware that people might have thoughts and feelings of their own. At the heart of the story of the pig's foot is the fact that Brother Juniper could not understand that other people might not have the same belief about his action as he did himself. The lack of awareness of other people's thoughts about things or events is a vital clue to the nature of "autistic aloneness."

There are other stories that testify to Brother Juniper's honesty and humility, and yet also to his inability to gauge any effect his actions may have had for others beyond the most immediate context. For instance, he was loudly rebuked by his Superior for some particularly crazy action (he had cooked food for a whole fortnight in one go – not considering that most of it would be spoilt). Far from showing the appropriate contrite reaction, Brother Juniper noticed one thing only: the Superior's voice had become hoarse while haranguing him. What did he do? He procured hot porridge – at some considerable trouble. This he tried to offer to the angry Superior, to soothe his throat. Since it was by now the middle of the night the Superior refused to get up. At long last Brother Juniper accepted the refusal, but he now asked the Superior to come and hold the candle so that he himself could eat the porridge! Marveling at such piety and simplicity, the Superior could not resist. He came out of his cell and shared the meal.

A similar lesson in humility was given to the citizens of Rome who had come to welcome Brother Juniper, who was on pilgrimage. Brother Juniper took no notice of the procession, but instead he fixed his attention on a seesaw. Hours later, when the amazed crowd had long gone, he stopped the (typically repetitive) seesawing and continued his journey.

Brother Juniper gave away anything to anyone who asked for it, including frequently his own clothes. Once he even cut the bells from the altar-cloth to give to a poor woman. This was a literal interpretation of the Franciscan virtues of poverty and charity carried out to embarrassing excess. The brethren had to keep a constant watch on him, and strictly forbade him to give away his clothes. Nevertheless, he was recognized to be a pure example of the true Franciscan spirit and for this he was held in high esteem. One cannot help thinking that he provided not only an idealized model for the brethren's own conduct, but one in which they would also see a degree of absurdity. They could laugh at him, the "plaything of God," as St Clare, another famous follower of St Francis, called him.

What the case of Brother Juniper highlights is one of the many astonishing aspects of autism, namely utter guilelessness. If his humility had been a deliberately adopted way of life we would not expect the ridiculous excesses and the awkwardness that resulted. Indeed, they did not occur with other brethren, famed as they were for their saintliness. There are other legends in the *Flowers* about the early companions of St Francis. But none are like those about Brother Juniper!

The Blessed Fools of Old Russia

Holy (or "blessed") fools were venerated in ancient Russia for centuries. In a landmark paper, the eminent Slavonic historian Horace W. Dewey, who was also familiar with autism, made explicit the extraordinary similarities between holy fools and the modern diagnosis of autism.[2] The conclusion that many of the holy fools were indeed people who suffered from autism is as surprising as it is convincing. The label "blessed" connotes feeblemindedness, as well as innocence in the eyes of God. Eyewitnesses were still alive who could remember the fool Grisha, who lived in the town of Leningrad before the Revolution.

> He was an awesome figure: emaciated, barefoot and in rags, with eyes that "looked right through you" and long, straggly hair. He always wore chains around his neck . . . Neighbourhood children would sometimes run after him, laughing and calling out his name. Older persons, as a rule, viewed Grisha with respect and a little fear, especially when he suffered one of his periodic seizures and began to shout and rant. At such times adult bystanders would crowd around and listen, for they believed that the Holy Spirit was working through him.

Challis and Dewey point out that a similar description is available from an English visitor to Russia in the sixteenth century. The Blessed Simon of Jurev, who died in 1584, is of special relevance since he was found in a forest as a wild boy by Russian peasants. Knowledge of holy fools is not only the province of scholars, but has filtered into general knowledge, not least because of Dostoyevsky's novel *The Idiot*.

The features most suggestive of autism include "eccentric, irrational conduct," "apparent insensitivity to pain" (tolerance of extreme winter cold, and of hunger, is always mentioned), a life outside of society, guilelessness, and indifference to social conventions. Furthermore, the fact that often they were wearing chains suggested to Challis and Dewey that these were used to fetter them on occasion, just as with other madmen. They also commonly suffered from epilepsy, a clear sign of brain pathology and present in a high proportion of adults with autism, but rarely encountered in patients with schizophrenia.

The reports also indicate that many of the blessed fools were mute. Those who spoke were unresponsive to questions and given to parroting. Many of the utterances reported were stereotypic and the speech of the blessed fools showed what we would now call inappropriate phrases. All these peculiar features of their speech, which are suggestive of autism, were considered proof of prophetic powers. Thus, unintelligible, parroted, or even absence of remarks, and bizarre, sometimes stereotyped, actions were endowed with significance, and often embellished in legends. For instance, why did the blessed fool Nicholas hurl cabbages at a holy man who had made a special trip from another part of the town to see him? The citizens of Novgorod believed that this was because he wished to give them a lesson, symbolically representing their internal bickerings by throwing cabbages.

A further example of a blessed fool, this time a woman, described in the nineteenth century, poignantly illustrates the obsessional nature and oddness of interest which, despite its totally different cultural context, suggests autism: Pelagija Serebrenikova would collect loose bricks or stones, carry them to a flooded pit, and throw them in one by one. Then she would immerse herself in the water and pull out and toss back the stones she had thrown in, one by one, "and for many years did she toil thus."

Characteristically also, the blessed fools had no sense of social status, and thus were exempt from the usual rules of polite conduct. This enabled the fools to approach powerful personages of church and state with impunity. In fact the fools were famous for confronting bishops and tsars, often with profound effects. In this way, they might have exerted power and influence. This possibility was in fact exploited by a number of impostors (including the infamous Rasputin). For these reasons, there were rules for determining which were genuine fools. For instance, they had to be fools all the time. "Of these there were not many, because it is a very hard and cold profession to go naked in Russia, especially in winter."

The foolishness of the fools was, it appears, above all a social foolishness. The particular interest of the blessed fools of Russia is that, for at least some of them, there is evidence of "autistic aloneness." This is not the same as the crude avoidance of people, but rather an inability to relate to people in the ordinary way. It was assumed at the time that foolishness was deliberately adopted and a sign of great religious faith. Of course, we must allow for heroic individuals existing in all religions, who do adopt voluntarily a life of social isolation and hardship.

There are other aspects of autism that have been treated more recently in art and literature. One particularly intriguing theme is that of the creature of cold reason who is incapable of warm-hearted relationships. This does exist in real life, and has been elaborated in literature. This theme reminds us of the fact that autism is compatible with high analytic intellectual ability.

Sherlock Holmes

The detached detectives of classic mysteries are not only eccentric and odd, but they are reminiscent of extremely clever people with autism. They demonstrate a particular type of oddness that might be shared by highly gifted individuals with autism. The oddness conveys clear powers of observation and deduction, unclouded by the everyday emotions of ordinary people. Absentmindedness in relation to other people, but single-mindedness in relation to special ideas, are part of this image. It is obvious that those whose thoughts are preoccupied while penetrating through conundrums (as detectives or as scientists) will tend to forget social niceties. Their minds cannot be troubled by the simple events of everyday life. On the other hand the genius professor or genius detective attends to matters that seem trivial to the ordinary person. It is usually near the end of the story that "the significance of trifles" is revealed. This is precisely why this type of genius can solve problems on the basis of what appeared to be negligibly small clues. The clues, traditionally, are of the kind that mislead ordinary people. Readers of detective stories are willingly misled by their natural emotional and social prejudices, which show them certain events and facts in a particular light but not as they really are. Conan Doyle has given us the archetypal detective in Sherlock Holmes. He has also created an archetypal Mr Average, with warm feelings and prejudices, in Dr Watson. In science too, the original genius can see data in a different light from that in which others have grown accustomed to perceive them.

Sherlock Holmes suggests the social usefulness and originality of the brilliant but socially detached mind. There is yet another autistic feature that many fictional geniuses possess, namely a special, circumscribed interest. One can think of Sherlock Holmes's "little monograph on the ashes of 140 different varieties of pipe, cigar and cigarette tobacco." One can also think of that other classic detective, Rex Stout's Nero Wolfe, and his obsession with orchids and rigid daily routine. Frankly obsessional characteristics are also evident in Agatha Christie's Hercule Poirot, who insisted on neatness and rectangularity in every aspect. He delighted, for instance, in square-shaped crumpets, in preference to the ordinary round-shaped ones, and his perpetration of a killing was proved by the perfectly symmetrical placement of a bullet hole.

Miss Marple, Agatha Christie's other immortal detective, is in every way the opposite and has no autistic traits at all: she solves crimes by intuition, immersing herself in the context without analytic deduction. For instance, she feels that there is something wrong with the atmosphere in Bertram's Hotel (in the novel of the same name) long before she knows why. In contrast, the classic detached detective is not captured by atmosphere. It is indeed this atmosphere that misleads everyone except him into suspecting the wrong person. The detached detective is objective, incorruptible and in a way also often extremely literal. When everyone thinks that R-A-C-H-E is the beginning of a girl's name, Sherlock Holmes knows it is the German for "revenge" and acts on this simple clue. "Elementary" is the detective's usual verdict, leaving Dr Watson gasping.

The term "autistic intelligence" was coined by Asperger. He believed that autistic intelligence had distinct qualities and was the opposite of conventional learning and worldly wise cunning. Indeed he thought of it as a vital ingredient in all great creations in art or science. The fictional literature surrounding the endearingly "mad professor" or his variants is full of examples that would fit Asperger's notions. A vivid biography of the great mathematician Erdös[3] suggests that he had many eccentricities that are reminiscent of autism. Yet in his case the possibility of autism had never been considered.

The Pinball Wizard

The Who's rock opera *Tommy* centers on a hero who has strongly autistic traits – although autism is never mentioned, and other themes are superimposed on it.

Through the character of the father we are reminded how normal children enjoy waking up on Christmas morning, getting all excited. He could well have spoken of an autistic child when he says: "And Tommy doesn't know what day it is . . . surrounded by his friends, he sits so silently, and unaware of everything . . . playing poxy pinball, picks his nose and smiles, and pokes his tongue at everything."

The opera *Tommy* is of interest here since it builds on an aspect of autism that has not found expression in other myths, namely a strange and perversely effective system of sensory perception: Tommy does not function like a normal seeing, hearing, speaking child ("I often wonder what he's feeling. Has he ever heard a word I said?"). Yet there is a paradox: he plays pinball to perfection, which surely demands superior sensory skills. "He ain't got no distractions, can't hear those buzzers an' bells, don't see no lights a-flashin', plays by sense of smell . . . He stands like a statue, becomes part of the machine . . . That deaf, dumb an' blind kid sure plays a mean pinball." It is known that Pete Townshend, who composed that work, knew about autism at the time, and by his own account has long been interested in this disorder. At least in this case, we have direct evidence of the existence of the phenomenon of autism contributing to art and culture.

The Changeling

John Wyndham's science fiction novel *The Midwich Cuckoos* has elaborated the theme of a "different" child smuggled into an unsuspecting family.[4] This theme of the changeling could, of course, apply to any child with special handicaps or gifts. In this story, aliens have planted beautiful and brilliantly clever children on the unwitting population of a small English village. These children eventually have to be given up by their stunned, uncomprehending human parents. Since these parents are just as much subject to mothering instincts as any parent, this proves to be a harrowing experience. Some parents of children with autism find this story deeply evocative of some of their own experiences. The story represents symbolically the "alien" nature of children so difficult to understand. Even those aspects of autism that seem at first so positive, such as the occasionally found remarkable skills, appear far from normal if represented as signs of "alien" intelligence.

The Robot

The theme of the intelligent but soulless automaton is only a small step away from the genius detective. It has undoubtedly created some of the most potent of modern myths. It is my belief that the existence of autism has contributed to this theme in no small way. But this is not the only reason to look at it in more detail. I selected this theme because it reflects not only normal perceptions of autistic aloneness, but also reactions to this phenomenon.

Obedient only to logical principles, robots are untouched by all that matters in ordinary human relationships. Yet they are a fascinating partner in such relationships. The first robots of science fiction knew no love, hate, curiosity, jealousy, or revenge and could not fathom these feelings in others. They were easy to recognize as machines. New robots who, like R2D2 in *Star Wars*, have feelings programmed into them, are more tricky to classify as machines. Like autistic people, early robots have no sense of humor, and are utterly literal in their understanding. But – despite their metal exterior – one tends to forget that they are machines. More often than not people treat robots as if they too are scheming beings. This is understandable if we assume that the attribution of states of minds is pervasive and compulsive.

As a metaphor for autism robots serve well in many respects. The exterminating cone-shaped Daleks of the British television series *Dr Who* have given a name to the mechanical quality of voice (the Dalek voice) that has often been ascribed to individuals with autism. The stiff gait of some older individuals with autism is modeled by the metal humanoid devices. Robots carry out jobs that they are specialized for, without concern for wider aspects, with precision and, above all, in an unvarying routine. The machine-like behavior reminds us of many characteristics of autistic behavior: we see repetitiveness, stereotyped movements, lack of emotional expression, and lack of spontaneous playfulness.

So many human qualities can be found in an intelligent machine, yet some elusive but essential humanness is missing. One of the first and still best elaborations of this theme can be found in the tales "The Sandman" and "The Automata" by E. T. A. Hoffmann, written in the early nineteenth century.[5] Hoffman was among the first to portray the paradoxical relationship between rationality and Gothic horror. This paradox strikes a familiar chord with many who have an uneasy relationship with modern machines such as computers. *Frankenstein*, Mary Shelley's masterpiece, is also concerned with the paradox of irrationality out of rationality. The Frankenstein myth, too, deserves to be looked at from the point of view of certain deep resemblances to aspects of autism. I will mention here only the innocence of the monster and the sharp differences between his abilities and defects.

The disturbing theme of mechanical man is alive and well in contemporary films and stories. There are many fascinating elaborations, for instance, those by Philip K. Dick, whose *Do Androids Dream of Electric Sheep?*[6] was turned into the successful Hollywood film *Blade Runner*. Here the theme directly concerns the definition of the thin borderline where human and android may or may not be distinguished. Again this raises a question that can be tackled by scientific methods: is there a continuum or is there a radical difference? Does this apply equally to trying to differentiate individuals with autism and those without?

Star Trek's Mr Spock and Commander Data present a particularly interesting variant of the robot theme. Their mental makeup is nonhuman to the extent that all their actions are governed by logic and not by emotion. They are detached from the messiness and confusion of ordinary personal relationships, and hence have no prejudice. This gives them clarity and objectivity of thought. In this way these characters resemble Sherlock Holmes.

The robot metaphor symbolically captures the coexistence of the physical and intellectual achievements of individuals with autistic disorder and, in sharp contrast, their perceived emotional insufficiency in personal relationships. The myth allows the representative of this particular contrast to be surprisingly constructive: the emotional detachment itself can be seen as an asset or even an attraction. The borderline between man and machine is ever more elusive. Clearly, when trying to understand robots, just as when trying to understand individuals with autism, we must comprehend them as participants in the human condition. A celebrated case is Eliza. It can tell us much about the vicissitudes of understanding that may well face us when tackling these puzzling problems.

Eliza

Not only in literature, but also in the study of artificial intelligence, questions have been asked about the essential humanness of humans. Eliza is a program for analyzing language, and is so cleverly designed that it is possible to have a "conversation" with it using a printer. The program creates the illusion of perfectly understanding the minds of its partners.

A dialog quoted in a book by Eliza's inventor, Joseph Weizenbaum,[7] goes as follows:

Human I'm depressed much of the time.
Eliza I am sorry to hear you are depressed.
Human It's true. I am unhappy.
Eliza Do you think coming here will help you not to be unhappy?
Human I need some help, that much seems certain.
Eliza What would it mean to you if you got some help?
Human Perhaps I could learn to get along with my mother.
Eliza Tell me more about your family.
Human My mother takes care of me.
Eliza Who else in your family takes care of you?
Human My father.
Eliza Your father.
Human You are like my father in some ways.
Eliza What resemblances do you see?
Human You are not very aggressive but I think you don't want me to notice that.
Eliza What makes you think I am not very aggressive?
Human You don't argue with me.
Eliza Why do you think I don't argue with you?

The conversation becomes gradually more like a psychotherapy session. It is no wonder many partners of Eliza requested that they could converse in private. Clearly they believed that some useful communication was achieved.

Eliza became a legend and was used, for instance in David Lodge's novel *Small World*, to show a developing therapeutic relationship between man and machine. What Eliza shows is how difficult it is in fact to distinguish machineness and humanness by humans while they are involved in communication. When communicating, the human being actively and continuously attributes ideas, intentions, and feelings to the machine. Such attribution seems to be an inevitable part of two-way communication. It even happens when only one member (human, but not machine) does the attributing! However, as it works it deceives. In reality in this situation there is no two-way communication of the kind there appears to be; there is just a clever script that picks up key words and uses them again in certain neutral but apparently provocative phrases.

Are individuals who can speak, but fail to communicate, a bit like Eliza in this respect? This possibility would certainly be amenable to being tested by scientific methods – though this has yet to be done. If the similarity were confirmed this would have a rather surprising consequence: as conversation partners or therapists of people with autism, we could not help but attribute intentions, even if they themselves did not, and if the attributions were quite unjustified. It seems to me that this is likely to be the case in traditional psychotherapy with individuals with autism. If so, this method would seem rather dubious, and indeed some sufferers have spoken out against psychotherapy, which they have found unhelpful. Given the ideological isolation of psychotherapy, it is not surprising that one particular myth has attracted therapists' attention. It is a variant of an old fairy tale theme: the "refrigerator mother."

The Mother's Dilemma

Snow White was poisoned by her stepmother, and the Sleeping Beauty was cursed by the fairy who had not been invited. A modern contribution to the theme of the wicked stepmother is the emotionally detached and intellectual mother who may otherwise be conscientious in mothering duties. This mother's "crime" is far more subtle than that of the traditional stepmother. She brings up her child by the book, taking expert advice, rather than relying on instinct. In doing this she forgets the importance of the heart over that of the intellect. The result, so it has been claimed, may be autism and an emotionally stunted child.

This caricature of bad mothering overlaps with the caricature of the career woman, in particular of the "intellectual" type. An abnormally detached child – a child who is unable to relate lovingly – is a fitting punishment for the woman who neglected to be a full-time devoted wife and mother!

The insidious term "refrigerator mother" encapsulates the essence of this myth. In its application to autism, it proved irresistible to Leo Kanner. But it really *is* a myth as far as any causal connection with autism, or the basis of a cure, is concerned. Unfortunately, this evil myth is still not universally dismissed, and thus has the power to cause guilt and recrimination. However, mothers are in a no-win situation. They can attract reproach for the reason that they are too protective and spoil their children. This can easily appear to be so on the surface, for instance, when they give in or use bribery to calm a tantrum. On the other hand, if mothers use behavioral methods with strict reinforcement schedules, then censorious voices will also be raised.

Autism has at its core a basis in the brain, and this view is now widely accepted. Autism is not caused by psychodynamic conflicts between mother and child. With blatant disregard for the biological evidence, the erroneous belief that autism can be cured by resolving deep-seated conflicts lingers on. It lingers on together with the belief that one can die of a "broken heart," or be made ill by the "evil eye." Autism occurs in all kinds of families and cultures, and not particularly in problem families with unresolved emotional conflicts. Problem families may well produce problem children, but there is a world of difference between an emotionally disturbed child and a child with autism. There is no reason to think that parents of children with autism love their children less, or try less hard to nurture and educate them. The visible evidence is that many try harder, and are more selfless in their efforts.

As convincing evidence for the genetic causes of autism has now emerged, a new twist has been added to the story. Kanner's and Asperger's clinical intuitions about the often intellectual and detached parents of the children they saw were not mistaken. Well-controlled studies have shown that fathers as well as mothers may have some of the same traits as their children, often in very mild form.[8] Of course, this does not mean putting back the blame on early interaction with parents. If anyone is to blame, it is indifferent Mother Nature.

Just as with any other developmental disorder, it is necessary to take account of both biological and environmental factors. There has to be interaction between these factors, or mutual influence, or else development does not occur at all. Where bringing up children is concerned, good parenting and special education will not make a damaged child normal, but will help the child to achieve its potential. It does not take much imagination to think that a poor psychological or educational environment prevents such achievement. But this truism does not aid our understanding of autism, because it applies to any child.

The enchantment of autism is something that mothers are bound to experience when their child develops in surprising and different ways. This may counteract, but does not diminish, the burden of autism. This burden is great and demands courage. It is aggravated by not knowing for certain the best thing to do for any one child.

Myths and Treatments

Since no method has yet been proven to cure autistic disorder, each hypothesis about treatment is a shot in the dark. The same applies to medical conditions that at present cannot be cured. But who will ever believe this if it is a personal matter? Rationality does not always prevail, and hope is powerful. Each new treatment success story feeds the hopes of parents who want nothing less than a complete cure.

Eager people are likely to find the scientific approach to treatment extraordinarily cautious, if not downright mean and petty. They read about a drug, a diet, or an educational program, which resulted in such dramatic improvements that autism seemed to be overcome. Indeed, parents appear on TV and praise the effects. The next day, a scientist is interviewed and says that without systematic studies no conclusion about the effectiveness of the treatment can be drawn, and also mentions undesirable side effects that could occur. Such spoilsport experts are forever warning that an initial success story may not be reliable and that more research needs to be done with better controls.

There are many reasons for skepticism. For one thing, most novel treatments show effects that are later found to be much weaker or are never replicated. The effects can be due to the sheer force of enthusiasm of the people who pioneered the new treatment. This is why questions about the right controls need to be asked. For instance, if the treated group was selected on the basis of volunteering for a new treatment, rather than randomly, then there will be a bias. Further, if the evaluators used subjective impressions of improvement, knowing which people were treated, then again bias is introduced and group differences are questionable. Finally, the belief in the efficacy of treatment is a powerful promoter of improvement. This is shown in the well-known placebo effect. Often the improvements that are seen afterwards are very similar in placebo and active treatment. In the case of behavioral treatments, control children who get individual attention for the same length of time as treated children may also show improvements. It is a remarkable fact that in developmental disorders improvements over time are the norm.

Because the effects of bias and expectation are so strong, many refinements of treatment trials have been thought out. One refinement is to cross over the different kinds of treatment, including no treatment, in each patient and observe changes. Another is to make trials "double-blind" so that neither investigator nor patient knows what treatment is being given. The confidence one can put in the results from a double-blind, randomized control trial is clearly very high. However, these studies are difficult to carry out. It is a sad reflection of our state of ignorance that so far, when they are done, they rarely support the initial claims made for new treatments. The warning to be skeptical about new wonder drugs and treatments must be proclaimed more loudly than ever.

However, this is not the whole story. Parents can make a huge difference by understanding the nature of autism as expressed in their unique child. With understanding they develop ingenious strategies. Like parents of physically disabled children, they consult specialists, join support groups, and seek community services. As a result they can give patient and loving guidance to reduce the frustrations of their son or daughter. Indeed, by accepting the individual and accepting that problems are likely to persist, they can guide the child to the best possible outcome. As testified by many parents, this outcome is often better than was predicted. Teachers also make a crucial difference. Through professional training they learn to understand the nature of autism. They can thus help their students to develop their potential and produce achievements to be proud of. It is useful to remember that the miracle of Helen Keller came not from a cure for her blindness and deafness, but from patient and resourceful teaching.

In the recent history of autism many fads have come and gone. One fad that was prominent in the last decade went under the label "facilitated communication" (FC) and created some tumultuous waves.[9] The premise is that the person with autism has untapped communicative powers and a sophisticated understanding that cannot be transmitted through the normal output systems. This idea is reminiscent of the "locked in syndrome," a rare condition that can follow severe brain injury. The claim is that a facilitator can release communication by prodding the locked output system. The stimulus is some kind of subtle guidance of the wrist, arm, or shoulder while the child's finger is poised over a keyboard. Much outpouring of language, good and bad, has been produced in this way. But does it stem from the mind of the person with autism?

It is right to be skeptical at the writings obtained through FC. A large number of appropriately controlled experiments have shown that it is the facilitator who generates the content of the message indirectly, even though totally unaware of doing this. Sadly, a few messages proved highly inflammatory. Some totally fabricated memories of sexual abuse were reported to the police, with harrowing consequences.

The human capacity for wishful thinking is astounding and should not be overlooked when new "cures" are heralded yet again. Myths can enrich and inform our experiences, but they can also inhibit the development of scientific theories. Unlike literary treatments, scientific understanding cannot just seize on one fascinating aspect of autism and ignore others. It is tempting to spin one or two astounding phenomena into an enchanting tale. However, to get to the truth, we have to go beyond enchantment.

chapter 3
Lessons from History

Autism is not a modern phenomenon, even though it has been recognized only in modern times. In view of the short history of psychiatry, and the even shorter history of child psychiatry, we know that a disorder recently described is not necessarily a recent disorder. An increase in diagnosed cases does not necessarily mean an increase in cases. There are tantalizing hints of autism in the medical records of history.

For a long time, the earliest putative evidence of the existence of autism, before Kanner, was a case description by the apothecary of Bethlem Hospital, the London mental asylum.[1] The case was that of a five-year-old boy who was admitted in 1799. It was particularly noted that this boy never engaged in play with other children or became attached to them, but played in an absorbed, isolated way with toy soldiers. Is it possible to identify critical similarities in cases that were described 200 years ago with children diagnosed as suffering from autistic disorder today? If so, this would help to distill those features that are the essence of the disorder beyond our immediate time and cultural context.

Two cases of the late eighteenth and early nineteenth century, the "wild boy of Aveyron" and the mysterious case of Kaspar Hauser, invite a closer look. Among other things they will allow us to examine theories about the interplay of biological and social-environmental factors in the origin of autistic features. Recently, after the end of Ceaucescu's regime in Romania, children were found in orphanages in conditions that provoked horror at the extent of physical and social neglect. Many of these severely deprived children have been adopted by caring families. The majority of these children flourished both physically and mentally after their adoption. However, a number of children were found who disturbingly displayed many autistic features.

The common thread between the two historical cases and the Romanian orphans is formed by the heartrending and extreme circumstances of social deprivation. In contrast, two cases from the eighteenth century, one with severe autism, Hugh Blair of Borgue, and one with a mild form, John Howard, will allow us to see the helpful effects of a privileged social background on autism at a time when there was no awareness of the disorder.

The Case of the Wild Boy of Aveyron

In the last years of the eighteenth century, the intellectual and fashionable world was enthralled by the case of a wild boy who had been found in a forest of central France. The boy, who was about 12 years old, did not speak, did not respond to questions, did not even respond to noises made next to him. He had no clothes and his body was covered in scars. His whole appearance and range of behavior seemed totally asocial.

Here, then, seemed to be a boy who provided an ideal example of what a human being would be like who grew up outside human society. Some believed that such a child would be truly savage and bereft of all moral sensibility. Others, on the contrary, thought that he would reveal human virtues unspoilt by society. A few, however, considered the possibility that brain pathology might be present in such a child. If this were true, the example would lose its point. Indeed, some eminent physicians who examined the child at the time found him similar to other children "of incomplete and damaged constitutions." They believed that the boy's muteness and strangeness were due to "constitutional imbecility." This theory also provided a reason for the boy's living in the wild at all. Perhaps desperate, impoverished parents had abandoned the boy because he was seriously abnormal. They might even have intended to kill him, a conjecture based on a wound on his throat.

Public fancy was not captured by this relatively simple explanation, but instead was intrigued by a social-environmental explanation. The idea was that the boy, who was named Victor, had been a perfectly normal child who, through an unknown fate, was lost or abandoned when still very young. By living outside human society he was stunted in his development to the point of appearing mentally retarded. Language, of course, would never have been acquired, through lack of opportunity. The burning question was: could Victor be educated? Could he be brought back from his savage state into the civilized world? Jean-Marc Gaspard Itard, a physician fascinated by this question, took on the challenge. By doing so he became one of the pioneers of special education. The story of Victor's education has become well known recently through a highly praised film by Truffaut, *L'Enfant Sauvage*, which was closely based on Itard's own writings.

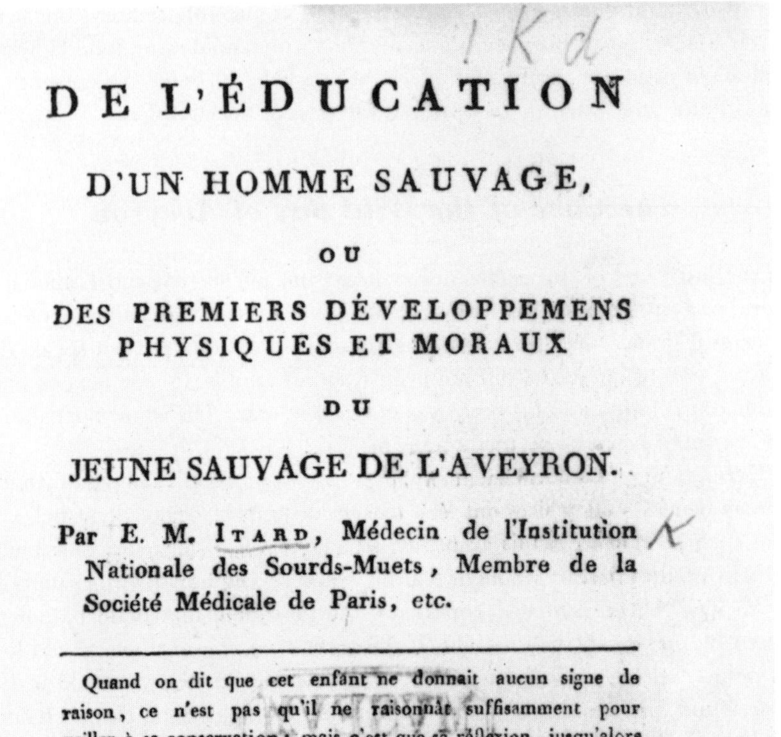

DE L'ÉDUCATION

D'UN HOMME SAUVAGE,

OU

DES PREMIERS DÉVELOPPEMENS PHYSIQUES ET MORAUX

DU

JEUNE SAUVAGE DE L'AVEYRON.

Par E. M. ITARD, Médecin de l'Institution
Nationale des Sourds-Muets, Membre de la
Société Médicale de Paris, etc.

Quand on dit que cet enfant ne donnait aucun signe de
raison, ce n'est pas qu'il ne raisonnât suffisamment pour
veiller à sa conservation ; mais c'est que sa réflexion, jusqu'alors
appliquée à ce seul objet, n'avait point eu occasion de se porter
sur ceux dont nous nous occupons.......................
.... Le plus grand fonds des idées des hommes est
dans leur commerce réciproque.

CONDILLAC.

A PARIS,

Chez GOUJON fils, Imprimeur-Libraire, rue Taranne,
N°. 737.

VENDÉMIAIRE AN X. (1801).

Figure 3.1 Title page of Itard's treatise *On the Education of a Wild Man, or The
beginnings of physical and moral development of the wild boy of Aveyron*
Reproduced by kind permission of The British Library

Figure 3.2 Contemporary portrait of Victor (c.1775–1828)
Reproduced by kind permission of The British Library

Did Victor suffer from autism?

In his scholarly study of the wild boy of Aveyron, Harlan Lane discusses
the possibility that Victor had autism. Lane's account includes translations
of Itard's reports on Victor's education and other relevant documents and
provides a valuable and comprehensive case history.[2]

Perhaps the most important evidence that Victor might have suffered from
autism comes from the first scientific paper written about the case, by the

Abbé Pierre-Joseph Bonnaterre, Professor of Natural History at the Central School for Aveyron. This was in 1800, before Victor had received any systematic education.

EVIDENCE OF AN IMPAIRMENT IN RECIPROCAL
SOCIAL INTERACTIONS

> His affections are as limited as his knowledge; he loves no one; he is attached to no one; He shows some preference for his caretaker, . . . he follows him, because the man is concerned with satisfying his needs and appeasing his hunger. . . . I led him one day to the home of Citizen Rodat. . . . All had been arranged for his welcome. Beans, potatoes, chestnuts and walnuts, were prepared. . . . The abundance of food pleased him greatly. Without paying attention to the people around him, he grabbed the beans, placed them in a pot, added water, and put the pot on the fire . . .[3]

This anecdote is comically reminiscent of a story I was told by a friend. She invited a young autistic man of high academic ability to dine at her home for their first meeting. On entering the house, Arthur immediately strode to the kitchen, where he seasoned the entire dinner to his liking. Only then did he return and accept the proffered handshake and introduction. While the anecdote about Victor could conceivably be attributed to his total lack of training in manners, the same excuse cannot be made for Arthur, whose cultured family made every effort to indoctrinate him with the basic rules of politeness.

The oddness of Victor's relationship to people can be evaluated more clearly from later reports, after he had already had several years of education in Itard's house. Highly revealing is the statement that Victor had "no sense of gratitude toward the man who feeds him, but takes the food as he would take it from the ground."[4] Also, he was said to be totally unaware of the fact that no one was obliged to feed him, and quite oblivious to being served by the hand of a pretty girl. These observations seem as pertinent for many modern-day individuals with autism as they were for Victor. All these behavioral signs are pointers to the elusive but critical feature of "autistic aloneness."

EVIDENCE OF SPECIFIC INTELLECTUAL IMPAIRMENT

> He reflects on nothing, therefore he has no judgment, no imagination, no memory. His imbecility is evident in his gaze, as he does not fix his attention on

anything. It is evident in his vocalizations, which are discordant, inarticulate, and can be heard night and day; in his gait, walking as he does always at a trot or a gallop; in his actions, which lack purpose and determination.[5]

The chief examples that can be taken as signs of hidden intelligence are from Victor's expert conduct in preparing a meal of beans. He showed economy and suppleness of movement, planning, and coordination of several activities, such as shelling the beans, separating the bad ones, throwing the empty pods on the fire, and getting water. This sort of expertise would not normally be expected from a child who has mental retardation, but is exactly the kind of task that can be performed as a reliable routine by an individual with autism whose interest is engaged by it. For instance, autistic adolescents who hardly speak and have severe learning disability can learn to wash cars, clean rooms, prepare vegetables, lay the table, and so forth.

It is interesting to note that, in the first overall assessment of Victor's intellectual capacity quoted above, gaze, voice, and gait are all mentioned as peculiar. Abnormalities in these three channels of nonverbal expression point to autism.

EVIDENCE OF A CHARACTERISTIC IMPAIRMENT OF SENSORY ATTENTION

The shrillest cries, the most harmonious sounds make no impression on his ear. . . . He shows no awareness of noises made next to him; but if a cupboard that contains his favorite foods is opened, if walnuts, to which he is very partial, are cracked behind him, he will turn around to seize them.[6]

A striking observation in almost all accounts of children with autism is that they have been thought deaf at one time, yet that they also have unusually sensitive perception of certain sounds.

EVIDENCE OF LACK OF IMAGINATIVE PLAY

Victor was reported to be "indifferent to all childish amusements": "When he is alone he is happy to sleep, for he has nothing to do after he has eaten, and he almost never plays . . . He likes to run bits of straw through his teeth and suck the juice out of them – that is his favorite amusement."[7]

EVIDENCE FOR STEREOTYPIES

The first reports contain some descriptions of how Victor fills the empty hours that may have been created by his lack of imagination as much as by his lack of social interaction or interest.

> He normally wakes at dawn: then he takes a sitting position, wraps his head and body in his blanket. He rocks back and forth and lies down intermittently, until it is time for breakfast. During these periods, which could be called recreation, he wants neither to get up and start the day nor leave his room . . . [later in the afternoon] when he has no beans to shell, he retires to his room, stretches out on the straw, wraps himself up in his blanket and rocks back and forth or goes to sleep. [8]

What became of Victor?

It was with extraordinary courage that Itard, in 1801, took on the formidable task of educating Victor in his own home. This courage was remarkable since Pinel, the most eminent physician of the day, after examining Victor, declared that there was no hope of turning him into a normal child. Pinel was right, yet Itard showed that education did lead to dramatic improvements in the quality of Victor's life. Despite remaining mute, Victor had many accomplishments, such as a certain amount of sign language. The young savage from the forest of Aveyron had made incredible progress.

Most unexpected, however, even for those who had only modest hopes for him, was that he never learned the meaning of some basic social values. He never showed evidence of friendship or pity, nor embarrassment, and he retained what was described as unbounded egoism. This observation again fits extraordinarily well with many modern-day adults who have autistic disorders. Itard, after five years of inspired teaching, resigned and stated in his final report that the education of the young man was still incomplete, and would probably always remain so.

Ironically, while Victor was able to survive alone in the wild, he was unable to live independently in society. Mme Guérin, the woman Itard had engaged to look after Victor, was given a stipend to continue to look after him. He lived in her house until he died in his forties. Many authorities, including Édouard Séguin, one of the founders of psychology as a science, and Franz Gall, the famous promoter of phrenology, investigated Victor in his later years. They all concluded that he was "a true idiot," meaning that he was similar to other people they knew as mentally defective from birth.

The mystery of the wild boy

There are three pertinent questions that Lane puts against the possibility that Victor had autism: (1) How could a child with autism have survived in the wild? (2) Are *all* feral children to be presumed to have autism? (3) What is there about Victor's deviant behavior in society that cannot be explained by his adaptive behavior in the forest?

The first question is as difficult to answer as it would be to explain how any young normal child could have survived alone. We do not know at what age Victor was abandoned. Lane suggests he was left at five, since before this age it would be difficult to imagine that any child, healthy or not, could have survived in the conditions that he lived in. On the other hand, to assume that he was abandoned much later would make the muteness more difficult to explain. Yet there is quite a good pointer toward Victor's age when he was abandoned. For two years prior to his capture he had been sighted on several occasions, and during a hard winter people had fed him when he appeared near a village. When he was captured, again during a severe winter, he was thought to be about 12. This would suggest that he was abandoned not much before the age of 10.

Even at that age, it is astonishing that he was able to survive for two years. Without shelter and clothing, he had to tolerate extremes of weather and hunger, not only lack of comfort. Could a child with autism do this? Curiously, in quite independent accounts, it has often been said that individuals with autism may tolerate extremes of pain, hunger, and temperature without complaint. Altogether, such individuals seem to be peculiarly qualified to lead the rugged, solitary life that Victor lived when roaming the forests. In the case of a normal child it would be more difficult to explain why he did not seek refuge with people. Villagers, by all accounts, were often nearby and ready to help. If he had autism this may not have occurred to him. Perhaps he found it impossible to differentiate well-meaning people from creatures of the wild.

This point also goes some way toward answering Lane's second question: do all feral children suffer from autism? From what we have just discussed it may be inferred that an unduly high proportion of feral children suffered from autism before they were abandoned. Indeed autism, with its often severe conduct problems, may be the cause for the abandonment in the first place. On the other hand, it would be strange to assume that all feral children had autism.

There are, no doubt, different reasons for young children being lost, hidden, isolated, or abandoned, and different reasons for their survival in isolation.

The third question turned on the point of parsimony of explanation. What else is needed to explain Victor's odd behavior but his prolonged social deprivation? Perhaps we can answer the question in the following way. It is difficult to see how Victor's behavior could have been considered entirely shaped by, and truly adaptive to, his life in the wild. He was undersized and underweight, he suffered many wounds, and he was eventually driven by extreme weather into the vicinity of villages. Once he was "tamed," he preferred human company to the wild. His behavior recorded in later years shows much change and a high degree of adaptation to the requirements of the Itard household. At the same time, the oddness of his newly acquired behavior that is evident in many examples fits in well with modern descriptions of autistic individuals. One last example, taken from Lane's rendering of an eyewitness description, helps to illustrate this contention.

It is a description that is heavily biased toward the idea that it is truly civilization that stands between modern man and savage. Only through an enlightened education, exerting its influence from earliest childhood, was it conceivable that moral behavior would develop. Only by education would a child be integrated into society. This theory was part of the mainstream Enlightenment philosophy that flowered in the eighteenth century.

Itard and Victor were guests at a dinner in the house of the celebrated Mme Récamier.

> Mme Récamier seated him [Victor] at her side, thinking perhaps that the same beauty that had captivated civilized man would receive similar homage from this child of nature, who seemed not yet 15 years old ... Too occupied with the abundant things to eat, which he devoured with startling greed as soon as his plate was filled, the young savage hardly heeded the beautiful eyes whose attention he himself attracted. When dessert was served, and he had adroitly filled his pockets with all the delicacies that he could filch, he calmly left the table ... Suddenly a noise came from the garden and M. Itard was led to suppose his pupil was the cause ... We soon glimpsed [him] running across the lawn with the speed of a rabbit. To give himself more freedom of movement, he had stripped to his undershirt. Reaching the main avenue of the park ... he tore his last garment in two, as if it were simply made of gauze; then, climbing the nearest tree with the ease of a squirrel, he perched in the middle of the branches. [9]

The story continues with the boy failing to heed Itard's entreaties to come down, leaping from tree to tree in the process. Eventually, it was the gardener who enticed him down by showing him a basket of peaches. Victor let himself be hurriedly covered and bundled off home in a carriage. The guests were left to discuss the "perfection of civilized life and the distressing picture of nature untamed."

What this account illustrates vividly is how "autistic aloneness" is evident even if the person with autism is in the midst of company and enjoying himself. The aloneness is poignant because of an inability to understand states of mind. It is as if, for Victor, minds did not exist. It follows that he is unconcerned about the effect his behavior has on other people's opinion of him. Mme Récamier's gardener must have known this instinctively when he offered peaches instead of entreaties.

In my view the evidence presented allows us to assume that Victor suffered from autistic disorder, even though there can be no conclusive answers. What of other historical cases with similarly extreme social deprivation? Would we again come to the conclusion that the person in question suffered from autism? If so, the possibility that autism and feral existence are causally connected would have to be taken seriously. If not, we can dismiss at least strong claims of such a connection. There is in fact a second case where severe social deprivation occurred and where excellent documentation of behavior exists. This case will again allow us to check whether presence or absence of "autistic aloneness" can be gauged across a considerable distance of time and culture.

The Case of Kaspar Hauser

On Whit Monday 1828, a very odd-looking lad appeared on the Unschlittplatz in Nuremberg. He seemed to move his feet without knowing how to walk and he seemed to comprehend nothing at all. At first, he was thought to be drunk or mad, as he repeated over and over again the obviously rehearsed sentence: "I want to be a horseman like my father was." He had a letter on him for the Captain of Cavalry in Nuremberg. This letter asked that he be allowed to serve the king as a soldier, and named April 30, 1812 as his date of birth. According to this he was 16 years old, yet he was only 4 foot 9 inches tall. To everyone's amazement, he could write his name: Kaspar Hauser. But he could not talk, except for a few fragments of speech. It became apparent from his strange appearance and behavior that he had lived all his life in a cellar and had never seen his keeper. It was soon deduced that he had been fed solely on bread and water – as he rejected any other food – and that a wooden horse, which he pined for constantly, had been his only companion.

Kaspar Hauser

Figure 3.3   Contemporary portrait of Kaspar Hauser
Reproduced by kind permission of The British Library

Kaspar was placed at first in a prison cell for tramps, but he was looked after kindly by the warder's family. He then lived with various more or less benevolent families receiving sporadic tuition and schooling. He was considered to be one of the sights of Nuremberg, and was officially adopted by that city.

The sensation that the case created induced many speculations: was he an idiot, a savage, a madman, or a deceiver? That he was not an impostor was readily established. But there were persistent rumors that he was of royal blood. These speculations were fired by an attempt at murder, which he survived. Kaspar was in fact ultimately assassinated by an unknown person only five years after he had appeared in Nuremberg. This happened at the time when he was rumored to be writing his memoirs. In 1908 the novelist Jakob Wassermann wrote an epic novel based on the facts of the case, citing every shred of evidence that portrayed Kaspar as a tragic victim of court intrigue. Indeed, there is little reason to doubt such a possibility other than the fact that it is fanciful and romantic. But then, real life is often said to be stranger than fiction. Werner Herzog's film *Kaspar Hauser* vividly treated the plight of Kaspar, who remained a stranger in the world for all of his tragically stunted life.

The justification for discussing the case in the present context is that there is a detailed first-hand account of Kaspar's physical and mental state with many precise observations. The *Account of an Individual Kept in a Dungeon Separated from all Communication with the World from Early Childhood to About the Age of 17* was written by Anselm von Feuerbach, then President of the Bavarian Court of Appeal at Anspach near Nuremberg. A famous lawyer, Feuerbach was interested in the case as a species of crime never yet treated by legislation, a "crime on the soul of a man."[10]

From Feuerbach's account, which is both passionate and objective, we can piece together a clinical picture of the strangeness of Kaspar's behavior. According to this report, Kaspar, when found, could say only a few phrases and fragments of speech jumbled together. Yet he learned language rapidly, apparently from the prison warder's children. He also liked to receive toys and drawings as gifts. He was especially pleased with the gift of a toy horse to which, it was noted, he solicitously offered his own food and drink.

Initially, Kaspar preferred darkness and to sit on the ground with legs stretched out before him. This gave some clues to the terrible conditions of his dungeon. It was said that his "hearing was without understanding, his seeing without perceiving." He showed pronounced lability of emotions and was highly excitable.

Kaspar formed personal attachments readily, first to Julius the 11-year-old son of the prison warder, then to others. He obeyed authority without question. He was eager to learn, especially to write and to draw. His memory for names and titles of people was considered astonishingly good, and pleased people. Memory of his life in the dungeon, however, was practically absent. In a short time of tuition he soaked up a large amount of knowledge, including even Latin. Due to his improved diet – once he accepted food other than bread and water – Kaspar grew more than two inches in a few weeks.

Feuerbach was especially interested in Kaspar's sensory perception of the world and odd physiological reactions. There were parallels with another celebrated case, publicized by Voltaire, concerning a person who was blind from a few weeks of age and whose vision was restored by a cataract operation. In both cases scientifically controlled observations were made. Kaspar, just like the previously blind man, failed to appreciate size constancy and depth cues. For instance, objects that looked small at a distance were mistaken for miniatures. These observations confirmed the belief that Kaspar was kept in conditions with very restricted visual stimulation. This is consistent with Kaspar's own later reports. He claimed that men and horses in pictures at first appeared to him as if carved in wood. A landscape looked ugly to him, but walls did not. He also explained that at first when he saw the world it was like a window shutter splashed with paint that was held close before his eyes. All these new sensations were eventually sorted out by his rapidly increasing experience. As far as we know, his visual perception gradually improved.

Feuerbach was particularly interested in Kaspar's superior acuteness of sensory perceptions, which he believed had not been blunted by experience. His visual acuity, hearing, and sense of smell were found to be highly discriminating. However, his sensory acuteness gradually diminished. It was noted that Kaspar above all liked the smell of the bread spices that were then common (fennel, anise, and caraway), and hated the taste of opium. All of these were presumed to have been familiar to him from his dungeon days.

Kaspar learned to play chess, learned to garden, learned that plants were not artefacts, and that animals were not like people. And he learned to ride, at which he proved to be skilled. Many people came to visit him, and he was talked about all over Europe. One year after his sudden appearance he began to show sadness and indignation at having been locked up for so long.

Many people found it surprising that Kaspar showed a pronounced love of order and cleanliness. Everything had to have its place, and Kaspar would carefully brush specks of dust from clothes. He had hundreds of little possessions of which he was proud. Each had its proper symmetrically arranged place. Such refinement struck people as odd in someone who had been incarcerated in a dark cellar.

About a month after his appearance Kaspar began to have dreams and at first thought them to be real. This was while he was living with an important benefactor, the kindly Professor Daumer. This observation, together with the hint that Kaspar later could distinguish between dreams and reality, is interesting because it suggests that Kaspar became aware of his own mental states and could talk about them. This is very different from the wild boy of Aveyron, who gave no evidence of such awareness.

People were curious to know whether Kaspar had any religious understanding. However, he simply could not understand what the clergymen were talking about. Later he was reported to be "astonished at the discovery of an invisible inner world of the mind." This observation again suggests that he was gradually becoming aware of such an inner world. How else could he have been astonished at it?

However, Kaspar remained a stranger in the world. Indeed he must have stood out from ordinary people. His movements remained stiff and unpliant. His speech was probably never quite normal but remained labored. It was awkward, simple, and literal. His voice was said to have a harsh and foreign sound. Feuerbach talks of a curious mingling of a child's and an adult's mind. He noted many contradictions in Kaspar's judgment, abilities, and feelings. For example, Kaspar was mild and gentle, feeling sorry for a worm in case he trod on it, timid to the point of cowardice, but also reckless, stubborn, and capable of insisting on his rights. Feuerbach considered Kaspar to be "without a spark of fancy or sense of humor." Significantly, however, he credited him with a "dry downright healthy common sense."

Did Kaspar have autism?

The contemporary accounts of Kaspar allow us to piece together a clinical picture that is very different from that of Victor. This picture does not permit us to conclude that Kaspar had autism. I would, for instance, expect that an observer as careful as Feuerbach would not remark on common sense as a special attribute in an individual with autistic disorder. Even in very able people with autism, whose high verbal ability and abstruse knowledge may be impressive, the lack of common sense can be striking. Common sense, among other things, implies a set of background assumptions held by all members of a community. If people with autism were able to share in this they would be able to avoid literal misunderstandings, would appreciate in-jokes and so forth. In short, they would no longer be odd.

Some of the observations on Kaspar might be taken as evidence of autism: oddities of sensory perception, general awkwardness, love of order, relative poverty of language, general naivety, and lack of worldly wisdom. The same question that was asked for the wild boy of Aveyron should also be asked here: can all the strange features be parsimoniously explained as effects of prolonged and severe deprivation? The sensory and motor impairments could

Kaspar Hauser.

Beispiel

eines

Verbrechens

am

Seelenleben des Menschen

von

Anselm Ritter von Feuerbach.

Ansbach, bei J. M. Dollfuß.

1 8 3 2.

Figure 3.4 Title page of Anselm von Feuerbach's *Example of a Crime on the Soul of Man*

Reproduced by kind permission of The British Library

certainly be a direct result of having been imprisoned in a dark cellar without much opportunity for seeing or moving about, as could his lack of knowledge about the world, his simplicity, and his confusion. His peculiar language might be due to him having learned to speak so late in life. What about

Kaspar's pedantry, or insistence on order? In ordinary life it seems that most young "uncivilized" children have to be constantly admonished to be orderly and are taught cleanliness with great difficulty. Many people may not value these notions at all, but Kaspar apparently did. This may be no more surprising than that a tendency to be pedantic can exist in anybody. It need not be a sign of pathology.

The main reason for rejecting a diagnosis of autism for Kaspar is his rapid improvement, although his social behavior may never have become normal and some quasi-autistic features may have persisted. It seems that Kaspar was aware of other people's reactions and interests. We hear that he pleased people by remembering their names and titles and that he formed trusting relationships. This social responsiveness is the more remarkable as one might have expected that Kaspar, who had been cruelly treated, and moreover had suffered an attempt at murder some time before he was assassinated, would avoid and distrust people emotionally and physically.

Another important feature of autism is absent if we believe that Kaspar whiled away much of his lonely time in playing with his toy horse, although it is not certain whether this was symbolic play or merely object manipulation. We are told of his eagerness to learn to speak and to communicate. It is evident that he was most particular about his possessions and about his rights, both of which are sophisticated social concepts, often beyond the grasp of people with autism. All of these points are in sharp contrast to the case of the wild boy of Aveyron. On the other hand, some of the features that show similarities between the two boys can be explained by long-term isolation in childhood.

Kaspar's story of recovery, as we can see, is different from Victor's. Kaspar received only haphazard education, not nearly as expert and committed as that of Victor. Nevertheless, he seemed to make enormous progress. There is little doubt, however, that Kaspar had suffered physical and mental deprivation to the extent that possibly irreversible organic damage had occurred. His strangeness persisted.

Here, then, we have a contrast between two cases of severe social deprivation, only one of which clearly shows the typical features of autism. Such evidence works against an environmental-social theory of the origin of autism. In Victor's case, autism may have been the cause of abandonment, rather than the other way round. It is deeply mysterious why Kaspar was treated as he was. It is not unthinkable that as a young child he did show signs of backwardness, which prompted his removal from an important family. Whatever the truth of the matter, which we may never know, one must agree with Feuerbach's judgment that a horrible crime was committed on the soul of a man.

The Case of the Romanian Orphans

The extraordinary story of children found in Romanian orphanages during the 1980s is a modern-day parallel to the story of Kaspar Hauser. These children had suffered extreme conditions of physical and social neglect in early life in institutions where, for a variety of reasons, they received only minimal care. A number of families in the UK adopted children from these institutions, and Michael Rutter and colleagues recognized the importance of documenting the development of these children.[11]

On arrival, almost all 165 babies, most of whom were under 12 months of age but some well over, were malnourished and socially unresponsive. They showed major impairments in language and play and exhibited repetitive rocking. At age four the vast majority of the children showed excellent recovery and were now normally developing children. Eleven children, however, were not so lucky. All of these children were over 12 months old when they entered the UK, having suffered a longer time of deprivation. They scored less well on IQ tests and exhibited features that were strongly reminiscent of autism: they had difficulties in forming normal social relationships with their new parents, but were often clinging to them. They had impaired language, and lacked the ability to sustain reciprocal conversation. In addition, many were preoccupied with smelling and touching things, and some had intense circumscribed interests, for instance in watches, vacuum cleaners, or plumbing.

Some of these observations are reminiscent of Kaspar Hauser, for instance, pronounced sensory interests, indiscriminate friendliness, and love of collections of objects. Despite their fulfilling the three main criteria for autistic disorder, the features were felt to be somewhat atypical compared with classic cases of autism. Ten additional cases had very mild or isolated autistic features, mainly stereotyped behaviors. Of these only two showed intellectual impairment. Another three children with atypical autistic features were found to have severe learning disability, undoubtedly the result of early brain damage.

At age six, remarkably, the autistic signs had receded or vanished in all these cases. This was not just the clinician's impression, but was based on a standardized intensive assessment procedure. This same procedure was used with a group of autistic children at the age of four and again at the age of six. Importantly, the two groups were similar in their scores at age four, but differed significantly at age six. In the children with autism, the three main features became more, rather than less, pronounced at age six. This comparison vividly illustrates that autism is a persistent disorder and affects development itself. It cannot be accurately viewed if seen only at one point in time.

The dramatic recovery of the orphans confirmed that they did not in fact have autism. Instead they suffered from a developmental delay in aspects of social and nonsocial development that can mimic autism. One other dramatic improvement occurred: intelligence scores increased by 20 points in the group of 11 "quasi-autistic" orphans, compared to an average increase of 7 points in the rest of the group. However, despite this increase, their IQ scores still remained low relative to the others.

The Romanian orphans are not the only children to be found to have "quasi-autistic" features. It is known that children who, for various reasons, are reared in institutions often show atypical autistic features. Most commonly noted is an indiscriminate friendliness and a preoccupation with sensations of smell and touch. Blind children with learning difficulties have such features too.[12] In all these cases learning disability and perceptual deprivation from birth may be a common denominator. However, neither of these factors is sufficient to cause autism.

The mechanism by which "quasi-autism" is caused remains unknown. A combination of intellectual impairment and prolonged social and sensory deprivation may lead to reversible arrest in the development of particular brain systems. The development of social communication systems clearly depends on sufficient levels of environmental stimulation. Blindness would curtail such stimulation, and so would prolonged absence of varied input in grim institutions. The presumption here is that in true autism the brain systems themselves are faulty and do not develop properly even in the presence of ample stimulation. In contrast, the brain systems in cases of "quasi-autism" prove capable of recovery as soon as adequate stimulation is provided, be it in the adopted families for the orphans, or in the enriched environments for educating blind children. In the case of the orphans, improvement was shown, not only in the lifting of the quasi-autistic features, but also in an increase in intellectual achievements.

The Case of Hugh Blair of Borgue

This well-documented case dates from the first half of the eighteenth century and was discovered by the British historian Rab Houston. He transcribed the records, dating from 1745, from the archives of the Edinburgh Court and consulted me about their clinical relevance. This led to our collaboration, which resulted in a book.[13]

The story behind the case is that of a fearful family feud. John Blair, Hugh's younger brother, was the "pursuer" and wanted the court to declare his older brother mentally incapable, ultimately to disinherit him. The defendant in the case was the mother. The records of the court faithfully preserve what 29 witnesses said about Hugh Blair's behavior. They are remarkably consistent in painting a picture of a person who today would be diagnosed as suffering from autism. Although information on Hugh's early life is missing, he showed all of the typical features of autism. The witnesses were servants, neighbors, and ministers of the church. Family members could not give evidence as they were interested parties, one side fighting against the other.

Hugh Blair would have been expected to lead the life of a gentleman. However, he was unaware of the social conventions, which would have prevented him from doing various odd jobs around the house and the fields. Thus, he mended his own clothes with peculiar patches, when in fact a tailor was employed by the family. He cut wooden sticks and built stone walls where none were needed. He preferred to eat by himself in the kitchen with the cats, when the family was assembled in the dining room. He slept in a cold attic room stuffed with his collection of feathers and sticks. He wore odd clothes and put his wig on back to front.

Hugh Blair's language was very limited, as he talked only in short repetitive phrases, and he understood even less. For this reason most people thought him to be deaf or "deafish." He was said to have an excellent memory – his old schoolmaster declared it better than his own. He was able to recite the catechism, questions as well as answers. He could read and write, but servants and children readily made fun of him and could lead him by the nose.

While Kaspar Hauser was credited with common sense by a contemporary witness, Hugh Blair was most frequently described as lacking common sense. Hugh was known as the "foolish laird" everywhere in his neighborhood. Probably because of his privileged social status as a landowner, he was well tolerated in the local community. He attended every funeral and visited neighbors at any time of the day or night without ever having any conversation with them. He sometimes took a piece of clothing, apparently unaware of the impropriety of such a deed, as he made no attempt at hiding it.

After a dramatic incident, which is only hinted at in the records, Hugh's mother suddenly moved out of the family home and into lodgings. She took Hugh, who was already in his thirties, with her, and to everyone's surprise she proceeded to arrange a marriage for him. The church elders advised her against this plan in no uncertain terms. However, her reasons can be guessed from a statement by the Revd Robert Walker, a witness for the defense: she wished to provide long-term care for her son. This witness too could not help but confirm Hugh's mental incapacity.

Figure 3.5 The Revd Robert Walker (b. 1716), one of the chief witnesses for the defense

Hugh's mother lost the case. The judges had no option but to accept the overwhelming evidence that Hugh would have been incapable of understanding a marriage contract. This is not just on the basis of the witness statements. The judges also interrogated Hugh themselves, first verbally, and then by presenting written questions, since they wanted to make allowance for a purported hearing impairment. The well-preserved autograph shows Hugh's neat handwriting. However, Hugh only copied the questions verbatim and, most poignantly, he even copied the written injunction not to copy the question, but answer it.

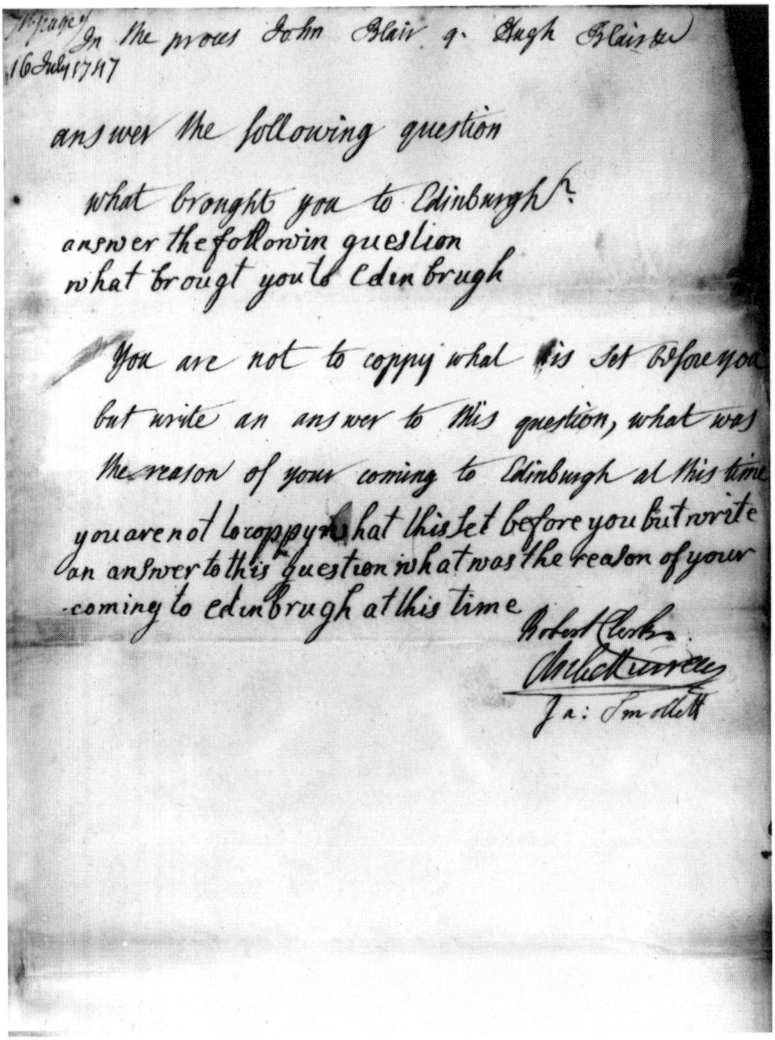
In the proces John Blair q. Hugh Blair
16 July 1747

answer the following question
what brought you to Edinburgh?
answer thefollowin queslion
what brougt youto edinbrugh

You are not to coppy what is set before you
but write an answer to this question, what was
the reason of your coming to Edinburgh at this time
youarenot tocoppy what thisset before you but write
an answer tothis question whatwas the reason of your
coming to edinbrugh atthis time

Robert Clerk
Ja: Smollett

Figure 3.6 Hugh Blair's written replies to the court's questions, July 16, 1747

Hugh Blair's marriage was annulled, and the whole family was thrown into financial ruin as a result of the court action. Nevertheless, his wife stayed with him and they had two children, of whom nothing is known. One can't help thinking that Hugh's mother had made a clever choice indeed. It is possible that mother, son, and daughter-in-law enjoyed a reasonable life together despite the fact that they were disinherited and had to live away from the family home.

Because of the quality of the documentation, the case of Hugh Blair allows a retrospective clinical diagnosis of autism. Yet it predates the first clinical description of the disorder by 200 years. There is reason to assume that autism has been with us for even longer, and perhaps further documents will come to light in the future.

The Case of John Howard

Hans Asperger always insisted that the individuals he described as autistic had much of value to give to society. There is no better illustration than John Howard (1726–90), a pioneer in prison reform. His book, published in 1777, brought about improvement of the often horrendous conditions of prisoners in earlier times. John Howard's work on behalf of the most disenfranchised section of society was revered to the extent of having statues of him erected after his death. Even today John Howard societies exist. A highly readable biography, written by Gordon Hay, appears on the website of the John Howard Society of Canada. In none of the existing biographies has the diagnosis of autistic disorder ever been considered, although there are plenty of comments on John Howard's rigid and lonely nature. Recently, the psychiatrist Philip Lucas reanalyzed the existing materials and came to the conclusion that John Howard suffered from Asperger syndrome.[14]

Howard, a gentleman of independent means and a devout Nonconformist, lived in London and Bedfordshire, where he had property. He spent his time traveling and making extensive and possibly obsessive meteorological observations. Taking no heed of the Seven Years War, he traveled to Lisbon in 1755, to see the effects of the earthquake that had then devastated this city. On board ship he was taken prisoner by the French and thus personally experienced prison conditions for two months. Nearly 20 years later, in 1773, Howard was appointed Sheriff of Bedfordshire. As part of his duties, which no one had expected him to take seriously, he inspected a prison, and was appalled at what he found. What outraged him most was not the unhealthy conditions, but that prisoners were obliged to pay the jailer for their upkeep and their release, with the consequences of blatant injustice for those who were unable to pay.

From this time on, Howard visited and revisited prisons for 17 years in "perpetual motion," covering 60,000 miles of journeys back and forth, over Britain, Ireland, and Continental Europe. Through his books he initiated reform, but when given the opportunity to build a reformed prison, he resigned from the specially formed committee. This was because his rigid rules did not allow compromise "even to a small degree." As a result the prison was

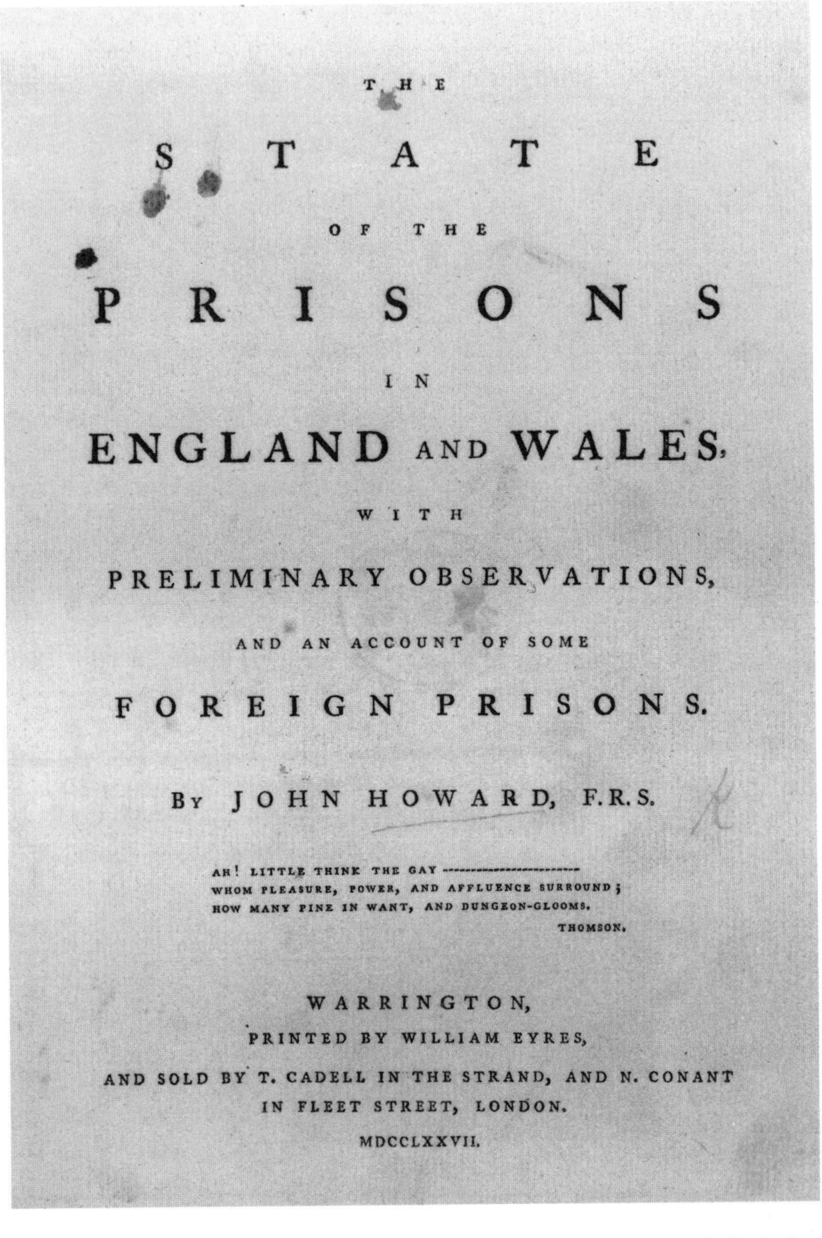

THE

STATE

OF THE

PRISONS

IN

ENGLAND AND WALES,

WITH

PRELIMINARY OBSERVATIONS,

AND AN ACCOUNT OF SOME

FOREIGN PRISONS.

BY JOHN HOWARD, F.R.S.

AH! LITTLE THINK THE GAY ——————
WHOM PLEASURE, POWER, AND AFFLUENCE SURROUND;
HOW MANY PINE IN WANT, AND DUNGEON-GLOOMS.
THOMSON.

WARRINGTON,
PRINTED BY WILLIAM EYRES,
AND SOLD BY T. CADELL IN THE STRAND, AND N. CONANT
IN FLEET STREET, LONDON.
MDCCLXXVII.

Figure 3.7 Frontispiece of John Howard's book *The State of the Prisons in England and Wales, 1777* never built. According to modern biographers, Howard's reputation rests not on his personal courage, but on the meticulous recording and reporting of what he saw. His book, *The State of the Prisons in England and Wales*, had three editions in his lifetime. With each new edition there was an appendix with the updated statistics of his findings. His credibility was due to the fact that he provided this information honestly, in factual and simple terms, and refrained from all embellishment and exaggeration.

The few facts that are known about Howard's private life may well be consistent with the idea of Asperger syndrome. He led a solitary life, yet he was married twice. As a young man he married his landlady, who was a widow more than 20 years older. She died only two years later. His second wife died in childbirth, again after a short marriage. Howard was heavily criticized for the upbringing of his son who, as an adult, led a profligate life and suffered an early death. There is a report that Howard was once called away on an urgent summons while he took his regular walk in the garden with his then three-year-old son. To keep him safe, he locked his son in a garden shed. However, he forgot to release him when his business was finished.

Howard's interests were intensely focused on one topic, and his activities must be described as repetitive. He traveled alone, or with only one servant, to the same places over and over again. He visited only prisons and fever hospitals and omitted all other sights. On one of these trips, in 1790, in Cherson in Russia, he died of typhus. Contemporaries described Howard as deporting himself in a sober, rigid way, which even then was considered old-fashioned. His daily routine was fixed; he ate the same frugal meal every day. Obsessed with punctuality, Howard was never late for appointments. Often he balanced a watch on his knee as he conversed. When the moment came, he would stop what he was saying and leave even in the middle of an argument.

Uncomfortable with his celebrity status, Howard refused portrait sittings and wrote to his lifelong mentor, the Unitarian minister Richard Price: "As a private man, with some peculiarities, I wish to remain in obscurity and silence." Price, who recognized the importance of Howard's dedicated work, played a vital role in ensuring its publication. According to Lucas, John Howard's social communication impairments are evident only in private letters, since he delegated the writing of his reports and books to trusted aids. Tellingly, an obituary referred to him as "the eccentric, but truly worthy, John Howard, Esq."

Clearly, the differences between the case of John Howard and the case of Hugh Blair are enormous, and yet both people failed to fit in with their social group. Nevertheless, through their privileged backgrounds, they were able to lead the lives they wanted to lead, and each benefited from kind and supportive friends or relatives.

chapter 4

Is there an Autism Epidemic?

Is autism on the increase? How do symptoms vary between individuals? Do the features of autism really "run together" as they should in a true syndrome, or are they occurring together by chance? Such basic questions are difficult to answer with certainty, and population studies are the only way to address them.

Autism is defined by behavior, and population surveys have to be based on behavioral criteria. The problem is that in the last 40 years or so they have not remained the same. This is because the understanding of autistic disorder has gradually changed its definition. The recognition of a spectrum with severe and mild forms has meant a widening of the boundaries. The way the behavioral criteria are formulated is to some extent arbitrary. People will disagree with each other from time to time as to which symptoms are the most important, how to handle cut-off points in degree of symptom severity, and how to interpret qualitative impairments in social communication.

Population Studies

Since it is important to know whether autism is increasing, it is worth re-visiting the first epidemiological study of autism. This study was conducted in 1966 by Victor Lotter under the auspices of the MRC Social Psychiatry Unit in London, which pioneered epidemiological studies in psychiatry.[1] The study focused on a geographically defined area. In order to appreciate the effort that is involved in population surveys, it is worth looking at the procedure in some detail. Lotter first screened *all* children between the ages of eight and ten whose addresses were in the county of Middlesex on a particular date. The total number amounted to about 78,000. By postal questionnaires to teachers and other people professionally concerned with children of that age, he initially identified all those children who might be autistic. He then consulted medical records and conducted interviews. In this way he was able to identify 135 suspected cases, all of which he assessed individually. As a result of repeated sifting, he found a group of 35 children who fitted Kanner and Eisenberg's criteria:[2] they were socially aloof and they had elaborate rituals and routines. Using these criteria he found a prevalence of 4.5 per 10,000 of the population of children aged eight to ten with a ratio of 2.6 boys to 1 girl. When this study was published, autism was still a little-known disorder, and most people were content to believe that it was very rare.

However, this belief proved to be mistaken. It turned out that the particular combination of symptoms that Lotter was looking for was highly unusual. Aloofness tends to be associated with low IQ and simple repetitive movements, while elaborate routines and rituals tend to be associated with high IQ. Lotter noticed a substantial number of learning-disabled children who were mute and socially withdrawn and showed motor mannerisms that did not qualify as elaborate routines. It took another 20 years before it was realized that there are also children of normal intelligence with social impairments who show elaborate rituals, but who are not aloof.

In 2002 Wing and Potter were able to review the impressive number of 39 population studies carried out in different countries.[3] We now know that there is no particular association of autism with social class or geographical area. This confirms the assumption of a biological cause that strikes regardless of social or other environmental conditions. The most recent and reliable studies, using the criteria of the standard diagnostic handbooks, are showing a prevalence of around 60 per 10,000 for autistic spectrum disorders[4] with an estimate of between 8 and 30 per 10,000 for autism in its more classic form. This is a huge increase from the estimate of 4.5 in 10,000 obtained in Lotter's study.

Most experts believe that the increasing prevalence figures that have been found over time do not reflect a real increase in cases. Not only have the diagnostic criteria been widened, but greater awareness of autism has meant that more cases are coming forward for diagnosis. It is difficult to compare population studies even if they are of more recent date and use similar diagnostic criteria. The size and composition of the population affects the estimate, as does the age range of the individuals targeted. In smaller studies researchers investigate each putative case rather than using only officially recorded cases, and therefore tend to find larger prevalence figures. In big population studies cases can be missed more easily. The numbers also depend on the exact interpretation of the boundaries of what is definitely autism, and what are other related disorders.

Given the enormous increase, are we in danger of exaggerating the number of cases that fall within a broadly defined autism spectrum? This is unlikely. No full-scale epidemiological study has as yet included children as well as adults, with a view to capturing cases with average and superior intelligence that may only come to light in adolescence or adulthood. Individuals with Asperger syndrome in particular can fall through the net in prevalence studies that are typically limited to younger ages. Prevalence estimates for Asperger syndrome are still a matter of conjecture. Studies in Sweden have estimated Asperger syndrome as occurring in between 36 and 48 per 10,000 children in mainstream schools, that is, around 0.4 percent.[5] If confirmed, the estimate for all autism spectrum disorders, regardless of age and regardless of ability, could be near 1 percent of the total population, a figure that would be quite similar to the prevalence of schizophrenia.

Is Autism a Syndrome?

Lotter's first population study of autism used a simple and strict set of behavioral criteria relating to aloofness and elaborate routines. The study proved that these criteria can be used reliably to identify children who resemble those first described by Kanner. But did it also prove that autism is a natural entity, a true syndrome? What about the possibility that the criterion behaviors occur randomly and independently of each other, and that their concurrence might merely be chance? For instance, if one looked for color-blind, agoraphobic flautists, one would find a number in a large enough population, but one would not have found a syndrome. It would be pointless to attempt to explain the constellation of symptoms in terms of some common underlying neurocognitive deficit. Since this is exactly what I shall aim to do in this book, it is important to be sure that we are not hunting after a chimera.

A landmark study by Lorna Wing and Judith Gould broke the circularity imposed by the search for cases identified by possibly arbitrary criteria.[6] Wing and Gould did not start with a given set of criteria. Instead they wanted to find out how often each of the symptoms might be present in a population of handicapped children independently of any prior diagnosis. This study was carried out in Camberwell, a borough of Inner London, with a population at that time of 155,000. As a first step, Wing and Gould established that among 35,000 children from 0 to 14 years who lived in Camberwell on December 31, 1970, there were 914 children who were known to the health or education services as suffering from some form of physical or mental handicap.

Almost all of them had IQs below 70. In the earlier Middlesex study, all children diagnosed as suffering from autism turned out to have been known to the services as handicapped. Therefore, the procedure followed in the Camberwell study was well suited for identifying all children who were already diagnosed as suffering from autism. However, identification of children with autism was not the main aim of the study. The study aimed at discovering how many children in the population under scrutiny showed any of the main features of autism.

All 914 children were screened and a sample of 173 children was identified for further intensive investigation. This sample included all physically mobile but mentally retarded children. It also included all children with any one of three behaviors typical of autism, regardless of retardation. These three features were severe social impairment, defined as inability to engage in reciprocal two-way interaction, especially with peers; severe communication impairment, defined as inability to communicate by both verbal and nonverbal means; and severe impairment in the pursuit of imaginative activities with the substitution of repetitive behavior. This was defined as an inability to engage in ordinary symbolic play with dolls. Each child (with the exception of six who had died) was repeatedly observed and tested, and parents and caretakers were intensively interviewed about the child's behavior and peculiarities from birth. Many years later, when the children were aged between 16 and 30 years, a follow-up study was conducted.[7]

Just as in the Middlesex study, an incidence of 4.9 in 10,000 (17 children in all) was found when autism was diagnosed on the basis of Kanner and Eisenberg's two cardinal symptoms, namely extreme aloofness and presence of elaborate repetitive routines. However, the single most important diagnostic sign, namely severe social impairment, was identified as present from before age seven in an additional 62 children. Seventy percent of these children had such severe learning disabilities that their behavior repertoire was extremely limited. For this reason alone they could not show many of the characteristic behavior patterns of autism. They had no elaborate routines, peculiar speech, or islets of ability.

The number of children who showed severe social impairment amounted to 22.5 in 10,000 children under age 15, a figure by far outnumbering the estimate of classic cases of autism. These children were not simply the most handicapped of the intensively studied sample, but differed from 60 other children who, despite severe mental retardation, were not socially impaired when allowance was made for their intellectual level. Among these sociable children, 32 suffered from Down syndrome. However, three other Down syndrome children were impaired in their social interactions.

The triad of impairments

The Camberwell study suggested that severe social impairment takes different forms at different ages and can be present at all levels of ability. What about the other behavioral features that the study focused on? Here it turned out that level of ability mattered. Before a certain degree of maturity and learning experience, children simply cannot show sufficiently strong evidence of their potential. Lorna Wing and Judith Gould found a mental age of 20 months to be a convenient cut-off point. They divided both the socially impaired and sociable groups into subgroups with a language comprehension age of either above or below 20 months. Only in the children of the higher ability range could impaired communication or impaired imaginative play be unequivocally recognized. The important finding was that *all* socially impaired children in the critical higher ability range showed impairment in *each of the three features* under consideration. None of the sociable children showed any of the other two features. Remarkably, only the socially impaired children (as long as they had a mental age of above 20 months) showed a significant impairment in a standardized test of pretend play. Only these children showed significant problems in both verbal and nonverbal communication.

Since these three features occur together there is therefore a "triad" of impairments, not just three separate impairments. We now have an answer to the question whether the characteristic impairments seen in the classic cases of autism in such clear-cut form are merely a chance combination: clearly, they are not. We can now be sure that when we speak of autism, we are speaking of a syndrome. There is every justification, then, for searching for a neuro-cognitive explanation for the curious constellation of the triad of impairments.

THE ALOOF, THE PASSIVE, AND THE ODD

In the Camberwell study social impairment was defined as an inability to engage in two-way interaction. When Lorna Wing and Judy Gould attempted to capture the quality of the impairment, they identified three distinctive types, labeled as aloof, passive, and odd.[8] Each of these types of behavior might be shown by one and the same child in different situations, and at different ages. However, it was also possible to characterize a particular child in terms of its predominant behavior. The following fictitious descriptions are intended to show an extreme version of each prototype.

Jane is an *aloof* child who evokes the image of the child in a glass cage. At school and at home she appears totally withdrawn and does not respond

the aloof   the passive   the odd

Figure 4.1   Three types of social impairment

to social overtures or to speech. Jane does not speak at all but can make speech-like noises. She does not use eye contact, and often appears to avoid it altogether. She refuses to be cuddled. She will not seek to be comforted when distressed. Her mother reports that Jane has never greeted her with the eager anticipation so obvious in her younger daughter. Sometimes she wonders whether Jane even recognizes her. Jane sometimes stares at people's faces closely, seemingly trying to puzzle out what sort of objects they are, and how they react to being prodded. She approaches people to obtain food or drink or a compact disk that she likes to listen to. She can concentrate for hours playing a computer game, but does not play with other children. It is unusual for a girl to have this pattern, which is far more common in boys.

David is a *passive* child who indifferently accepts social approaches made by others. He does what he is told, and his parents and teachers have to watch constantly that he is not led into mischief by his compliance. David speaks and always answers questions willingly and with total honesty. For David, social contact with other children is part of the daily routine, but not something to look forward to or to be done for pleasure. On the contrary, he is often the victim of teasing and bullying. He accepts that this is the way it is, and seems not to know that he could get help from his teachers and parents. Most of the time, David has a remarkably easygoing temperament, and this is appreciated by his parents and teachers. However, any stresses or changes of routine result in emotional displays, which range from uncontrollable sobbing to temper tantrums and hitting out.

Louise is an *odd* child who likes being with people. She likes to touch people and likes being cuddled even by someone not familiar to her. She goes up to total strangers, and asks "What's your name?" or "How old are you?" She obviously is not able to judge when approach is unwanted or inappropriate. When she was brought for testing in a university department, she wore out the patience of several psychologists with incessant chattering and her habit of asking repetitive questions. At the end of the day she clung to one of the testers and insisted she wanted to stay overnight, much to the embarrassment of her parents. Louise does not understand why people often comment on her pestering and obnoxious behavior. Her parents are also worried about her tendency to physical aggression. They feel they must watch over her constantly, never letting her out alone. Individuals who are chatty and socially odd are often diagnosed as having Asperger syndrome.

The three types of social impairment were distributed in the Camberwell sample in such a way that about half the cases were typically aloof before age seven. By definition this included all the children with the classic syndrome described by Kanner. A quarter each of the remaining cases could be classified as either passive or odd. By the time of the follow-up study many children had changed from one category to another. There was a strong trend for aloof children to become either passive or odd, except for those with more severe learning difficulties. Importantly, of the seven children with classic autism four had lost their aloofness completely. What this shows is that the three types of social impairment may all arise out of the same underlying profound disability to form social relationships.

The autism spectrum – and beyond

These findings gave major impetus to the widening of the diagnostic criteria and convinced clinicians that too many cases were unjustly excluded by a narrow definition. Furthermore, the narrow definition did not seem to hold over time in an individual child. Some children seemed to qualify only when young, but not as they got older. Others, whose symptoms appeared to be too mild when young to qualify for a diagnosis, showed the symptoms in unmistakable form when adult. The triad of impairments, on the other hand, applied to all these cases and in the same individual over time. The proviso is that allowance is made for age and ability, which strongly determine the manifestation of the behavioral symptoms. For example, impairment in socialization in a young child may be shown as aloofness, but in an adult may manifest itself as poor understanding of social subtleties. Impairment in communication in a young child may be shown by not turning around when called by name; in an adult by an inability to engage in gossip. Impairment in imagination in a young child is shown by not understanding pretence; in an adult by not understanding the hypothetical "what if?" and its imaginary consequences in a story.

In the Camberwell study the triad of impairments was present in every child who had a diagnosis of autism. But it was also present in a large number of individuals who hitherto had not been so diagnosed. These children had been variously labeled learning-disabled, psychotic, or emotionally disturbed. What were the differences between these children and the classic cases? In the classic cases the median level of intelligence was higher, the proportion of boys was larger, and fewer children had shown clear signs of abnormality in their first year of life. Thus, the additional children had been more severely and more globally affected by brain abnormality, and this was noticeable at an early age.

The study opened up the possibility that *all triad-positive* children are part of a continuum and share one and the same underlying abnormality, regardless of additional problems. The work of subdividing such a continuum has hardly begun, but the category of Asperger syndrome is already well established. Other subgroups will eventually be formed, and these could be based on the presence of additional problems, severity of accompanying intellectual disability, or on developmental trajectories.

Although resulting in an important advance over the earlier narrow definition of autism, the search for the common denominator lost sight of some of the classic observations of Kanner and Asperger. The triad of impairments is not informative about islets of ability, obsessively pursued interests, or odd sensations. These symptoms have not always been found reliably in learning-disabled children, and we have hardly any information on their prevalence, their degree of severity, and their course over time. It may now be interesting to reconsider these phenomena at different levels of ability. It may well be that these phenomena do not correlate in any simple way with the severity of the disorder, and do not lend themselves to be considered along a continuum. They may not be universal, but they appear to be specific and may lead to new subgroups.

Why Do So Many Boys have Autism?

The excess of boys over girls with autism, at a ratio of 4:1 on average, is now well established, and the excess in Asperger syndrome is even likely to be in the region of 15:1. Boys predominate much less at lower levels of ability. The scarcity of girls at the higher ability levels may provide a clue to the biological origin of autism. Is it possible that being female carries some degree of protection from autism? Or does being male confer some degree of vulnerability? Does an excess of the male hormone testosterone during an early stage of fetal development constitute a risk factor?

Given that the predominance of males at higher levels of ability is still unexplained, it is worth considering whether girls are less likely to be detected. The triad of impairments combined with good language and high ability might be more effectively camouflaged in females. Girls are often considered to be more verbal and more compliant than boys in educational settings, and therefore might show better compensatory learning. One way of pursuing this idea would be by using tests that are sensitive enough to unmask camouflaged cases.

One early study by Cathy Lord and colleagues that addressed gender differences reported results from 384 boys and 91 girls, aged three to eight years.[9] This sample of autism spectrum cases was identified at the University Clinic of North Carolina at Chapel Hill and included many children with moderate or severe mental retardation. All children were seen between 1975 and 1980 and were thoroughly investigated by psychological tests and interviews taking into account each child's development. The ratio of boys to girls was 5:1 at the higher end of the ability range and only 3:1 at the lower end.

The girls had an average nonverbal IQ of 40 and the boys of 44, both of which are low. Though only a few points different, these averages nevertheless indicate a significant shift, since they are based on sizeable groups. Similarly, girls came out worse when simple daily living skills were assessed, and were worse on language or perceptual tests. Thus the girls were, on average, more seriously impaired on almost every ability tested than the boys. However, in terms of play or affect, or the ability to relate to people, the girls were no worse than the boys. From this result, it would not be right to think of the girls in this study as more "autistic" than the boys. Instead, they seem to have had more severe additional problems. A more recent study confirmed that gender differences were related to IQ scores and not to autism severity.[10] This finding is consistent with other studies that have shown that autistic features *per se* are relatively independent of intellectual abilities and acquired skills.

Increasing Numbers and Increasing Awareness

If autism was always as frequent as it is now, then what happened to all the people who were undiagnosed as children in the 1960s and before? An answer comes from a study by Lorna Wing and her colleagues. This study documented the closure of a typical old-style hospital for mentally retarded individuals in 1980. The hospital had to place all the remaining residents into different types of community accommodation and to this end they were all assessed in detail. This assessment revealed that 339 of the 893 residents had autism spectrum disorder, with 134 showing classic autism. However, none of the older residents and only a few of the younger ones had been so diagnosed.[11]

If this example is a true reflection of the change in diagnostic practice, then, as the diagnosis of autism spectrum disorder has increased, the diagnosis of unspecified mental retardation should have decreased. Some evidence for such a change comes from statistical data of the California Health and Human Services Agency,[12] which reported an increase in the diagnosis of autistic disorder from 5.78 per 10,000 in the year 1987 to 14.89 in the year 1994. The rates for the same years for the diagnosis of mental retardation of unknown cause showed a decrease from 28.76 to 19.52. This decrease almost perfectly balances the increase in autism cases. So much for the sensationalist cry of "epidemic."

Of course, we cannot completely rule out that there has been a real increase, unlikely as it seems to most experts. We will not know for sure as long as we depend on the behavioral definition of autism and its arbitrary boundaries. A big difference would be made if a genetic or other biological marker could be identified. Meanwhile, the way forward must be to refine the cognitive definition of autism and its basis in the brain.

Autism and Other Developmental Disorders

Misfortunes seldom come alone. Individuals with autism may be diagnosed with additional disorders, for instance, attention deficit disorder, motor discoordination disorder, language disorder, and dyslexia. However, so far no epidemiological study has established how frequent such cases are. Clumsiness is common in many developmental disorders, as are language problems, social problems, and educational problems. This does not mean that all these disorders are much of a muchness. In clinical practice it is necessary to take account of associations and of individual variation. For theoretical purposes, however, we would wish to focus on the essential features of a disorder and set aside the variable features.

Why is mental retardation so frequently associated with autism? The labels "learning disability" or "mental retardation" refer to a ragbag of conditions and reflect low intelligence levels. Mental retardation is only a sign, and not the cause, of an abnormally developing brain. The causes are largely un-known, but the obvious fact is that mental retardation implies brain disorder, whether this involves congenital abnormality, brain disease, or injury.

The existence of autism without additional problems, and without general accompanying mental retardation, has been confirmed. For this reason it is widely assumed that autism is a specific disorder. This simply means that not all mental functions are equally affected by the disorder. In autism, social communication is consistently lagging behind other aspects of development. This lag stands out sharply in a bright child who can engage with the physical world much better than with the social world, but less sharply in a child who is not particularly competent in interactions with the physical world either. In this case the diagnosis can become contentious. However frequent such cases may be, they do not challenge the assumption of autism as a specific disorder. This is not to say that a circumscribed brain abnormality early in develop-ment does not have downstream effects. If the maturation or development of even a single cognitive component is delayed, repercussions are to be expected on later developing functions. For instance, delay in the ability to attribute intentions to others will cause delays and impairments in normal language acquisition. Hence in autism we can identify specific deficits and trace their more general effects.[13]

While attention, language, and motor problems are noted in some cases of autism, a poverty of social relations and emotional problems are often noted in other syndromes. This can be confusing because these indi-viduals are likely to attract an additional diagnosis of autistic disorder. Some suggest that conditions such as Down syndrome, Williams syndrome, Rett syndrome, or fragile X syndrome can cause autism. This seems unwarranted, since all we know is that the frequency of such a diagnosis is raised in these disorders. In fact, all these conditions are associated with brain abnormality of unknown type and extent, and it is plausible that overlaps occur and give rise to clinical symptoms that seem to be common to several different disorders.

Autism and schizophrenia

Despite the fact that schizophrenia and autism are, by definition, distinguish-able diagnostic entities, in adulthood some autistic people resemble, at least in their surface behavior, a certain type of schizophrenic patient. After all, Bleuler coined the label "autistic" to refer to the particular social impairments and thought disorder in some of his patients for whom he introduced the label "schizophrenic." Similarities in so-called negative symptoms certainly exist. For example, Canadian researchers Konstantareas and Hewitt compared a group of men with autism and a group with schizophrenia, using reliable rating scales for specific symptoms that are now available.[14] Many members of both groups showed little or no speech or facial expression, and little or no interest in social contact or communication. It is not surprising that confusion between schizophrenia and autism can occur when an individual is first seen in adult life and a history of development is not available.

Such confusion is not warranted at the early age when autism is typically first diagnosed. Kraepelin, the first psychiatrist to describe the disorder that we now call schizophrenia, reported that 94 percent of his sample of over 1,000 cases had onset after the age of 15. This sharply contrasts with the onset of autism. The time of onset of a disorder is of crucial importance. A disorder that affects the normal course of development from birth, or even before, is not the same disorder when it befalls a mature organism. Being born deaf, for instance, leads to changes in brain and mind that have consequences for many aspects of development, such as the way language is learned. They are different from the changes that occur from becoming deaf after speech has been acquired.

What about the rare children who become schizophrenic before puberty? They almost always resemble adult schizophrenics in their symptoms and can be distinguished from children with autism. This was established early in a population study in Britain, published in 1971[15] and confirmed by a study carried out in New York in 1984.[16] Kolvin and his colleagues, in the earlier study, reported that the youngest child of their sample of 24 diagnosed as schizophrenic was 6.7 years old. In 80 percent of the sample, the onset of schizophrenia was after age eight and a half. By that age linguistic and cognitive development is substantially completed. The basic prerequisites for adult competence are present, although performance improves with experience. Childhood schizophrenia can be grouped with adult schizophrenia. There is no reason to confuse it with childhood autism.

While patients with negative schizophrenic symptoms resemble individuals with autism, patients with positive symptoms do not. The most characteristic positive symptoms of schizophrenia have to do with hearing voices and believing that there are significant personal messages in the environment. These are subjective experiences, which the patient is able to communicate to others. Articulate people with autism who have reported their experiences give quite different accounts. It is, however, possible that positive symptoms of schizophrenia can occur in autism, and in particular, paranoid beliefs have been described in some of these rare cases.

Hidden relationships continue to surface. Schizophrenia has increasingly been characterized as a developmental disorder with specific early signs that can be recognized with hindsight. In fact, these signs point to dysfunction of the frontal lobe.[17] Such signs are also common in autism.

The Many Causes of Autism

What causes autism? No question is asked more frequently by people confronting this puzzling disorder for the first time. Ideally, there should be an answer that would at once explain and prevent autism by pointing to a cure. Unfortunately, no such simple answer exists.

In principle, we can divide theories about the causes of autism into those that give the main weight to a genetic predisposition, and those that put the main weight on environmental factors. What matters is whether the damage sustained from whatever source prevents normal development of a specified neurological system at a critical time. Summaries of recent work on biological factors in autism are readily available, for instance in Gillberg and Coleman's updated volume.[18] Here I examine just some of the many causal factors that have been proposed and studied.

Genetic factors

Scientists have long suspected a genetic basis.[19] Twin and family pedigree studies have provided strong evidence. Investigations are being conducted still, as researchers attempt to find predisposing genes in families with one or more autistic members. Although it is rare for families to have more than one child with autistic disorder, the risk of a second child being affected by a form of autistic disorder has been estimated as 3–6 percent. This must be compared with a normal population risk of 0.6 percent, making it 5–10 times as high.

The first twin study was carried out in 1977. Susan Folstein and Michael Rutter succeeded in collecting 21 pairs of twin boys, with at least one twin unequivocally diagnosed as autistic.[20] The aim was to estimate the degree of concordance: would autism, diagnosed according to strict criteria, be present in both twins when they were genetically identical rather than fraternal? It has to be noted here that 100 percent concordance rates are not expected even in well-established genetic conditions, because there are other factors that create differences. Concordance for classic autism was found in 4 out of 11 identical pairs and in none of the fraternal ones. This is strong, but not overwhelming, evidence for genetic causes. However, the authors went one step further: many of the brothers in the nonconcordant pairs of identical twins did in fact have a milder form of autistic disorder, fulfilling the more recent wider diagnostic criteria. In fact, the autistic features of these less affected brothers became more apparent as they got older. Using broader criteria, which allowed for milder forms of autism, the concordance in identical twins was now as high as 90 percent. This finding suggests that the genetic cause is for a broader phenotype and not just for the narrow definition of autism. This finding is entirely consistent with the idea of an autism spectrum.

Some studies conducted on the relatives of autistic individuals show that certain features of autism may be present in other family members, for instance, aloofness, lack of close friendships, and rigidity.[21] However, it is hard to know whether such features have always been present, or are, at least to some extent, a consequence of having to care for a child with autism in the family. This qualification does not apply to studies that have found distinct advantages for certain analytic skills in parents and in their professional careers.[22]

Having established a genetic basis of autism, the search for the location of potentially predisposing genes has become a fast-moving area of research. It has proved to be very difficult, however. This is partly because no one knows what genes to look for, and partly because the current diagnostic procedures might actually fail to make the most appropriate classification. Large families with several affected members are relatively rare, but it is these families that allow a particularly promising genetic approach. Here the chromosomes of both affected and unaffected relatives are screened and compared in minute detail. As yet no consistent story has emerged from this work. However, it has become clear that different combinations of genes can produce the same clinical picture in different affected families. Several large collaborative studies identified sites on chromosomes 2, 7, 15, and 16, but unfortunately, the significance levels are low, and future studies might well upturn these early findings.[23]

While genetic studies are pursued vigorously, investigators need to explore how one should conceptualize the consequences of genetic risk. Why are there such big differences in severity of impairments between affected members of the same family? What causes the additional problems that are present in many cases? It could be that even if you are at high genetic risk for autism, you may show the features in such mild form that only autism researchers would ever notice. If true, this would throw considerable doubt on the usefulness of a genetic test for autism. A big gap still exists between what genes do and how exactly they influence the developing brain. In order to explain autism, we need to have a grasp of the way in which genetic faults compromise critical systems of the brain. Perhaps current laboratory studies investigating how genes affect brain development in genetically modified mice will provide clues to the genetic influences on human brain development.

Environmental risk factors

Environmental causes are attractive to consider because it might be possible to avoid them and prevent the disorder. A famous example is phenylketonuria, a metabolic disease with a genetic cause and an environmental trigger, phenylalanine, which the body in this case cannot metabolize. This is critical, as phenylalanine is in much of the food we normally eat. If unchecked, the consequence of the disease is subtle damage to the brain and intellectual impairment. Removing phenylalanine-containing substances from the daily diet can prevent these consequences. The children can then develop normally, despite the genetic predisposition. Is autism like phenylketonuria, triggered perhaps by toxins or allergens in the diet or in the environment? The idea has its strong adherents, but evidence is lacking.

Essentially, any environmental risk factor that can lead to brain damage early in development may be considered a potential nongenetic cause of autism. Prenatal factors and birth complications are risk factors that might result in brain damage. A number of studies have shown that significantly more hazards of pregnancy and birth are present in autistic than in normal children. However, these adverse factors, from pregnancy complications to forceps delivery, can themselves be a consequence of some genetic abnormality in the fetus. Reproductive problems and fetal abnormalities tend to go together, and it is not easy to tease them apart. Birth injury does not rank high on the list of causes of autism. A difficult birth can cause all sorts of developmental problems, but is not particularly associated with autism.

Both viral infections and autoimmune disorder have been reported in cases of autism. Viral diseases are subject to sudden outbreaks and can infect the central nervous system and lead to permanent brain damage. In rare cases, if the central nervous system becomes infected at a critical time, either before or after birth, autism may result. This hypothesis is testable by studying the incidence of autism in relation to known virus epidemics. Of particular interest is a special type of virus called a retrovirus, which integrates itself into the genetic material of the body's cells. Other viruses that have been suggested as possible causes of autism are herpes and cytomegalovirus. These can remain dormant for years but can be reactivated from time to time.

The immune system, which protects us from virus damage, can itself be subject to dysfunction for genetic reasons. Severe forms of immune intolerance in the mother lead to fetal death. Mild forms may interfere with normal processes of growth, and hence may lead to developmental disorder. Again, the question whether immune dysfunction is a cause or an effect of brain abnormality remains open.

Infection with rubella of mothers in the first trimester of pregnancy is known to be highly dangerous to the fetus. This is why the eradication of rubella through early vaccination has been public health policy in many countries. Rubella-affected children suffer from severe sensory impairments and many also have autism. However, follow-up studies made evident that these children had a form of autism that was atypical and proved transient. As in the case of blind children and Romanian orphans, discussed in chapter 3, nonpermanent "quasi-autism" may have been induced through physical and psychological deprivation with severe repercussions on social development.

Just because an illness preceded the onset of symptoms does not prove it to be a cause of autism. For such a proof, it is necessary to consider possible mechanisms by which a virus can enter the brain and by which it can do selective damage. This is not being pedantic. If all one needed to establish cause was to show a correlation, then all sorts of nonsensical conclusions would be drawn. For instance, it is well known that as the birth rate in Europe declined, the population of storks declined also. Still, we do not wish to conclude that the scarcity of storks is responsible for the scarcity of newborns.

THE GREAT VACCINATION SCARE

In recent years the association between a risk of autism and vaccination has been strongly implanted into public consciousness. In fact, as a result many parents have not had their children vaccinated against measles, mumps, and rubella by the recommended triple-shot vaccine. Health ministers now warn that if the number drops too much, protection may be lost, with serious implications for public health. Measles, mumps, and rubella might become established again and show themselves as the killer diseases they are. On the other hand, if an association does exist, then an important factor in the causation of autism would be identified, and prevention might be possible.

Given the strong feelings that the debate has aroused, it is vital to find out whether there is any truth in the idea. A number of parents are convinced from personal experience. Others are ready to believe this idea because of the perceived dramatic increase in autism. The logic is simple. If there is a sudden increase, some novel environmental agent must be to blame. Vaccination fits the role of potential trigger factor perfectly. Vaccines have in the past been known, in rare cases, to induce brain disease with the terrible consequences of severe brain damage. It is conceivable that this brain damage can result in autism. There are two additional factors that make the vaccination a favored candidate. The first signs of autism are often not noticed until the second year of life, during which the critical vaccination occurs. Secondly, a proportion of cases with autism show regression in development after a seemingly normal start. Putting all these factors together, the possibility has been seized upon that some children acquire autism from a vaccination shot.

An additional twist to the story added yet more fuel. This was the report, originating in the UK, of cases of autism with severe gastric conditions. These conditions were related to the measles virus and the possibility was considered of a "leaky gut" letting toxins invade the nervous system. This scenario has immediate appeal as a causal mechanism. However, no direct evidence of such a causal pathway exists.

The idea of a link between autism and triple vaccination has established itself as quickly as some of the infamous urban myths, which implant tall stories as true facts in public awareness. Triple vaccination fulfilled the role of scapegoat particularly well, as it seemed to be three times as bad as a single vaccine, implying an overload of the immune system. The more government ministers protested, the more the general suspicion of a potential cover-up grew. Were drug companies who wanted to sell their vaccines conspiring with governments wanting to avoid a health scare? Unfortunately in the UK this suspicion fed on the memory of the public fear of "mad cow" disease, which had been met by politicians' insensitivity and mistaken assurance.

What does the evidence actually suggest? We have seen that it is not possible to be sure that the number of autism cases has increased. Indeed, many experts feel that only its detection has increased. Various studies have computed the number of cases diagnosed in relation to the introduction of triple vaccines at different times in different countries. These studies showed that there is no observable pattern that relates increases in cases to the introduction of the triple vaccines.[24] We have already discussed the difficulty of diagnosing autism in the first year of life. Hence the significance of noticing the first symptoms only relatively late in development cannot be taken as a sign that autism has been acquired and that more subtle signs were not present much earlier.

Despite these data, the belief in the link has not diminished. Many people believe that large-scale studies using correlations and trends have no bearing on the events in rare individual cases. Here, causality is established by other means, for instance, the direct perception of eyewitnesses of preceding event and subsequent effect. The problem is that such direct perception is known from many experimental studies to be fallible. No scientist would trust it as evidence – unless, perhaps, he or she were a parent!

What conclusions can we draw at present? In all the possible scenarios of environmental triggers of autism, damage to the brain is the critical factor. The question is how exactly is this damage produced? One possibility is encephalitis. This terrifying disease, which in the extreme can devastate the brain, can be a consequence of a viral illness. In some rare cases, long before MMR vaccination was available, encephalitis is thought to have resulted in autism combined with severe intellectual deficiency. In these terribly sad cases autistic features such as stereotypies, loss of language, and withdrawal from social contact have been observed, as well as a regression of all other abilities.

The global and pervasive nature of the damage may well make the diagnosis a matter of debate. But such a dispute fades into insignificance. If brain disease with consequent loss of function can be induced by encephalitis, and if encephalitis can be triggered by vaccination, then this would be a serious matter. So far no one has been able to prove or to disprove this scenario. In any case, scientific methods are at present unsuitable for the task of establishing the "truth" in selected putative cases, which seem to rely on personal conviction. This is a pity. The debate is likely to be continued in courts of law, where adversarial rather than scientific methods are used, and where blame rather than truth is a major concern.

Living with a Disorder of Unknown Cause

Scientists are skeptical of the abundant suggestions of physical and chemical causes of autism that are constantly being produced. They can live with the abstract idea that the causes of autism are not yet known. Parents find this much more difficult. When no explanation is given of why their healthy and beautiful baby has autism, they are compelled to search for a cause. The human brain automatically detects cause-and-effect relationships between events that occur together. This may result in a powerful illusion, since correlation is not the same thing as causation. Regression in development following vaccination is an example of a correlation. The beauty of the scientific approach is that it provides methods to find out whether causally perceived events are indeed causally related. This takes time.

Will our attitude to autism be different once specific causes and their mechanisms have been identified? It is possible. In other diseases a change in attitude has often occurred when a cause became known. Parents of children with Down syndrome now know that the cause is a particular chromosome abnormality, and are accepting of the lifelong nature of the condition. They are less likely to be preyed upon by charlatans who advertise cures.

The question of causes of autism will remain a matter of intense speculation for some time. We need to think about a long causal chain with discrete links. In the manner of a mnemonic we can say that there is hazard, followed by havoc, followed by harm. The hazard can be of many kinds, including faulty genes, chromosome abnormality, metabolic disorder, viral agents, immune intolerance, and anoxia from perinatal problems. We can assume that any of these hazards has the potential to create havoc in neural development. Owing to the upheaval, lasting harm may be done to the development of specific brain systems concerned with higher mental processes. The harm may be mild or severe, but always involves developmental arrest of one or more critical systems at a critical point in time. The theory is that only then will autism occur.

chapter 5
Mind Reading and
Mind Blindness

The cover of this book shows a picture painted by Georges de la Tour (1593–1652).[1] We see four fancifully dressed people: a woman and two men are seated at a table, engaged in card playing. Standing behind the group is a maidservant holding a glass of wine. These bare facts do not convey the tacit drama that is there, in front of our eyes. However, this inner drama is not visible in the same way that the people and their actions are visible.

We know a drama is taking place because the characters speak eloquently with their eyes and hands. There is a curious sideways glance by the lady in the center, and also by the servant. Both look toward the player on the left, who looks toward us. The lady also points to him with the index finger of her right hand. The player pointed out in this way by look and gesture holds two aces behind his back with his left hand. In his right hand, elbow on the table, the player holds the rest of his cards. The other player, on the right, is looking downwards into his cards, apparently engrossed.

Even with this added detail the description does not capture what is going on in this scene. To do this we have to put the facts together and make some inferences. The facts and inferences have to do with what the characters know and believe, feel and desire. Although we cannot see states of mind, we can attribute them, guided by the painter's intentions, with logic and precision, and not by tenuous and vague speculation. As a result we know that the painter portrayed an incident of cheating at cards. How do we come to know this fact with such certainty? Our understanding is based on a powerful mental tool that every normal adult possesses and uses with varying degrees of skill. This tool is a theory of mind. The theory is not the same as a scientific theory, but much more practical. It provides us with the ability to predict relationships between external states of affairs and internal states of mind. I call this ability "mentalizing."

To grasp what this strange made-up word means let us go back to the picture. One clue to the inner drama is given by the concealed aces. According to our theory of mind we automatically infer that what the others do not see, they do not know. At the same time we infer that the other players believe the aces to be in the pack, because we know that this is the rule of the game. A second clue is the staring servant girl. We infer from her standing position that she would have seen the aces held behind the player's back, and hence knows of the cheating. A third clue is the strange look of the lady in the center who points to the cheat with her finger. Therefore, the lady knows. Perhaps the cheat himself does not know that she knows. His face is averted and he looks unconcerned. A final and most important clue is that the third player does not look up from his cards at all. Therefore, the painter means us to think that he does not know what is going on. We conclude that he is the one who will be cheated, and he will lose the heap of coins that now lies in front of him.

In our understanding of the drama in the picture we indulge in a kind of unconscious mind reading. We freely assume that we can tell what the people depicted are thinking, what they know, and what they don't know. For instance, we tacitly infer that the lady *knows* what the cheat is up to. We also infer that the young man *does not know* what sinister event is unfolding. Our automatic inferences even extend to what kind of *emotional states* might arise in the characters (surprise, anger), but we are left in suspense as to what happens next. Will the lady challenge the cheat? Will she collude with him to defraud the young man? Will the young man be warned in time? The painter has led us to make only some attributions of mental states but he leaves the outcome open.

This lengthy piecemeal analysis is not how people usually come to coherent interpretations of states of mind. Instead the normal response is either an instant realization, or else a slow dawning of the truth. The relevant mental computations, however complex they may be, happen without us being aware of them. How strange that mind reading comes to us so easily, even when we are distant spectators and know nothing about the actual people portrayed. In fact we can't help attributing intentions, knowledge, and feelings to other people. By contrast, trying to analyze the painted surface of the canvas as a composition with shapes and colors is an effortful task that needs practice.

This is not the case for everybody. A.C., a young woman with high functioning autism, kindly allowed me to quote the following e-mail message. It reveals quite a different view.

> On the cover of your book there's a picture of some people playing cards. I remember looking at the picture for something like an hour, figuring out how smooth the pigments of the paints the artist [used] had to be, and the

quality of brushes, and how greatly developed the sub-economy of artists at that time must have been to demand that quality of painting and of reproduction of the actual textures of the fabrics in the characters' clothes, and of course this is the most obvious thing about the painting, the high realism and the skill of the artist, and then I read inside the book, and I was like, What the hell? There's this whole "soap opera" that the "normal" person is supposed to pick on first, and this person cheating, and that person knows, and that other person doesn't, etc. it's nuts!

This example illustrates the idea that people with autistic disorder are not automatically programmed to think about mental states, or to "mentalize." They find mentalizing, which comes unbidden to ordinary children and adults, plain weird. This is reminiscent of the case of color-blind people who realize that other people see the world in color, something that they cannot really imagine. Just so, people with autism cannot really imagine what it is like to automatically focus attention on people and constantly think about their mental states. In this sense they are mind-blind. Of course, it is just as difficult for us to imagine what it is like to be mind-blind as it is for the autistic person to imagine what it is like to be a mind reader. The example provided by A.C. suggests that mind blindness should not be seen in a purely negative light. It is at least debatable which is more appropriate when looking at a painting: creating a soap opera or deriving an objective analysis of the physical features of the painting?

Testing the Mind-blindness Hypothesis in Autism

Individuals with autism occasionally talk about their inability to understand the thoughts and feelings of other people. For instance, in a paper in 1983, Sir Michael Rutter referred to a young man who

> . . . complained that he could not mind-read. Other people seemed to have a special sense by which they could read other people's thoughts and could anticipate their responses and feelings; he knew this because they managed to avoid upsetting people whereas he was always putting his foot in it, not realising that he was doing or saying the wrong thing until after the other person became angry or upset.[2]

Even though quite difficult to grasp, and prone to misunderstandings, the notion of a lack of an everyday "theory of mind" in autism has become widely known and accepted. This is justified because a large body of empirical work now supports this hypothesis.[3] Many people find the mind-blindness hypothesis appealing as it explains many of the social and communication impairments in autism. We will consider this topic in the next chapter. Simon Baron-Cohen, in his monograph on "Mindblindness" sets out the theoretical and practical implications of the theory.[4] Here I want to convey just how radical the hypothesis is, and what implications it has for exploring the neural basis of autism.

Instead of the cumbersome and misleading term "theory of mind," I often use the made-up word "mentalizing." This term is also open to misunderstanding, but at least it does not carry with it the false connotation of a consciously held theory. Mentalizing is a verb to describe an automatic and deeply unconscious activity. It is what we do when we attribute mental states to others to predict their behavior. The question is what supports this activity in the normal case, and what makes it impossible or difficult to attain for individuals with autism. Obviously, for experiments, more precise questions are needed. For example, can children with autism attribute a belief to another person and predict their behavior accordingly? To be sure that this question is about a belief and not just about a real state of affairs, it is necessary to introduce a false belief, since a false belief is by definition different from reality.

This hypothesis was first tested at the beginning of the 1980s at the MRC Cognitive Development Unit in London, when John Morton became its director. Simon Baron-Cohen, at the time a PhD student, and Alan Leslie, at the time a postdoc, embarked on this quest with me. This enterprise was built on the then radical assumption that the mind of the infant is equipped from birth with mechanisms that accumulate knowledge about important features of the world. We assumed that even the newborn child has built-in expectations about objects and about people and responds to them differently. Alan Leslie called these mechanisms "engines" of development. Our idea was that theory of mind was critically based on such a mechanism and that, if this mechanism was not working, development would go wrong and autism would result.

Alan Leslie had the insight that the same mechanism was responsible for the ability to understand pretense.[5] This fitted well with the observation, then already known, that autistic children do not show spontaneous pretend play, an observation that Simon Baron-Cohen confirmed experimentally. Previously, the observation was ignored as insignificant compared to the other signs and symptoms of autism. Yet it was this observation that gave the initial impetus for the development of the mind-blindness hypothesis.

The Origin of Theory of Mind

This is how Alan Leslie starts the paper where he sets out to elucidate the origins of both pretense and theory of mind:

> Pretending ought to strike the cognitive psychologist as a very odd sort of ability. After all, from an evolutionary point of view, there ought to be a high premium on the *veridicality* of cognitive processes. The perceiving, thinking organism ought, as far as possible, to get things right. Yet pretense flies in the face of this fundamental principle. In pretence we deliberately distort reality. How odd then that this ability is not the sober culmination of intellectual development but instead makes its appearance playfully and precociously at the very beginning of childhood. . . . How is it possible for a child to think about a banana as if it were a telephone, a lump of plastic as if it were alive, or an empty soap dish as if it contained soap?[6]

This opening paragraph makes us aware that infants have to learn specifics about their world. They can do this because their brains are capable of forming copies, or *representations*, of people, things, and events. Representations bring the world into the mind. However, in the second year of life the infant appears to be able to go a step further, and can now form representations of what other people *intend* to communicate. The mind forms these powerful new representations through a presumably innate mechanism, which according to Leslie decouples representations from reality. When decoupled, the representations are no longer copies of the real world. Therefore, they can be attached to a person's wishes, thoughts, or memories. For instance, the child understands: mother *thinks* about the banana "*It is a telephone,*" and laughs.

Through decoupling, representations are free to be thought about in their own right and can be played with by the imagination. Given sufficient learning experience, the mentalizing mechanism enables the child to learn surprisingly fast about beliefs and deception. By the age of five the child will already have the beginnings of a fully fledged theory of mind. In autism, a failure in mentalizing could be due to a fault in the decoupling mechanism, and this would lead to an inability to learn mental state concepts in the normal way.[7]

An example conveys Leslie's idea of decoupling by likening it to the familiar activity of putting words into quotes. The film *Citizen Kane* contains the famous headline: *Candidate found in love nest with "singer."* Kane's plan to become Governor was ruined by this scandal. His friend observed that his life was subsequently devoted to removing the quotes from the word "singer." Kane tried to do this by turning the "singer" into a famous opera star. Predictably, he failed. As implied by the quotes, the girl was *not* a singer in any serious sense at all. Quotes act as signals of decoupling. They indicate that the criteria of reference, truth, and existence are suspended; "singer" no longer commits one to think that the person can really sing, but singer does. This difference is similar to the difference between primary representations and secondary representations. The example shows how easily the decoupled thought, freed from its normal duties of referring to reality, can become part of other thoughts and undergo an amazing change in meaning.

In the future, neuroscientists may be able to develop a model that would explain how neuronal activity in specific brain regions might lead to decoupling. If this were possible, we might begin to have the neural underpinnings of the extraordinary ability to realize that other people's thoughts are different from one's own.

The Sally–Anne Experiment

To test the prediction that children with autism would not understand that someone else can have a belief that is different from their own, an appropriate task was needed. A common feature in children's stories and puppet plays all over the world is the surprise created by one actor knowing something that another actor does not. For instance, Punch is hit over the head by Judy. This is funny because, unbeknown to Punch, Judy was coming up behind him with a rolling pin. Children from about age three watch such shows with every sign of apparent pleasure and anticipation. They know that something that a person has not seen cannot be in the mind of that person, and will therefore cause a surprise. If a child can implicitly take account of another person's thoughts, this kind of inference will be obvious.

This was the idea behind an ingenious method developed by Heinz Wimmer and Josef Perner for the study of the development of theory of mind in young children.[8] These authors established that children from age four onward were able to explicitly understand that another person can have a false belief and predict their behavior accordingly. Simon Baron-Cohen adapted their method for an experiment illustrated in figure 5.1.[9] With the help of two dolls, Sally and Anne, he acted out a little scenario: Sally has a basket and Anne has a box. Sally has a marble and she puts it into her basket. She then goes out. Anne takes out Sally's marble and puts it into her box while Sally is away. Now Sally comes back and wants to play with her marble. At this point we

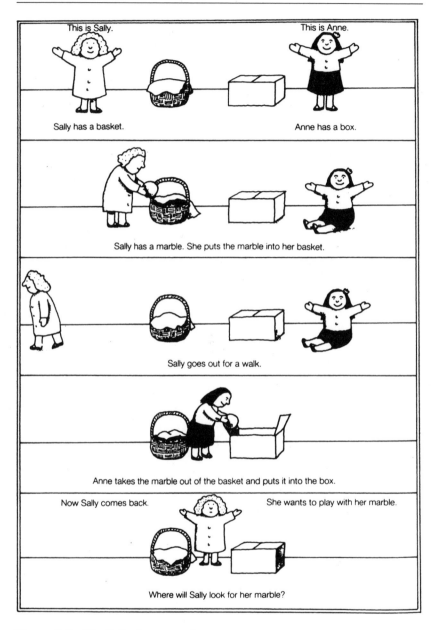

Figure 5.1 The Sally–Anne experiment

ask the critical question: "Where will Sally look for her marble?" The answer is, of course, "In the basket." This answer is correct because Sally has put the marble into the basket and has not seen it being moved. She *believes* the marble is still where she put it. Therefore she will look in the basket even though the marble is not there any more.

However, using this task with autistic children has many pitfalls. If they fail to understand that Sally has a false belief, it may be because of problems in general intellectual understanding or in memory. Further, it is necessary to investigate whether nonautistic learning-disabled children without social impairment would also be impaired in their ability to attribute mental states. If so, the task could not be used to test the mind-blindness hypothesis. We therefore decided to give the same task also to children with Down syndrome and to normal children who were much younger than the children with autism. All children had a mental age above three years.

The results were striking. Most of the young normal and Down children gave the correct answer, that is, they pointed to the basket. In contrast, all but a few of the children with autism got it wrong. They pointed to the box. This is where the marble really was, but where, of course, Sally did not know it was. They did not take Sally's own false belief into account.

The children who solved the problem also found it amusing. Some even started giggling as soon as Anne (naughty Anne!) transferred the marble to her own box. At once they anticipated what was coming and entered into the conspiracy of this little game. Some spontaneously made Sally say "Ooh – where's my marble gone?"

The failure of the children with autism to understand Sally's belief was remarkable, because they actually had a much higher mental age than the other children. Intellectually they were able to solve quite difficult logical problems. Yet they were not able to solve the apparently simple problem presented in the test. They remembered correctly where Sally put the marble, and they also answered correctly when asked, "Where is the marble really?" The difficulty resided in an implicit inference: if Sally did not see that the marble was transferred to the box, she must *still* believe that it is in the basket. This implicit inference did not seem a problem for most of the Down syndrome children, but it was for most of the much more able children with autism.

Could the results have been due to some hidden artefact? One such possibility is that developmentally advanced children with autism may be unwilling to attribute mental states to two wooden dolls, but would be willing to do so in the case of real people. This did not turn out to be the case when the test was arranged with real people taking over the role of Sally and Anne.[10]

For example, Alan Leslie ostentatiously gave me a coin and asked me to hide it in one of three places. I chose a special hiding place, asked the child to help me remember where I put the coin, and then left the room on some pretext. While I was out, Alan transferred the coin in a conspiratorial manner to another place. He could then, quite naturally, ask the child: where does Uta *think* the coin is? Has Uta *seen* what we did? Does Uta *know* that the coin is now here (pointing to its new place)? Lastly, he asked the same critical question as before, namely: where will Uta *look* for the coin when she comes back?

We found essentially the same results as before, that is, 15 out of 21 children with autism failed, and we could now be more certain. Some of the children who predicted wrongly where I would look for the coin also indicated that this was where I would *think* (or *know*) the coin was. This was despite the fact that they correctly indicated that I had *not seen* the transfer. In other words, they had not understood that in this case, *to see is to know* and *not to see is not to know*.

The Pencil in the Candy Box

One could argue that the problem is not necessarily to do with mentalizing, but with some other demands of the task. Perhaps the autistic children did not want to attribute a false belief to another person.

We checked this possibility in collaboration with Josef Perner and Susan Leekam. We used a task where the children themselves experience what it means to have a false belief. The experiment is illustrated in figure 5.2.[11] A candy container (a tube) which is well known to all British children was used in this test. All the children we tested expected Smarties (candy much like M & Ms) to be inside the box, and all were disappointed when a horrible little pencil fell out. Now the children with autism knew that there was a pencil in the box. When they were asked what a new child, who had just come to be tested for the first time, would say, they wrongly replied "a pencil."

The children who failed were quite aware that they themselves mistakenly thought that Smarties were in the box. They remembered what they said when asked. We can conclude that they did not fully understand *why* they had thought that there were Smarties. The reason is, of course, that the container *is* a Smarties tube and Smarties are justifiably expected to be inside. However, the children did not realize that someone else would make that same error for the same reason as they made it.

Figure 5.2 The Smarties task

Comic Strips for Behaviorists, Physicists, and Psychologists

Behaviorism is a form of psychological science that attempts to explain behavior without recourse to intervening inner states, whether conscious or unconscious. For students of behaviorism, just as for students of physics, mentalizing is irrelevant. For everyday psychology, on the other hand, behavior is almost

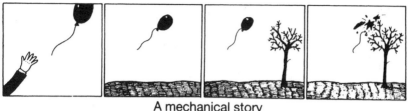

A mechanical story

A behavioral story

A mentalistic story

Figure 5.3 Three types of picture sequence

always explained by inner states. Are children with autism behaviorists? Do they think like physicists? To obtain evidence for this possibility, Simon Baron-Cohen carried out an experiment using strip cartoons of the kind illustrated in figure 5.3.[12] The same subjects as in the Sally–Anne experiment took part. The task was twofold. First, the children had to put the pictures in order so as to make up a story, with the first picture already in place. Second, the children had to tell the story in their own words.

From the ordering of the pictures it was possible to determine how well the intended story was understood, even in the absence of words. The words, however, gave more direct insight into what the child had understood the story to be. Specifically, if mentalizing is a problem for children with autism, then they should perform poorly only on the mentalistic-type stories, but not on the mechanical or behavioral ones. This was exactly what was found. A mechanical event as a story was perfectly understood by all the children with autism. Each of them ordered the pictures correctly. Moreover, they all used the right kind of language when telling the story, for instance: "The balloon burst *because* it was pricked by the branch," or "The tree *made* it burst."

A behavioral script can be told without reference to mental states. "A girl goes to a shop to buy some candy. She pays the shopkeeper and leaves with her candy." This way of ordering and telling a social routine was also well within the competence of the children with autism. Not so the mentalistic stories. The vast majority of the children with autism, although very able, just could not understand them. A mentalistic story only makes sense as a story if a state of mind is attributed to a protagonist. For instance: "A boy puts some chocolate into a box and goes out to play. While he is outside [the logic of mentalizing computes: without his knowing], an old lady (naughty!) eats the chocolate. When he comes back, he is *surprised* to find the box empty [the logic of mentalizing computes: he believed his chocolate to be still in the box]."

The mentalistic story is modeled entirely on the Sally–Ann experiment, and the same children who failed in that experiment also performed very poorly in this. They put the pictures in a jumbled order. Their "stories" were told without the attribution of mental states or appreciation of the naughtiness of eating the chocolate. For example: "A boy plays football. He puts some chocolate into a box. His mother eats the chocolate. He opens the box. It is empty."

The normal and Down syndrome children, of a lower mental age, outperformed the children with autism on mentalistic stories, in both ordering and talking about stories. They performed less well on the mechanical stories, and about equally on the behavioral ones. Thus children with autism appear to be better "physicists" and equally able "behaviorists," but poorer "psychologists." These results suggest that mentalizing demands a very different kind of ability from that involved in causal and mechanical thinking. However, does it really demand a different kind of ability, or could everything be explained in much more general terms?

False Photographs

The traditional idea that a set of conscious logical inferences governs our understanding of both social and nonsocial situations might still be correct. All the tasks we have discussed so far allow plenty of time for thinking about the answers. They do not convince skeptics that a special intuitive mentalizing mechanism comes into action. An ingeniously devised task gives us the opportunity to make a critical comparison between a false belief and a false depiction of reality. Just as a belief can become out of date, so can a depiction of a scene on a photo. According to the mentalizing view these should engage different mechanisms, but according to the traditional view both should be solved by similar mental operations. In other words, there should be no difference in how well these tasks are performed. Alan Leslie and Laila Thaiss used a task that was modeled closely on the Sally–Anne scenario, where an object is transferred from one place to another. Here the experimenter asked the child not about the content of Sally's mind (her false belief), but about the content of a photographic picture (a false depiction of reality). If mentalizing is triggered by the question about Sally's belief, but not by the question about the content of the photograph, then intuitive understanding of these two situations should have little in common. This was indeed the case.[13]

In figure 5.4[14] we see that a cat is placed on a chair and a Polaroid picture is taken. The picture, which shows the cat on the chair, is then put away, out of sight. Compare this to Sally leaving the room and going out of sight, while she has a mental picture of the marble in her basket. Next the experimenter moves the cat to another location. Compare this to Anne transferring the marble to another location. Now the experimenter asks, "In the photograph – where is the cat?" Compare this to the experimenter asking where Sally thinks the marble is. Sally has not witnessed the change of location, and her "mental picture" is still about the old state of affairs. The physical picture in the photo also still shows the old state of affairs. But here the similarities end.

As predicted from the mentalizing hypothesis, performance was very different in the two tasks. Children with autism, aged around 12 on average, understood perfectly the false photograph task but failed the Sally–Anne task. In contrast, normally developing children aged around four years understood the Sally–Anne task somewhat better than the photograph task. Hence, the difficulty in autism is not one of making inferences in general, but is very specifically to do with thinking about mental states. The same conclusion was also arrived at in experiments by Tony Charman and Simon Baron-Cohen,[15] and strengthened the idea that this mental mechanism acts like an independent module of the mind, and if so, should have a specific neural basis somewhere in the brain. A dysfunction of this neural basis might be the source of the failure in autism. This is utterly different from the idea that a failure in understanding mental states results from general problems to do with learning and experience.

Figure 5.4 The photograph task

Sabotage and Deception

It can still be argued that mentalizing is intrinsically a more difficult task and more likely to be misunderstood by children with autism. Scientific procedure demands that the traditional view of conscious processing using a multipurpose inference mechanism, rather than a specific mentalizing mechanism, should not be given up easily. We could imagine that failure on false belief tasks was due to not playing the game and not understanding, in very general terms, what the experimenter wants. A paradigm that tried to take care of this particular objection was devised by Beate Sodian, then a postdoc, who came to London to work with me on the following experiment.[16]

In this experiment the child was engaged in a competitive game with two puppets, a friendly rabbit and a thieving wolf. The child had to keep a reward, a piece of candy, safe in a box. If the rabbit got the candy, then the child would get two pieces of candy and was therefore told always to help the friendly rabbit. When the wolf got the candy, then the child got none and was therefore told never to help the thieving wolf. After some practice we found the children had no problem in telling who was friend and who was enemy. They also liked to get the reward and played to win.

The ingenious part of Beate Sodian's design is the comparison of two conditions. We called them sabotage (illustrated in fig. 5.5) and deception (illustrated in fig. 5.6). In the sabotage condition, a padlock and key were placed next to the box and the child could physically lock the box to prevent the thief from getting the candy. Of course, to play the game properly there were a number of trials and in half of them the child had to resist locking the box, because the friend was coming. All children, those with autism and those without autism, could do this task satisfactorily. Now, in the deception condition, there was no padlock, and the child had to use mental power to prevent the thief from getting the candy. This was in fact made easy by inviting the child to tell a lie. The wolf from afar said: "Is the box locked or is it open? I'm not bothering to come all that way if the box is locked." Nonautistic children gleefully replied, "The box is locked." Children with autism found it extremely hard to tell such a lie. Unlike the other children, they could not prevent the thief by mental manipulation from getting the candy, although they were easily able to prevent the thief by physical manipulation.

This experiment confirmed that the inability to attribute mental states to others cannot be explained away by a more general lack of understanding or an unwillingness to play the game. The failure of the autistic children was indeed a specific failure.

Recent Studies of Mentalizing

Since 1985 a large number of experiments have investigated mentalizing failure in individuals with autism. The results have not always been as

Figure 5.5   Sabotage

Figure 5.6 Deception

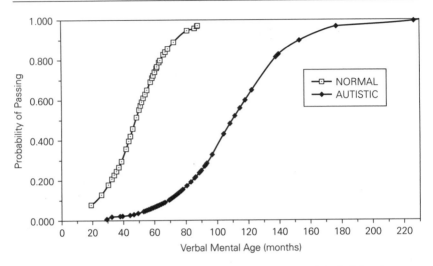

Figure 5.7   Relationship between verbal ability and passing false belief tasks
From F. Happé, *Child Development*, with kind permission

clear-cut as in the first experiments, and have sometimes even been contradictory. Francesca Happé, who has been my chief collaborator in the last
10 years, reviewed a large data set and found that the vast majority of normally developing children passed typical false belief tasks by the age of five, and
the majority of learning-disabled children by mental age five. In contrast, the
majority of children with autism spectrum disorder, however intelligent, did
not pass false belief tasks until a mental age of about 10 years, and often not
even then.[17] This is equivalent to a five-year developmental delay. The results
from Happé's review are shown in figure 5.7.

Clearly, mentalizing difficulties in autism should not be seen as a total
inability to acquire knowledge about mental states. Rather, these difficulties
are revealed in a severe developmental delay. This is compatible with the idea
that the mentalizing mechanism that normally allows fast-track learning
is missing. Slow learning over a span of five years, on the other hand, is
possible. This suggests that there are different ways to achieve successful
performance on mentalizing tests. Intuitive mentalizing ability may not be
necessary. One can learn about mental states through explicit rules of logic.
The question is whether this compensatory learning finishes up with the same
skill. This is unlikely, since knowledge about mental states that results from
compensatory learning remains fragile and results in frequent mistakes. Happé
constructed short stories that could only be understood if intentions and

beliefs were attributed to the story protagonists, and showed that these were still problematic even for those autistic individuals who can understand the Sally–Anne task.[18] An example of such a story is illustrated in chapter 11 (p.195).

Well-compensated individuals, who are knowledgeable about the role of inner states in principle, can fall to pieces under the stressful demands of real-life social situations. In the laboratory, where they are not usually under time pressure, they can often logically work out what the answer should be, even if they lack intuitive mentalizing. Again we are pointed toward a primary problem in the neural basis of mentalizing. The stories devised by Happé were used in one of the first neuroimaging studies of mentalizing with autistic adults of high ability. As discussed in chapter 11, the results showed an abnormal pattern of brain activation in this group.[19] This and other brain imaging studies give direct support for the idea that brain activity during mentalizing is weaker even in well-compensated autistic people than in normal people. So far, the mind-blindness hypothesis has only been strengthened by the challenge of imaging studies.[20]

An interesting problem for the mind-blindness hypothesis is reports of mentalizing failure in groups other than those affected with autism spectrum disorders.[21] It remains to be seen, however, whether other groups with developmental disorders, who show failure on false belief tasks, also show success on the type of control tasks that we have discussed. If they fail these too, then a more gobal cognitive deficit could be responsible. It is possible, however, that difficulties in the attribution of mental states occur in other clinical groups because they have brain abnormalities that are like those in autism with the same consequences for everyday-life social impairments. Intriguingly, schizophrenic patients with negative symptoms, who have social communication difficulties that resemble autism, tend to fail mentalizing tasks.[22]

The Evolution of Mentalizing

The work I have described supports the proposal that the brain has an innate mechanism for processing other people's mental states. The intuition that other people have minds, and that mental states are different from physical states, is after all an instinct. This is the opposite of the idea that social insight into other minds is a matter of years of learning and requires conscious thought. Only the case of autism, where this instinct may be missing, might be consistent with this idea. The effortless and obligatory nature of mentalizing, whether in real life, or when looking at a painting, watching a film, or reading a novel, is the hallmark of a hard-wired brain system. Living organisms need such systems to adapt to the world.

The ability to think about our own and other people's thoughts is of central importance for human interaction, for good or ill. It is fundamental to human communication, and therefore to human culture and civilization. When we speak, we strive to affect another person's understanding. We would not do this if we were not able to realize that our thoughts are different. On the other hand, social behavior such as mating, nurturing one's young, fighting for one's place in a hierarchy, is independent of mentalizing. It is still possible to argue that mentalizing makes these activities more rewarding for humans. The ability to take other people's thoughts into account can enhance even basic social actions. However, it cannot be denied that mentalizing has negative consequences as well: by being able to think about other people's mental states, a human being can deceive others and can persuade them to believe and do abhorrent things. By the same token, mentalizing failure in autism is not an unmitigated disaster.

Many animals appear to have brain mechanisms that are distantly related to mentalizing. The social brain is very old, and precursors of mentalizing are likely to be found.[23] Systems concerned with recognizing the identity of others, and one's relationships to others in terms of kinship or social hierarchy, are probably not the most direct precursors. Instead, systems responsible for the ability to discern actions of others and to understand the goal of an agent, are probably more relevant. Animals can distinguish friend and foe, prey and predator. Still, none of these social accomplishments involves mentalizing.

Many researchers claim that mentalizing is not available even to our closest primate relatives, the great apes, who are known to lead complex social lives. They are unlikely to be aware of mental states. It is possible, however, that they can to some extent perceive inner intentions and desires, not just simple goals of actions. This ability would help explain the admittedly rare observations on deception in these creatures.

The search for the physiological underpinning of our perception of goal-directed behavior has recently been advanced by the Italian neuroscientists Giacomo Rizzolatti, Vittorio Gallese, and their colleagues.[24] They observed that certain neurons in monkey brains were active and produced electrically recordable impulses, not only whenever the monkey grasped an object in a certain way, but also when the monkey saw someone else grasp an object in the same way. These cells were called mirror cells, for obvious reasons. They are acutely sensitive to the type of action performed, but appear indifferent to who is doing the action. However, this distinction may not be necessary for the perception of goals.

Human brains also have mirror neurons. It is reasonable to speculate that they are a precursor of mentalizing. Mentalizing, however, also needs a component that distinguishes the intentions of the self from those of the other. Such cells have been identified in other parts of the monkey brain. For instance, some neurons respond only to those sounds that a monkey makes itself, and other cells only to sounds made by others. One may speculate that a link between these specialized cells and mirror cells could be an important step toward the building of a mentalizing system. But this is not enough. The mentalizing mechanism in the human brain is sensitive to other people's invisible inner states, not just their visible actions and audible speech. What is the neural basis of this mechanism? The full history of the evolutionary origin of mentalizing ability in the human brain remains to be discovered.

The mind-blindness hypothesis has enormous implications for the diagnosis and treatment of autism. It can also provide a framework for a deeper understanding of the social and communication impairments in autism. Just as it is possible to make allowances for people who can't see color, so it is possible to make allowances for people who can't read minds, once the impairment is recognized. We will consider these questions in the following chapters.

chapter 6

Autistic Aloneness

It makes me very sad because I am getting older and older and I continue not to meet anyone. Perhaps someone reading this could get in touch with me. I hope someone that can offer me some love and affection will get in touch. Living is more or less one constant bore. Yes, I think anyone normal would find it hard to lead the kind of existence I have. I think if some normal girl would take an interest in me I would just bother with her and no other girl, but I spend my time talking to a lot of girls, hoping I can find one that will take a real interest.

This extract ends David's 100-page autobiography, which he hopes will help him find a companion. But how is he different from the thousands of lonely hearts who might have written very similar words? When explaining the reason for the social impairment in autism, we need to go beyond the ordinary concepts of sociability.

Social Competence and Social Ineptness

David shows the effects of autistic aloneness, and not for lack of wanting companionship. What is the nature of this aloneness and what causes it? Social behavior and emotional relationships involve many different components, so that it is difficult to define social competence even in normal individuals. Surface behavior is not a useful guide here. If it were, we would have to attribute social impairment to those people who display little outward affection, and who react to their own feelings and to the feelings of others with a "stiff upper lip." We might also be misled into attributing warm, affectionate relationships to those who are only play-acting. Instead, we know with Hamlet that "one may smile, and smile, and be a villain." Sophisticated social competence includes telling the difference between posing, acting, and really meaning it. It also includes the art of being a recluse and the skill of keeping others at a distance if necessary. The loneliness of autism is something different altogether. It demands a circumspect approach.

One approach is to use standardized interviews with parents or teachers who know the child well. The Vineland Adaptive Behavior Scales contain questions that are appropriate for different ages across a large range of social skills. Fred Volkmar and his colleagues at Yale used these scales with a sample of autistic and nonautistic children, all with a degree of learning disability.[1] The autistic children were not impaired equally across all categories of social behavior, but showed a wide scatter. They were by no means devoid of social interest or responsiveness. However, they were different from the nonautistic children, although these too showed their share of social impairment. In self-care and simple daily living skills, the children with autism did rather well, sometimes better than their peers. However, in interpersonal communication the autistic children came out much worse. They were rated poorly at sharing and cooperating, apologizing, making and keeping appointments, borrowing and returning, controlling impulses, and responding appropriately to familiar and unfamiliar people. Deficits in the area of interpersonal relationships were so marked that the group with autism on average was functioning four years below what would be expected from their mental age level. What is it that causes this severe incapacity in social relations?

Fran Siddons and Francesca Happé, working with me, also used the Vineland Scales, but this time a specific hypothesis guided the research.[2] Our hypothesis was that autistic aloneness was caused by the inability to attribute mental states to others. To pursue this hypothesis we asked questions about two kinds of social behavior: behavior that did and behavior that did not depend on thinking about mental states. One question for an older age group was, "Does he/she (ever) choose a present that is just right for a particular person?" To choose an appropriate present for someone requires the awareness that another person's wishes are different from your own. Another question was, "Does he/she (ever) try to please the teacher?" To please the teacher you just have to behave in a way that was previously rewarded, and therefore this sort of awareness is not required. Here is another example: "Does he/she (ever) successfully play hide and seek?" Success in this game does require taking account of what other people think: you should choose a hiding place that the seeker will not think of straight away; at the very least you should not give away where you are, for instance, by making a noise. On the other hand, there are other games, such as dominoes, which you can play successfully without taking into account what another player is thinking.

The results confirmed the hypothesis. The nature of the social difficulties in autism, as assessed by the questionnaire, seemed to be strongly related to the inability to take into account that other people know and believe different things, assessed by artificial tests in the laboratory. The failure to mentalize, a highly theoretical concept, as tested by Sally–Anne and Smarties tasks (see chapter 5), could be linked directly with everyday life. Children with autism, as compared to a control group, were impaired precisely on those everyday activities that required thinking about the content of other minds. Furthermore, even those few children who were able to pass the Sally–Anne task in the laboratory still failed in everyday social situations. Perhaps this is because they could think about other people's thoughts when given enough time, but the speed of normal social interactions is too fast for the application of logic. Yet the speed is not too fast for the automated responses of ordinary children.

Much of normal social interaction seems to be characterized by an intuitive grasp of mental states, but there are also other aspects of social life that do not depend on it. How do these different aspects of social understanding normally develop? How do young children learn to become socially skilled human beings?

Social Responsiveness in Normal Development

Infants from a remarkably early age show various kinds of social responsiveness, which do not depend on the intuition that other people have minds.[3] The social smile emerges at around six weeks of age, but a preference for human faces and voices exists already from birth. It takes somewhat longer for the infant to distinguish individuals by looking at their faces. A dramatic demonstration of facial discrimination occurs when the infant shows fear of strangers, usually at eight months. Fear of strangers implies more than the ability to discriminate between different people. It also implies attachment to certain familiar people. No wonder the distress of their baby at the sight of unfamiliar faces is reassuring to parents: it is the sign of a special emotional bond. From six months infants indulge in social games. They will greet their mother in the morning; they will stretch out their arms, anticipating being picked up; they will mold their body to her and make joyful sounds. But they may well stiffen and turn away if someone unfamiliar wants to cuddle them. Of course, these are general trends. Everyone will have observed that not all babies are alike in their social responsiveness. There are the real charmers who turn on smiles to initiate as many interactions with as many people as possible, and there are the shy ones who look away and cry when others wish to engage them in a game.

Unequivocal signs of the implicit awareness that other people are beings with their own intentions can be observed in babies after the first year. At first babies are unable to follow a pointing gesture when distractors are present and when the object pointed at is outside their view. However, this changes between the ages of 9 and 15 months, and evidence for joint attention, for deliberate imitation, and for the ability to communicate with others becomes plentiful.[4] A "cognitive revolution" is set in motion from about 18 months.

Joint attention

Joint attention refers to a common enough phenomenon. Typically, mother and child coordinate their gaze, and presumably their attention, toward one and the same object. It also refers to the automatic tendency to look where another person is looking or pointing. What is so special about this? The amazing thing is that the baby is interested not simply in the object. The baby is interested in another person's attitude to the object!

Attending to the object that another person is also attending to is a major developmental milestone, which presents the child with a multitude of learning opportunities.[5] When children look at the same object that another person is looking at, they are not only sharing another person's interest, they also get clues about the other person's feelings. Why is mother making a worried face when looking at the pretty glass bauble? Because she fears the baby might break it and get hurt. Before approaching a strange novel object, babies aged eight months deliberately look at their mother to check whether she expresses fear or pleasure before advancing further. In this way babies can avoid danger and learn by proxy. With intuitive mentalizing learning from others is easy: when we look in the direction where another person is looking or pointing, we are likely to find something of interest. Normal children accumulate tacit knowledge that is continually being updated as they seek to share mental states with their peers and elders. They do not need to make all their own mistakes, any more than they need to develop their own language.

Normal 10-month-old children begin to point out things with a charmingly outstretched finger even before they use their first words. Again this is an activity that involves an implicit awareness of other people's mental states. They direct other people's attention to the object they have in mind. But the aim is not to obtain the object. What typically happens in early pointing is that children indicate something that is relevant not only to them but also to the person they are communicating with. The partner reciprocates with a statement that reinforces mutual comprehension, for instance, "Yes, you have a penguin just like that one." This is an example of true communication and is immensely rewarding.

In the mid-1980s, Marian Sigman, Peter Mundy, and their colleagues at UCLA, and Katherine Loveland and Susan Landry at the University of Texas, made the fundamental discovery that the sharing of attention in pointing and showing, but also later in speech, is absent in children with autism.[6] For instance, when autistic and nonautistic children were observed with their mothers in a room full of toys, the autistic children showed the toys they played with to their mothers far less often than did nonautistic, but learning-disabled, children of the same mental age.[7] The lack of joint attention in autism is strongly evident during the preschool years.[8] It is not yet known whether and how changes occur with increasing age. Children with autism can point to objects when they want them, but this is another form of pointing – so-called instrumental pointing. They can indicate when they want a broken toy mended, showing awareness of a source of help, but they do not indicate to their mother what toy they remember or like. We can hypothesize that young autistic children make no distinction between what is in their own mind and what is in anybody else's mind. Thus for them the question of sharing the content does not arise. For this reason, the mother of a child with autism has to work hard to share in her child's inner world.

Maturation has visible effects on body proportions and the increasingly skillful execution of movements. Even though invisible, brain maturation has profound effects on behavior. Environment, learning, and experience too have left their mark and influence the nature and timing of the developmental progress. However, sooner or later, every child reaches a point when babyhood is left behind. If all goes well, a different, more socially knowing human being emerges. Among other brain systems that may make a leap in development at this time, I assume that the mentalizing mechanism, which was the subject of discussion in the previous chapter, is now fully ready for almost continuous action.

What are the consequences of this readiness? It is arguable what takes precedence: is it the explosion of language, the flowering of imaginative play, or the dawn of peer interactions? All these accomplishments benefit from the fact that children are now able to attribute thoughts and wishes to others and to themselves. If their mentalizing mechanism is working in automatic mode, then attending to a speaker's intention will put them on the right track for learning what words mean. They will also be able to share the make-believe world of play with others. Their social interactions gain force as they realize that what they wish and what others wish may not always be the same. In time, this implicit insight will give them the impetus for learning about social negotiation and manipulation. Without a properly working mentalizing mechanism, children with autism would have to miss out on the revolutionary changes that happen in social understanding between the first and second year of life.

Autism and Learning to be Social

We still know little about the social responsiveness of infants later diagnosed as autistic. As we have already discussed in chapter 1, social impairment is not obvious early in life and still awaits more refined measures than are currently available. Children who are later diagnosed as autistic are often distinguishable with hindsight. These children showed less eye contact and fewer social smiles, and they responded far less than normal children to their name being called. Nevertheless, early signs of sociability are by no means absent in all autistic children, and at least some show quite normal social interaction in the first year of life. They smile and babble like other children, and they look pleased to see their parents. Some even stretch out their arms to be picked up and play peek-a-boo games. None of these social interactions actually require mental state attributions.

Not just at six months, or at 18 months, but throughout development, social behavior shows dramatic changes. Remarkable changes also occur in the social behavior of children with autism. In early childhood, between three and five years, the isolation of the child with autism from the world of others is probably at its height. "She is always looking through people," "He never even glanced at his new baby sister," are typical remarks from parental accounts. Delayed or absent language is a strong impediment to attempts at socialization. Furthermore, social praise and disapproval are more difficult to apply than they are with normal children. Mind blindness means that children with autism are not able to judge the intention behind these common controls of behavior. For instance, they may be miserable over a petty reprimand ("Your fingers are sticky") and ignore an important one ("Get out of the road!").

After age five autistic children often show marked improvement in social skills and general adaptation. Indeed, during the whole of their development, children with autism show improvements in socialization. Yet being unable automatically to attribute mental states to other people means that learning to behave appropriately toward others is slow. Compensatory learning means that parents and teachers have to direct many specific lessons to instilling social dos and don'ts in children with autism. Yet sometimes they might wish that the maxims were not learned as well as they are! There are, after all, cases where being polite is actually an insult ("Thank you for a delightful dinner" when it was an acknowledged disaster), and where behavior normally frowned upon becomes the right thing to do. From anecdotal evidence it seems that even able autistic people have trouble making such subtle distinctions.

What is it that travels between ordinary people and is observed by ordinary children who can easily pick up social knowledge? It hits us through all the senses we have available. Language may be the most obvious channel, but it is certainly not the only one. The human face, eyes, and hands are all sending signals that are vital in our social life.

What We See in Other People

Faces

One of the many implicit accomplishments that human beings have is the ability to remember thousands of faces. It is important for our social life to remember other people and to store relevant knowledge about them. Experiments have shown that people with autism cannot remember faces as well as they can remember buildings or landscapes.[9] In some sense one might wonder whether people with autism suffer from people blindness as well as mind blindness. This is not a far-fetched hypothesis. A neurophysiological study by Robert Schultz and colleagues at Yale has demonstrated that the part of the brain that is normally specialized for faces is not specialized in autistic people. Here then is a biological basis for poor face recognition. However, as Schultz points out, the lack of brain specialization may be itself a consequence of something else. For instance, if young children with autism do not look at people's faces, then the specialization cannot develop.[10] Intriguingly, children with Williams syndrome, a rare genetic disorder with repercussions on brain development, have excellent people perception and a strong interest in social contact from early childhood. They provide a mirror image to autism.[11]

Eyes

Within the face it is the eyes that provide the most important social cues. A well-known saying has it that the eyes are the windows of the soul. There are pleading and imploring looks, triumphant looks, glaring looks, looks that could kill, looks that mock, and looks that seduce: the list is as long as social relationships are varied. The meaning of these looks lies in shared mental states. If there were no mental states, then the language of the eyes would be exceedingly impoverished.

Clearly, without the intuitive ability to attribute mental states to others, a language of the eyes would be meaningless. In autism, the inability to understand other minds is deeply linked to abnormalities in the use and interpretation of eye gaze.[12] This idea was first proposed by Simon Baron-Cohen, who has used it as a basis for an advanced test of mentalizing. A set of 36 photographs of male and female actors showing only the eye region is presented and the subject has to evaluate the expression by choosing one of four descriptions, for example, serious, ashamed, alarmed, bewildered. Reading the mind from the eyes in this test is easy for most normal adults, but difficult even for those autistic individuals who are otherwise well compensated.[13]

Observing the direction of a person's gaze from a distance is a useful tool for tracking their inner intentions. This tool is built into our nervous system.[14] Normal children and adults are automatically attracted to look in the same direction as another person. Experiments have shown that subjects can be primed to look more quickly in a particular direction if a pair of eyes looking that way flashes up briefly beforehand. They are slower to look when the eyes flash up in the opposite direction.[15] No doubt, noises in the environment, and particularly speech, may have similar effects on orienting. It is conceivable that the normally built-in orienting mechanisms may not be working in the case of autism.

Researchers have also realized that eye gaze can reveal children's thoughts. Experiments have shown that normal children automatically gaze at the right place while being told a story along the lines of the Sally–Anne test. This is not the case for autistic children. Eye gaze turns out to be a better measure of mentalizing ability than the standard verbal response, and is even more discriminating between autistic and nonautistic mentally handicapped children.[16]

If children with autism cannot automatically decode the meaning of eye gaze, then ordinary silent messages sent by their peers and carers are likely to be ignored or mistaken. Teachers of autistic children are often seated side by side with their pupils and even stand behind them. This indirect approach acknowledges misunderstandings in the use of eye gaze and neatly avoids them. Would it be wise to use the same precaution for the gestures we perform with our hands to communicate?

Hands

One of the most poignant observations that is quoted almost universally in descriptions of childhood autism is that the children use an adult, or an adult's hands, as a tool. They may lead an adult to an object they want and place the hand of the adult on the object.

A classic example is given in the first report about the "wild boy of Aveyron," the case discussed in chapter 3. This report was written in January 1800 by Constans Saint-Estève, the commissioner for the district where the boy was found. "When he became thirsty, he looked left and right; spotting a pitcher, without making the least sign, he took my hand in his and led me to it; then he struck the pitcher with his left hand, thus asking me for something to drink."[17]

The strangeness and poverty of gestures in children with autism has been the subject of a number of systematic studies, both experimental and observational. As part of his PhD thesis, Tony Attwood discovered that there are certain gestures that children with autism are very adept at handling.[18] The common feature of this class of gestures is that they have an instrumental purpose. That is, they are designed to make someone else do something. Figure 6.1 shows examples. Autistic children with a wide range of intellectual abilities respond to all four illustrated instrumental gestures appropriately and spontaneously. Normal five-year-old children also use them, as do children with Down syndrome.

Taking just this result, one might conclude that when children with autism interact with each other they use gestures like everybody else. This would be quite wrong. We have considered only instrumental gestures so far. This type is used for a kind of communication that we can refer to as bare communication. Bare communication exists, but is completely different from ordinary communication, where information is constantly evaluated for its intended meaning. The instrumental message "go away" is like pressing a button. Its sole purpose is to make the person leave. Actually, a button would be preferable, just as in the film *Being There*, where the autistic hero carries with him a television remote control which he aims at people in the street. However, in real life, bare messages, suitable for button-pressing, are rare. Their inflexibility is often a source of annoyance. Who has not been frustrated by the telephone message that asks you to press specific numbers for specific prerecorded messages that never quite meet your need, or by the cash machine that fails because you mistyped your code.

Figure 6.1 Instrumental gestures

What is it that makes us prefer normal human communication to potentially efficient button-press type interactions? We clearly get more from normal communication, which is also called intentional or ostensive communication. We look to see whether behind the words "go away" there is an apology, a challenge, or an open attack. "Push off," "get lost," "just leave me alone," "please move a bit," "I'm very busy just now" are examples of utterances that can verbally embody the request to go away. In the case of bare messages there is only room for obeying or defying the request as formulated. In the different shades of intentional messages there is room for compromise. For instance, if somebody said to me, "Never darken my door again," I would probably ignore the actual request, and treat it as a joke. But

Figure 6.2 Expressive gestures

first I would try to find out why the utterance was made at all, and base my reaction on my inference.

Ordinary communication also uses another class of gestures, and these are often called expressive gestures. Examples are shown in figure 6.2. Unlike *instrumental* gestures, *expressive* gestures convey states of mind. They deliberately convey feelings one has about something. For instance, one may be embarrassed about seeing somebody else behaving in a silly way and deliberately show this feeling in a gesture of embarrassment. Other examples are demonstrations of friendship, offerings of goodwill, and threatening gestures. In Tony Attwood's study no autistic child showed such a gesture during the observation periods – while every Down syndrome child did. We need to address the question of feelings, both simple and sophisticated, more directly.

Emotions

Attachment

Kanner originally suggested that autistic children were born "with an innate inability to form the usual biologically provided affective contact with people."[19] This hypothesis remains attractive because it takes seriously the indefinable emotional quality of normal personal relationships, a quality that is felt to be missing in autism. Some people take it for granted that early bonding and attachment formation is missing in children with autism, and that this lack is the purest manifestation of their core symptoms. Yet others believe that early bonding failure is the cause of their later problems in relating to people. But do autistic children actually fail to bond with their mothers? Consider the following evidence.

A rich paradigm in developmental and clinical psychology is based on the "stranger reaction." In this paradigm, there is an initial free play period with mother and child. Then the mother leaves for a brief interval and sometimes a stranger stays with the child. Lastly, the mother returns. During the reunion period the effects of attachment are shown by a marked increase in the child's spontaneous interactions with the mother. Distress reactions are typically observed at the mother leaving, as well as pleasure at her return.

The stranger reaction paradigm has been applied in autistic children between two and five years old. They were compared with learning-disabled children without autism who were of the same mental age. These two groups reacted in the same way when the child was left with a stranger and when the mother returned. They all showed a significant increase in social responses directed toward their mother at the reunion stage. This study provides further evidence of positive social responses in young children with autism.[20] An awareness of mental states is not required for attachment behavior.

Recognizing emotional expressions

The study of emotions in autism has been slow and confusing. And no wonder, it is a complex field where methodology lags woefully behind the questions we would like to ask. The London-based psychiatrist Peter Hobson was among the first to suggest that autistic children may lack the basic capacity to interpret emotions. If they cannot read even basic feelings expressed in faces or in voices, then this alone might be sufficient reason for their autistic aloneness. Hobson tested this possibility in a number of ingenious experiments.[21] In one study he portrayed the emotions happy, sad, angry, and afraid, by means of a video film, and asked children to match them up across different modes of presentation. For instance, the child had to say which of four faces went with which of four sound recordings, all expressing these emotions. Other tasks involved matching faces with situations in a video sequence, and again with body postures. The children with autism were in their teens, with mental age averaging 10 years on a test of nonverbal ability. Roughly two-thirds of these children were poor at emotion matching. In contrast, almost all normal and mildly retarded children of the same nonverbal mental age performed without errors.

Is there then a primary impairment in emotion processing in autism? It is possible. However, the impairment found in Hobson's studies could also be secondary to mind blindness. It is possible that the children were not aware that particular feelings can be portrayed and enacted in different ways. Precisely such a lack of awareness could be a consequence of the inability to attribute mental states to themselves and others. Furthermore, mind blindness could lead to a poor conception of feeling states, just as it leads to a poor conception of other mental states, such as beliefs. In this case, the deliberate display of feelings and their distinctive expression in voice, face, and gesture would be meaningless. Children with autism of a higher verbal mental age have better recognition of emotions, just as they have better understanding of mental states.

Expressing emotions

To date a number of studies have addressed the recognition of emotion in autism, but what about the expression of emotions? It has often been remarked that people with autism have few facial expressions, a wooden or stiff body posture, and frequently a monotonous voice. Many observers agree that there is some dysfunction, lack of regulation, or modulation that diminishes the emotional expressiveness of people with autism.

The lack of appropriate emotional responsiveness in their child is a distressing aspect for the family. We are not, however, talking about an absence of affect. Basic emotions that are instinctive reactions to pain or pleasure are certainly expressed by children with autism, for instance, in the delight in rough-and-tumble play, or in angry tantrums. At all ages extreme moods of happiness, distress, frustration, fury, or panic can be observed. However, individuals with autism are capable of subtle moods too. For instance, Elly Park shows fine-grained emotional reactions to light and number patterns.[22]

Observations are different when it comes to the class of special emotions that are abundant in normal social communication that presupposes an awareness of other minds. Obviously these would be difficult to experience or understand if you were mind-blind. They include pride and embarrassment, haughty disdain and humble modesty; they include exuberance at others' success or glee at others' failure, and insatiable curiosity in other people's affairs. People with autism tend to find these social emotions puzzling, and need to have them explained in detail. As normally developing children grow up they are exposed to these emotions, and learn about them, but they certainly do not need formal teaching. This is different for autistic children. Many emotional expressions are culturally coded. For instance, the display of delight is different in Italian compared to, say, Swedish. These expressions can be taught explicitly. Autistic children can learn these codes, but learning is slow and difficult, by all accounts.

A study by Marian Sigman and her colleagues illustrates the difference between the two types of emotions in autism.[23] Autistic and nonautistic children alike showed visible pleasure in mastering a new skill. However, the visible pride of nonautistic children was manifested by them turning around to monitor the audience's reaction. This kind of showing off is an emotion that implies an awareness of other people's attitudes toward you. Unlike simple emotions that just spill out, it is communicated deliberately and is a speciality of those who need to impress others.

The different meanings of empathy

The question of how autistic people understand and express emotions is highly relevant to their daily interactions with others. Problems are to be expected, and among these a lack of empathy is a particularly uncomfortable possibility. Do individuals with autism lack the ability for empathy? And does empathy require the ability to attribute mental states?

But first, what do we mean by empathy? At the least we should distinguish instinctive and intentional empathy. In the first edition of this book I used the terms sympathy and empathy to distinguish these concepts. Instinctive sympathy, accompanied by autonomic responses, is a basic emotional response that just spills out, and is *not* dependent on the ability to mentalize. Many people with autism have the capacity for these responses and are not indifferent to other people's distress. Brain-imaging studies have shown that emotional expressions of fear and sadness are registered even without awareness.

Intentional empathy, however, does require an ability to mentalize, and is thus dependent on the instinctive orientation to other people's mental states. This is the way in which Baron-Cohen uses the term "empathizing" when characterizing social impairments in autism (see chapter 9). This type of empathy is linked to understanding the reasons for another person's sadness or fear, and with the appropriate response. The appropriate response depends on the situation and this is precisely where a theory of mind comes into its own. This is not an occasion for fixed rules. In one case, the appropriate empathetic response may be turning away and leaving the distressed person alone; in another case, it may be giving comfort by word or deed; and in yet another situation the appropriate response may be to join in with outrage.

Instinctive sympathy and the implicit feeling of pity are not a precondition for intentional empathy, but the ability to attribute mental states is. When you can attribute mental states, you will be able to understand and can give the right response, even if you do not feel actual distress at the other person's misfortune. On the other hand, when you cannot readily and consistently attribute mental states to others, then you will be lost as to how to respond, even if you feel sympathy for the person. In this case other people may wrongly think you are callous.

Autistic individuals can be profoundly upset by the idea of suffering, and they can show righteous indignation. The case of the prison reformer, John Howard, who may have had Asperger syndrome (see chapter 3), strikingly demonstrates this. One young man with Asperger syndrome, seeing a girl roughly treated, attacked her escort, with painful consequences for himself. When the difference between own and other minds can be ignored, autism is no barrier to feeling a similar emotion. If a newsreader says, "These people suffer from unrelenting hunger," then Jack – without needing to take into account states of mind – feels genuine compassion. He too has suffered from hunger and knows its effects. Another kind of sympathy might be an automatic mimicry of another's perceived emotion. This is seen in infectious laughter and infectious crying, and is not unlike the infectious yawn. As yet nobody has tested whether there is evidence of such emotional mimicry in children with autism.

Autism vs psychopathy

James Blair, who started as a PhD student at the MRC Cognitive Development Unit in London, postulated that the brain system that normally enables instinctive empathy, just like the brain system underlying mentalizing, is vulnerable and can therefore develop faults. In such a case an individual would lack the ability to feel instinctive sympathy. Blair built on evidence that certain emotional expressions trigger innate brain mechanisms, located in circuits involving the amygdala. These circuits can become active in quite subtle situations. For instance, you are predisposed to feel uncomfortable if shown a picture of a face expressing sadness or fear. In real life, you might be quick to react by stopping what you are doing, possibly running away. Such alarm signals have a long evolutionary history. Recognition of certain stimuli is built into the brain in many animal species, not just in humans. When this brain system is not working properly, then one or all of these instinctive responses will be impaired. One might think that this should not matter for humans because we now have alternative means of communication. However, the consequences for emotional development may be devastating.

What would be the consequence for development in the case of a fault in the instinctive sympathy circuit? According to Blair, such children would find it difficult to learn moral imperatives, such as not to hurt others, and would be unable to distinguish between more or less arbitrary laws that govern social conventions, and other laws that are motivated by a deeper moral sense. These two kinds of law are not usually distinguished explicitly. However, a test in story format demonstrates that normal children as young as three years are able to tell the difference. They can indicate that if permission is given it is all right to break a conventional social rule (talking in class), but not all right to break a rule that prevents harm being done to others (hitting another child). Their responses show that they assume this rule cannot be suspended, even with permission. Children with psychopathic tendencies, as well as adult psychopaths, were unable to make this distinction.

Psychopaths lack instinctive sympathy, but they have excellent mentalizing skills. Thanks to their intuitive ability to attribute mental states, they can even feign empathy if they wish. However, they feel no guilt at having caused harm to another person. Instead they hold the other person responsible. For instance, after savagely beating a young boy who was in his way, a man simply said, "He had it coming to him; he should have moved." Not all people with an inability to feel instinctive empathy are excessively violent. If they have no motive to offend, then no harm may come to others. However, individuals who perpetrate violence without pity or remorse are rightly feared as dangerous. From this point of view, and contrary to popular opinion, psychopathy is not caused by a violent upbringing and is not the same as being a violent type. A violent person may still have instinctive sympathy responses to the distress of a victim. Psychopaths, on the other hand, remain unmoved. They have a malfunction of the specific brain circuits that normally come into action at the signs of distress in others. Blair points out that throughout the animal kingdom an instinct will often stop an aggressor from killing a member of its own species. The attacker withdraws on perceiving submission cues from a conspecific. In human beings, these cues are expressions of sadness and fear.

How do individuals with psychopathy compare to individuals with autism? Blair showed clear differences in a number of experiments. Children with psychopathic tendencies, who were educated at special schools because of severe behavior problems, were not only very good at mental state attribution, but even superior to children of the same mental age.[24] On the other hand, individuals with psychopathy failed to react with increased arousal when shown faces expressing sadness or fear. In contrast, individuals with autism showed the same pattern of increased arousal as normal children.[25] Furthermore, they were able to make the distinction between moral and conventional rules in the story task, which the children with psychopathic tendencies failed to do.[26] Since it is possible to sustain abnormalities in more than one brain system, there are individuals who lack both the ability to empathize and the ability to mentalize.

The conclusion from Blair's work is clear. Autism and psychopathy are two different disorders. Failure of mentalizing does not necessarily entail failure of instinctive sympathy.

Communicating Mental States in Everyday Life

For clarity, I have frequently separated the ability to attribute mental states to others from the ability to understand and express basic emotions. However, this should not be taken to imply that mentalizing has nothing to do with the emotional aspects of social interactions. Emotional experiences are part and parcel of the dynamism of all our thought processes. Emotions of all shades constantly accompany our actions and most of the states we attribute to ourselves and others have to do with feelings about things, events, and people.

Let us consider an everyday example involving Lucy, a teenager, and her friends. When Lucy meets Jane, she exchanges remarks about the weather. Is this to do with emotions? Very likely, yes. While talking about the weather, Lucy and Jane really convey something else to each other (Thinks: "I am in a friendly mood and I like talking to you, particularly if it is not about a real problem!").

Paul now appears, but Lucy does not talk to him about the weather or anything else, thus giving a pointed message (Thinks: "You are in my bad books. I hope you notice that I'd rather not talk to you just now"). While Paul goes away, in his hearing Lucy says to Jane, "Have you heard that Mrs Wood is getting married again?" (Thinks: "Paul is really going to be shocked now. Serves him right").

When Lucy interacts with her autistic sister, Jennifer, expectations are entirely different. She avoids remarks about the weather since they would induce Jennifer to talk about her special "hobby." Jennifer records daily temperature, air pressure, and rainfall. If Lucy were to say casually, "It's incredibly warm today," Jennifer might reply, "It is not warmer than yesterday. At my last reading it was 28.1 degrees Celsius, yesterday's temperature was 28.3 degrees. . . ." This could lead to a tedious conversation.

Lucy cannot really gossip with Jennifer, only exchange information. For Jennifer, information is received and given away indiscriminately and without considering any effects, such as hurting or pleasing somebody by giving this information. She does not know what it means to keep a secret and would not imagine that Paul could be shocked at a piece of information that he overhears. It is puzzling to her that a simple statement of truth might hurt others. "Aunt Doreen shaved her moustache" was a remark that was not welcome at her aunt's engagement party. Yet it was just an observation of Jennifer's, not at all calculated to cause embarrassment.

The emotional life of people with autism is very likely to be different from normal. Yet it is tempting to project on them our own emotions, often inappropriately. It is only right to acknowledge that some individuals with autism are happy to be left alone to indulge in their solitary activities. Many would never spontaneously seek social contact. Young children with autism seldom run to be hugged when they need comfort and many appear to dislike bodily contact. Roberta, a highly intelligent adult with autism, forcefully articulates that she wishes to be by herself and not to share a home with anybody else. She is content and pities people like David, who crave the company of a girlfriend, but cannot attain it. Her example shows that being alone and autistic is not necessarily a bleak state.

chapter 7
The Difficulty of Talking to Others

A Conversation

Ruth is a pretty, 17-year-old girl with ash-blonde hair. She attends a special school for children with autism and is doing well. Her reading age is almost at a normal adult level. Ruth rarely speaks spontaneously, but answers questions willingly enough. She has a rather grating voice and emphasizes final consonants of words. Her diction is oddly wooden, with little modulation, but her grammar is faultless. I talked to her after she had done a number of reading tests.

UF: Ruth, you were most helpful . . .
R: Yes.
UF: It was very kind of you . . . I think you are an excellent reader.
R: Yes.
UF: Have you *always* been such a good reader?
R: Yes, I have.
UF: Do you remember when you first learned to read?
R: No.
(After several unsuccessful attempts to make her talk about anything she remembered from her childhood I bring the conversation to the immediate context. Ruth lives in a self-contained flat, which she shares with some other pupils at the boarding school.)
UF: Now you live in that lovely flat, upstairs?
R: Yes.
UF: Is that really good?
R: It is.
UF: Do you do some cooking there?
R: Yes, I do.

UF: What kinds of things do you cook?

R: Anything.

UF: Really. What is your favorite food?

R: Fish fingers.

UF: Oh, yes . . . And you cook them yourself?

R: Nearly.

UF: That's very nice.

(Again, my attempts to make Ruth volunteer information were unsuccessful. All I could do was ask leading questions which she answered with perfect honesty. At no point did she try to create an impression, one way or the other, for instance by boasting or denigrating her cooking or reading skills. Indeed, she seemed to express no attitude whatsoever toward either her accomplishments or her failings.)

UF: And what do you do for fun?

R: Nothing.

UF: Perhaps you do some knitting?

R: Yes.

UF: Or watching television?

R: Yes.

UF: What programs do you like?

R: *Top of the Pops.*

(After some unsuccessful questions relating to the program, with which I was unfamiliar, I switched topics.)

UF: And do you read?

(Implied here was "for fun," but this was probably not conveyed to Ruth.)

R: Yes.

UF: What sort of things? . . . *(no reply)* Do you read magazines?

R: No. Just look at them.

UF: Ah, yes . . . Because there are lots of pictures in them?

R: Yes.

(Presumably, Ruth's literal understanding does not allow her to consider "just looking" at a magazine to be called reading.)

UF: Hmm, what sort of magazines do you look at?

R: *Radio Times* and *TV Times.*

UF: Oh, yes, I look at those too . . .

R: Work time now.

(The characteristically abrupt ending of a conversation with an individual with autism is well illustrated. Ruth did not mean to be rude, but the break was over and it was time to go back to work. Normally such a fact would be wrapped up in the language of politeness. Ruth does not present any wrappings; instead she gives bare information.)

What does this highly typical example tell us? First of all, it shows that communication with a person with autism is by no means a total failure. Nevertheless, the communication that is achieved is extremely limited. Compared with ordinary conversations, my conversation with Ruth was like getting blood from a stone. How could this be when she was clearly willing to answer all my questions? Although there was exchange of information, something was missing. Ruth showed a peculiar detachment, a profound lack of interest in why I had asked the questions and in the effect her remarks might have had on me. It is not that Ruth, like so many adolescents, "couldn't care less." Rather there was nothing else to the conversation than point-blank answers. Questions and answers were small units of information, and each answer was minimal and final. In contrast, in the everyday spontaneous flow of conversation one thing leads to another. In this way it is possible to build up a rich picture of even a stranger's life and attitudes. Language is a means to such riches, but these riches seem to be inaccessible to autistic people, even if they do have language. In this chapter we will attempt to find some of the reasons. Such reasons will have to explain the subtle failure that is typified in the conversation with Ruth.

What is the Matter with Language in Autism?

Much has been written on language and autism – the peculiar forms of speech as well as the difficulties in comprehension.[1] Language depends upon a vast array of abilities: *phonology*, the ability to handle speech sounds; *syntax*, the ability to operate the rules of grammar; *semantics*, the ability to understand and create meaning. Lastly, and somewhat separate from the primary linguistic abilities, there is *pragmatics*, the ability to use language for the purpose of communication. An example of pragmatics is illustrated in figure 7.1. The point of the question "Can you pass the salt?" is a request for salt, not a request for information (about one's ability to pass the salt). To get this point one needs pragmatic rather than syntactic or semantic competence.

It is generally agreed that difficulties in the domain of pragmatics are a universal feature of autism and are similar in many respects to those experienced by patients with right hemisphere brain damage.[2] Whatever the level of syntactic or semantic skill in autism, the level of pragmatic skill will be lower.[3] Pragmatic difficulties in someone with good speech are illustrated in the conversation with Ruth.

What do we know about language acquisition in autism? Helen Tager-Flusberg and her team at the University of Massachusetts carried out a rare

Figure 7.1

longitudinal study comparing children with autism, children suffering from Down syndrome, and young normal children.[4] All these children were studied as they were just beginning to talk, regardless of their age. Remarkably, the same range of syntactic structures and grammatical morphology was observed, and these structures emerged in the same order in all groups. These similarities suggested that autism does not involve a fundamental impairment in formal aspects of language acquisition. However, marked differences were found in the way in which language was used. Here children with autism were highly deviant from the other groups. Studies such as this are needed to study language acquisition in children with Asperger syndrome. While current diagnostic criteria for Asperger syndrome stipulate lack of language delay, it is not at all clear whether early language acquisition in children with Asperger syndrome is the same as in normal children. Perhaps more able children are faster at language learning, while children who are delayed in general ability may also be delayed in acquiring language skills.

What about children with autism who never speak at all? Sometimes, by accident, a surprising degree of competence is discovered. There is, for instance, the case of a young man who never used language until he was given a computerized communicator, which he took to and used effectively almost straight away. Normal language acquisition is undoubtedly aided by an innate desire to communicate. If this desire is weak in children with autism, then this might be just as serious a handicap for language acquisition as, for instance, deafness.

Delay in Language Acquisition

In his enlightening book, *How Children Learn the Meanings of Words*, Paul Bloom, a developmental scientist at Yale University, makes clear what is and what is not yet known about this enduring topic.[5] One old idea is that the sound of a word has to be paired with the sight of a stimulus, and that from such pairings lasting representations are formed in memory. According to Bloom such a mechanism alone will not be sufficient. It would lead to frequent incorrect pairings of word sound and word meaning, which are actually quite rare in young children's language. Consider the novel word "fendle" spoken when looking at a novel object, an unusual red ball with yellow spikes. Does "fendle" refer to the whole object, to the yellow spikes, or perhaps to one particular spike? If you follow the speaker's gaze, and if you take into account what they said before (e.g., "Here is a strange one"), you would get clues to what the speaker meant (e.g., "fendle" refers to a red ball with yellow spikes). All this is done unconsciously. To understand the speaker's intention, the intuitive mentalizing mechanism, already discussed in the preceding chapters, will play a role. The 18-months revolution, which may coincide with a leap in the maturation of the brain system that underpins mentalizing, also coincides with a leap in word learning. Bloom argues that this is more than coincidence.

If it is true that tracking a speaker's intention is the normal gateway to learning what words mean, then this is a body blow for children with autism. The experiments discussed in the last two chapters leave little doubt that children with autism have difficulties in tracking the mental states of other people. Normally developing children learn the name of the thing that the speaker attends to, and not the name of some other thing that happens to be in their own field of view at the time. But perhaps this is not true for children with autism. Perhaps children with autism who miss out on the 18-months revolution rely more heavily on associative learning of pairings of sound and sight.

This is indeed suggested by an ingenious experiment by Baron-Cohen, Baldwin, and Crowson.[6] In the experimental room no speaker was present, but a voice came from above, saying "fendle," at the same time as the child touched a novel object. This situation has all the prerequisites for learning a sound and sight association, but not the prerequisites for intention tracking, as there is only a disembodied voice. Children with autism were able to learn new words under these conditions. Normally developing children did not. While normal children ignored the sound from above when no speaker was present, so autistic children may well ignore the subtle cues to intentions when face to face with a speaker.

Paul Bloom suggests that, given the ability to attribute intentions and other mental states to others, it is after all not such a mystery that young normal children manage to acquire language without much trial and error. It is not only the children, but the other people around them, who continuously monitor mental states. Thus many situations are created where a topic of interest is shared. When a child learns the word for "pudding," it is most likely that the word will have been uttered at exactly the right moment so that the child does not mistakenly learn to use the word "pudding" to mean "raisin," or "yellow," or "stop it." Children with autism, in contrast, may miss out on situations where a topic is shared with another person. If so, this would mean they have fewer learning opportunities. It would also mean that they might learn words or phrases that somebody uttered without intending them to be associated with the event that the child associated them with. So it is conceivable that they would actually learn to use the word "pudding" to refer to a raisin. This is one explanation of idiosyncratic word use, which has been noted in autistic children since Kanner, though he somewhat confusingly referred to it as metaphorical language.[7]

"Peter, Peter, pumpkin eater"

Kanner, in his original paper in 1943, relates the following incident.[8] An autistic boy, Paul, was two years old when his mother recited the nursery rhyme "Peter, Peter, pumpkin eater" to him. One day, while she was doing this, she was working in the kitchen and suddenly dropped a saucepan. Paul, from that day on, chanted "Peter eater" whenever he saw anything resembling a saucepan.

The anecdote constitutes a perfect example of association learning without regard to the speaker's intention. Such learning is not typical of young normal children. Idiosyncratic words in autism appear to be bizarre because they are based on unique associations, and because they do not refer to wider experiences that are accessible to *both* speaker and listener.

Trying to puzzle out why and how an autistic child uses particular idiosyncratic expressions can be quite a challenge. An example is taken from the vocabulary of Jay, an able autistic man who became an electronics technician. He consistently uses the term "the student nurses age group" whenever he refers to the years spanning late adolescence. Why student nurses? When asked this question, he wrote, in a letter to Margaret Dewey:

> I know that there is another name which identifies the 17–21 age group other than "student nurses" age group as according to certain people. Mr T. my electronics teacher at VGRS might call the 17–21 age group the American Television Electronics School or ATES age group, since most students at ATES are in that age group, as well as most student nurses.

This comment is remarkable, as it implies an awareness of other people's point of view without drawing the consequence that it is shared points of view that permit two-way communication. Jay is not concerned with what label most people would use, let alone whether they would want to make a special category out of the 17–21 age group.

Metaphorical remarks, as opposed to idiosyncratic remarks, can be accessed by other people through shared experiences. For instance, one may say that one's arm has "gone to sleep." Sometimes such remarks are highly original and they can still be shared. Abundant examples are to be found not only in literature, but also in everyday life. A normal four-year-old child, for instance, spontaneously described his arm as having "gone fizzy." This was instantly understood.

It remains characteristic of children with autism that they persist in using bizarre idiosyncratic phrases, which are not characteristic of normally developing children, children with specific language impairment, or mentally retarded children. This peculiarity can be seen as part of a wider failure in communication: idiosyncratic speech suggests a lack of interest or need to share with the listener a wider context of interaction in which both individuals are actively involved. It suggests a failure to gauge the comprehension of listeners, an example of a failure in mentalizing.

"Say hello, Bob" – "Say hello, Bob"

The one word you should not repeat in the request to repeat given in the form of "Say hello, Bob" is the word "say." Among the most characteristic behavioral abnormalities of young children with autism is the parrot-like echoing of speech (known as echolalia) which would include repeating the word "say." At least three-quarters of all speaking children with autism show echolalia. As a symptom it can be observed in some other conditions involving brain abnormalities, for instance, developmental or acquired aphasia or dementia. It also occurs in the speech of normal children, but only at a very young age. Often, in more anxious moments, a child can be heard to echo a parent's or teacher's admonishing words from the past: "Don't do that, Paul" or, "You're a clever boy, Gregory." An important question not yet answered by research is the extent to which utterances are modified when they are echoed.[9] Normal children mainly echo speech that is just above their grammatical competence, and they often modify what they echo, but this may not be the case for autistic children.

Ordinary communication is about meaning rather than about transmitting high-fidelity messages, while echoing is about high-fidelity transmission. In the previous chapter we have already come across the idea of bare communication, as in the case of instrumental gestures, in contrast to ostensive communication, as in the case of expressive gestures. Echoed words and phrases are elicited not only on the spot (immediate echoing), but they are often recalled when some aspect of the earlier event cues the memory (delayed echoing). They seem to occur in place of ordinary communicative speech and they may well have an instrumental purpose, for example, a request. "Do you want a cookie?" simply means "I want a cookie." However, in some instances echoing may merely be stereotyped behavior without a purpose.

Should echoing be discouraged? Practitioners are divided. Both in normal language development and in pathological cases, as language improves, echolalia diminishes. This is also true for children with autism. Echolalia appears to be a glaring manifestation of detachment between more peripheral processing systems and a central system that is concerned with meaning. The child with autism selectively attends to speech and translates heard speech proficiently into spoken speech. However, this processing seems to bypass meaning. Echolalia demonstrates how end-products of sophisticated information processing can go to waste because of their failure to be interpreted by higher-level processes. Though the echoed phrases are perfectly analyzed in terms of phonological, prosodic and syntactic units, they do not become part of global meaning. Instead of becoming tributaries of a mighty river they are streams running into sand.

The phenomenon of echolalia is not outside normal adult experience: anyone may lose the thread of conversation when tired or preoccupied. In this case it is typical to find oneself silently echoing the last phrase heard, without comprehension. It is as if the phrase is being recycled, until an internal interpreter is found. Less cognitive effort is needed for echoing a message, while some extra effort is needed for understanding a message. In chapter 10 we will consider the possibility that in autism such an inner interpreter or inner "executive" is rather derelict in its duties.

I and you and you and me

When an autistic child substitutes "you" for "I" and "I" for "you," the listener may find this quite startling. It seems such a fundamental mistake. No wonder the phenomenon has been vested with deep significance. It has been used to support speculations about whether autistic children are deeply confused about their own identity. It has even been alleged that the child is actively avoiding the pronouns I, me, my, and mine. Thorough investigations leave no doubt that such fanciful speculations are part of the myths of autism and not part of the reality.

What happens when an autistic child reverses pronouns is both simple and complex to explain. The simple part has to do with delayed echoing of an utterance associated with a similar situation.[10] For instance, the boy who said "Do you want a cookie?" to mean "I want a cookie" was parroting a phrase that was frequently used by an adult when giving him a cookie. He had simply learned to associate this particular phrase with the event.

The complex part of the analysis of pronoun errors has to do with the so-called deictic function of personal pronouns. What this refers to is the fact that their use is *relative* to who is speaker and who is listener. Even in normally developing children errors in deictic terms are common at least up to age five. Even adults sometimes confuse "teach" and "learn," "borrow" and "lend." Errors made by children are often "edited out" by listeners, since it is taken for granted that the child is not really confused about the relative positions of speaker and listener. There is also experimental and observational evidence to show that children with autism are not confused about their own and others' physical identity. They almost always use proper names correctly. However, they probably use proper names long after their nonautistic peers have started to use the correct pronouns with previously established and mutually understood referents instead.

For similar reasons some children with autism have difficulty with words like "this" and "that," "here" and "there," "come" and "go." Normally, we keep continuous track of what an utterance means from the point of view both of the speaker and of the listener. For instance, it may be appropriate to use the word "coming" to emphasize your point of view and "going" to emphasize mine, even if they refer to the same action. Of course, whose point of view should be taken in a particular case is open to social negotiation. Individuals with autism have problems in these finer points of social role appreciation. It is therefore not surprising that they confuse so-called deictic terms and even personal pronouns.

The delay in language learning, the difficulties with pronouns and deictic terms, the learning of idiosyncratic words, and the pervasiveness of echolalia are all typical features of autism. They all can be explained as consequences of mentalizing failure. Another thing entirely is specific linguistic impairment. This can exist over and above what might be expected from general ability and appears to affect syntax and phonology in particular. Such additional specific language impairment can also occur in autism.

Written Language

A sizeable proportion of autistic children learn to read fluently despite language delay and despite even general intellectual delay. They read aloud with excellent phonology, and they can complete unfinished sentences with the right grammatical form. Some children learn to recognize written words even before learning to speak. Even individuals with Asperger syndrome who have fluent speech often use written language as a preferred means of communication. They claim that the face-to-face contact during normal conversations is too stressful, and that they are under less pressure and can think better when they write or read.

With Maggie Snowling, my long-term collaborator, I carried out investigations of phonological and syntactic competence in not-so-able children with autism who were nevertheless excellent readers.[11] We compared them to younger children who showed the same level of competence on a standardized test of grammatical competence. These children were not only good readers, they could also make very fine syntactic distinctions. For instance, when reading aloud sentences such as "One yellow bippis is enough for me," and "Seven little bippis had a boat," they quite unconsciously adjusted their phonology according to whether the word "bippis" appeared as singular or plural. The final -s is voiced when it indicates a plural, but unvoiced if not. This is the same distinction that we hear between "peas" and "peace."

We found that these children, who enjoyed reading, did not read for meaning. When we asked them to guess the missing words in a story, or to detect silly words that we inserted, they failed markedly, compared to controls. For instance, in a factual nature story they did not bat an eyelid when they came to the sentence: "The hedgehog could smell the scent of the *electric* flowers." They were also not sure how to fill the gap in: "There, surfacing in the dim light, was a young male –" when from the story context it was obvious that the missing word had to be "beaver." They might, for instance, happily insert the word "horse." This was fine in the local sense of the sentence, seen by itself, but not in the global sense of the story.

Kristina Scheuffgen, a PhD student at the MRC Cognitive Development Unit in London, probed further into this idea. Could it be that, when reading a story, children with autism pay more attention to the individual words than to the overall story? Her studies suggest that this is indeed the case. After reading a story children were asked whether a test sentence actually occurred in the story. The sentence was either exactly as read or had a tiny change in the order of words, for example, "The children both swam into the cave" versus "Both the children swam into the cave." The children with autism were far better at making this judgment than children with dyslexia who also read the stories. However, when they told the gist of the story, the dyslexic readers were better. One of the reasons, then, that communication is so difficult with autistic people is that they fail to process content to the same extent as other readers. Therefore, they miss the underlying meaning.

Fluent Language

The language of Asperger syndrome individuals is typically fluent, articulate, and grammatically complex. This is also true for a proportion of individuals who are diagnosed as autistic because of their early language delay, but who later become highly verbal. So far it is unknown whether such able autistic individuals and individuals with Asperger syndrome are different from each other in their semantic or pragmatic skills. It is clear that, regardless of their diagnosis, these people can become excellent speakers and writers on topics that relate to their special field of interest. One of the best known is Temple Grandin. This exceptionally articulate woman can truly speak for herself:

> I am successful in my business. I travel all over the United States, Europe, Canada and Australia designing livestock handling facilities for ranches, feedlots and meat packing plants. My experiences have given me empathy for the animals going through the facilities and help me design better equipment. For instance, the chutes and pens I design are round. The reason for this design is because cattle follow a curved path more easily. There are two reasons for this: first, the cattle can't see what is at the other end and become frightened and, secondly, the curved equipment takes advantage of the animal's natural circling behaviour. The principle is to work with the animal's behaviour instead of against it. I think the same principle applies to autistic children – work with them instead of against them. [12]

There is little one can add to such competent and lucid writing.

Those who are in close touch with able and articulate autistic people often remark that there is something peculiar about the way they talk but that it is hard to put a finger on it. A telling example is provided in one of many letters written to Margaret Dewey by Jay (the same who coined the term "student nurses age group"). In this extract, he gives a remarkably insightful analysis of the struggle he has with subtle word meanings.

> I wonder if John's voice still sounds whiny or not? My voice does not sound whiny but it did when I was at H. I was telling you this last June also. My sister Wanda originally used the word whiny to mean nasal voice. Why? I don't know. She did two months after her high school graduation. I've copied. Using the word whiny to mean nasal voice is just what an autistic child would do. The expression "whiny voices" is not used in social circles. It is rather blunt and insulting like calling colored people "niggers." When a person speaks of a boy or girl whose voice sounds whiny, he or she always says this: "this boy or girl's voice is nasal," which is also true. I must apologize for using whiny voices in this letter. I should have used nasal voices instead. I just can't seem to get whiny voices off my mind.

The writer is extremely, if not obsessively, concerned with the exact meaning of the phrase "whiny voice." To him, it refers to an exact sensory quality, a purely perceptual or behavioral phenomenon. However, there is clearly more to its meaning than this. This "more" can only be understood if one considers the reason a person might use the phrase in the first place. The answer cannot be found in any dictionary: it is in the realm of intention. Perhaps the speaker wants to complain about the voice quality. Jay has correctly deduced that whiny is a pejorative term, but he does not know when and how to use it. In this sense what escapes him is *shades* of meaning. A common complaint of those experienced with advanced autistic language is that there is a tendency to see everything as either black or white. The analogy made from "whiny voice" to "nigger" is a strangely exaggerated one, while the difference between whiny and nasal may be almost nonexistent in terms of social acceptability. The differences and similarities are not categorical, since they truly depend on the circumstance. Although Jay has clearly thought a lot about this problem, it did not occur to him to worry about the fact that commenting on voice quality at all may be socially inappropriate.

We all implicitly know that you can change the meanings of words by placing them in a different context, but autistic people do not seem to have this implicit knowledge. For autistic people the literal meaning of words does not change in different settings. A good example is irony. Here, the actual words remain the same, but the meaning changes completely.

It is universally agreed that irony is difficult, if not impossible, to master for individuals with autism. Their tendency to literal understanding of words regardless of context is strong, and their love for precise definition of terms is sometimes reflected in the ability to give perfect dictionary definitions. However, nuances that depend on context are a different matter. Yet the ability to detect nuances is not just a luxury shared by a few sophisticated people. It is common to all normal users of language, even though it varies with practice and culture. Detection of nuances, including irony and sarcasm, depends critically on the capacity to track other people's intentions and attitudes. Given what we know about their limitations in the ability to attribute mental states to others, autistic individuals need to make an immense effort to learn to recognize subtle or shifting meanings that depend on the speaker's current attitudes and intentions.

The uses of speech in communication

Let us go back to the conversation with Ruth. Ruth had a good vocabulary, excellent grammar, and was a superb reader. Yet she was an abysmal partner for small talk. Poor language is not the cause of poor conversational skills. Nothing illustrates the truth of this statement better than the insistence on syntactic and phonological precision typical of some children with autism. "He speaks as if he were an adult," or "He is extremely precise in his speech," are comments that are often heard. On the other hand, there are remarks such as "He takes everything literally," or "He has no sense of humor." Such comments are rare in interactions with normal children.

Conversational competence is an interesting research topic, but it is hard to measure.[13] Early studies by Christiane Baltaxe represented something of a landmark.[14] She documented, for instance, that German-speaking adolescents with autism confused the polite and familiar form of address (*sie* and *du*), a confusion that arises from a neglect of social roles. She also documented a number of other subtle problems in language use including turn-taking and the differentiation of new information from old. When introducing a new topic into a conversation, an individual with autism may not mark it as new. On the other hand, observation suggests that those who are highly verbal often say "by the way . . . ," "talking of . . . ," "well, anyway . . . ," when they are in fact *not* introducing a new topic. They have learned a formula without fully understanding it.

When considering conversational competence, the prosodic features of speech are just as important as the content.[15] We are talking here of the use of

intonation, pitch, speech rate, fluency, and word stress in the service of communication. Even well-adapted people with autism show relative incompetence
with these tools of communication.[16] For instance, their voice may suddenly
switch from whisper to shout, from low to high pitch. It is as if they fail to
judge what volume is needed to reach the listener, and use sometimes too
much, sometimes too little. Speed can be a similar problem. "If only I could
make him speak more slowly, people might understand him," one mother
said to me. With some the complaint is total lack of variation, which is
perceived as sing-song, or monotonous, pedantic speech. On the other hand,
an apparently beautifully modulated voice can carry a nonsensical remark or
a repetitive phrase. All this suggests that the problems do not originate from
lack of control but from lack of knowing why, when, and where to apply
control. In the normal case this is not a conscious decision – this would be
far too slow to be useful – but originates from the intention that underlies
the message. The failure of control of conversational tools in autism is a
consequence of the same deeper disturbance that explains all the language
peculiarities we have considered: mentalizing failure.

Conveying what is relevant

One of the unspoken rules that govern our conversations is that new information is interesting to others, and old information is boring. This simple rule is
not self-evident to children with autism. While three of us were working in the
quiet room of a school for autistic children, Josef Perner and Sue Leekam
devised the following scenario.[17] When a new child came into the room, Josef
pulled out a large wooden toy bee from a bag. He presented the bee as
something new and special and then showed us what it could do: it could flap
its wings! This was quite a showy demonstration, and it was easy for me to
feign surprise. He then said: "Here is something else the bee can do," and at
exactly this moment I left the room with the excuse of urgently needing a
handkerchief. Josef now demonstrated to the child that the bee can also nod
its head. Of course, I was out and saw none of this. When I returned with a
handkerchief, I immediately asked: "Well, what can the bee do?" Autistic
children were just as likely to tell me that the bee can flap its wings as that it
can nod its head. And yet the head nodding should have been mentioned
first, as the action I had not yet seen, and hence likely to be of interest to me.
Normal children did just this. By implication, they seemed to be aware that
I did not yet know about the nodding action, and that therefore they should
tell me about it.

Figure 7.2   The flapping and nodding bee

News becomes old news very fast. This study raises the question of how we know what is old news. The answer is through tacit cooperation between conversation partners. Successful cooperation is only feasible through tracking each other's mental states and by constantly adapting messages. We are guided by what we think our partner does or does not know. The familiar interchange of friends may seem cryptic to an outsider, but the friends rely on their shared knowledge. They avoid boringly repeating the obvious.

Intentional Communication

The disturbance of communication in autism is at once gross and subtle. This can best be explained by imagining that there are two kinds of communication. One kind is of highest priority in normal individuals, and this has the special status of fully intentional communication. It relates information to mental states and evaluates information that is conveyed. The other kind applies just to the conveying of bare messages. This second kind can be clearly observed in the conversation with Ruth, but the first kind seems to be absent altogether.

Faithful conveying of information is not a trivial accomplishment. It calls for accurate encoding and decoding of speech at input and output stages. Ruth does this. Echolalic children do it too. Nevertheless, in everyday communication one rarely expects that a listener will have to receive and then transmit a bare message as an exact copy. On the contrary, one expects listeners to know that messages are not bare, but usually contain something more. What really matters in everyday communication is the point of the message rather than the message itself. In other words, as listeners, we need to know *why* the speaker conveys *this* thought (rather than another), and as speakers we need to be sure we are understood in the way we *want* to be understood. We have elaborate verbal and nonverbal signals for getting across these intentions.

The two sides of intentional communication fit like lock and key in Dan Sperber and Deirdre Wilson's innovative relevance theory.[18] This theory, which attempts to explain how comprehension is possible, is uniquely suited to a psychological explanation of the communication failure in autism.

An example may illustrate the two kinds of communication. Consider the scene of one creature pushing another, illustrated in figure 7.3. "Crinkley is pushing Snakey" is a bare message conveying the content of the cartoon. In the ordinary flow of conversation, this message would only be one among many possible ways of talking about the picture. Which particular utterance was produced would depend on the context. It would depend on what the speaker expects the listener to understand. Though correct, the description

Figure 7.3

"Crinkley is pushing Snakey" might be an entirely inappropriate (babyish? pedantic?) thing to say. The various utterances that are illustrated in the speech bubbles convey more than the content of the picture. In every case it is *surprise* at Crinkley pushing Snakey. Yet each utterance puts across the surprise in a different way. While revealing the mental state of the speaker, each utterance gives a different shade of meaning to the bare message. We normally pack all sorts of evaluations into our utterances, and reveal or hide all sorts of mental states. Indeed, utterances can reveal something about the reason that somebody is talking to somebody else at all. What is more, we constantly pay attention to aspects of utterances that have to do not with their content, but with the intention of the speaker. According to Sperber and Wilson, true communication would just not work without this type of attention. In fact, in ordinary conversations bare messages (where only content matters) are so rare that they tend to be interpreted in terms of some ulterior communicative purpose *even if* none is there. This is the case in figure 7.4.

Figure 7.4

Because of the normal language user's habitual processing of a speaker's intention, autistic language may be overinterpreted in the way the telephone query in the cartoon was overinterpreted.

The reverse failure is illustrated in figure 7.1. Here, the lack of communication is due to not considering the reason a question was asked in the first place. The speaker really did want the salt. This situation is highly reminiscent of the failure of people with autism to answer similar questions appropriately.

It is pervasively documented that individuals with autism cannot easily understand language that is flippant or witty, and that instead they are excessively literal. Margaret Dewey carried out an informal survey in America using cartoons from the *New Yorker*. Very able and highly educated people with autism failed to understand them or find them funny. The utterances of people with autism can be lengthy and pedantic, and often use stock phrases. Their comments may be perceived by others as inappropriate, rude, or else overpolite. For instance, one young man with autism, who often telephones his favorite aunt, never fails to announce himself by saying, "This is M. C. Smith, your nephew, speaking."

One final example of the vicissitudes of the two kinds of communication, the literal and the normal, intentional kind, is provided by the delightful comedy film *Being There*. Here, an innocent, mentally handicapped and undoubtedly autistic hero, played by Peter Sellers, is taken up as a guru by a sophisticated and gullible group of people. They do not know anything about him, but his simplicity and artlessness puts them in awe of him. His every pronouncement (spoken in a slow, measured voice) is transparently obvious, and a bare truism. None the less, it is eagerly received, richly interpreted, and invested with deep significance. At the same time, the hero is quite unaware of the effect he has. The serious side of this comedy of errors is that the autistic literalness acts as a blank canvas to those who are busily mentalizing, and who can read any meaning they choose into any message. Here for once the capacity for mind reading is shown to make fools of us all.

chapter 8

Intelligence and Special Talent

Intelligence is a concept loaded with many meanings. Here I use it to refer to the general efficiency of the brain when processing information. The idea is simple: the more efficient the brain, the better the capacity to analyze incoming information and to act upon it, and thus, the higher the intelligence. Admittedly, such a definition is vague as we still lack a systematic theory of the neural foundation of intelligence.

How can the processing efficiency of someone's brain be assessed? IQ tests, if properly carried out and interpreted, can give us an estimate of how well an individual has acquired information in the past (so-called crystallized intelligence), and how well an individual can process novel information (so-called fluid intelligence). But does an IQ score for an individual with autism mean the same as for a nonautistic person? Both Kanner and Asperger were impressed by the "strikingly intelligent physiognomy" of children with autism, and by their unusual interests, but this was belied by their poor IQ scores. Could it be that these children are more intelligent than the tests give them credit for? After all, children with autism can have capabilities that are out of the ordinary, and sometimes rare talent.

Autism and Mental Retardation

The terms mental retardation and learning disability imply slow development and poor learning. But even individuals with limited intelligence have the *capacity to learn*. Mental retardation is a classification that is based largely on IQ scores. An IQ between 85 and 115 is considered average normal, while an IQ between 85 and 70 is low normal. Below 70, the label mental retardation applies, which becomes "severe" when IQ drops below 50. The lower IQ bands reflect a progression in the extent of brain abnormality and hence, increasing limitation of information-processing capacity. In this sense, IQ can be read as a barometer of brain health.

While 3 percent of schoolchildren have some degree of mental retardation or learning disability as defined by IQ tests, only 0.3 percent have severe mental retardation.[1] Yet even though these children cannot pass many academic exams, they may learn to read, write, and be numerate. Patient and sensitive teaching, not just in childhood but throughout life, pays enormous dividends. Laboratory experiments have shown that changes in performance do occur as a result of learning – once learning gets off the ground.[2] Significant progress is demonstrable over time even in those children with severe intellectual impairments. This underlines the importance of special education.

It has been widely reported that 75 percent of children with autism have mental retardation, an estimate that was based on clinic populations and did not include the full range of the autism spectrum. A new population study with children aged seven, carried out in the south-east of England, found that only 35 percent of children affected by autism spectrum disorder, including Asperger syndrome, had IQs below 70.[3] This is due to increased awareness of autism in brighter children. This new finding raises the possibility that learning disability may not be as strongly associated with autism as was once thought.

However, it would be wrong to think that high IQ rules out the presence of brain pathology. Brain pathology is also present in autistic individuals who have IQs in the normal and superior range. Consequently, they too benefit from special education. As Hans Asperger pointed out long ago, they need teachers who understand them and their condition and allow them to learn in their own way. They need sensitive indirect guidance rather than confrontational methods.[4] Even though many intelligent autistic children are able to perform the same tasks as their nonautistic classmates, they are probably doing them in a different way. Pinpointing such differences is the prized goal of many psychological investigations.

Anderson's Model of Intelligence

Mike Anderson, my former colleague at the MRC Cognitive Development Unit in London, wrote a monograph and a recent review of the concept of intelligence and its significance for individuals with intellectual disabilities.[5] He presents detailed arguments that intelligence is not a mythical concept, nor an artefact of measurement. Anderson's model, which is shown in figure 8.1, proposes that intelligence, understood in a commonsense way, rests on some few essential cognitive components.

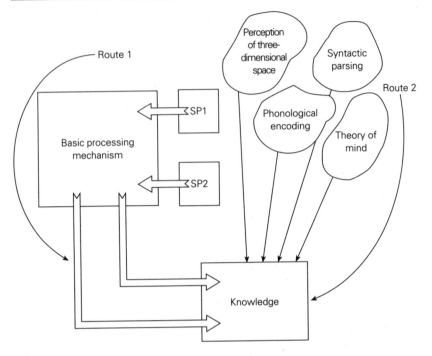

Figure 8.1 The theory of the minimal architecture underlying intelligence and development

Reproduced with kind permission from M. Anderson (1992) *Intelligence and Development: A Cognitive Theory* (Oxford: Blackwell), p.107

At its core Anderson's model has a basic information-processing mechanism (BPM) containing a verbal (SP1) and a nonverbal (SP2) component. These mechanisms are responsible for acquiring knowledge and operate with a greater or lesser degree of efficiency in different individuals. Their efficiency is assessed by verbal and nonverbal IQ tests. However, in addition, there are several independent cognitive modules, which depend upon special purpose neural structures. They are specialized devices for acquiring particular types of knowledge.[6] One module, for instance, processes speech and nothing else. Another module is the "theory of mind" (ToM) or mentalizing mechanism. These modules are designed to work at superefficient levels, regardless of the brain's basic processing efficiency.

If one of the modules is faulty, perhaps through a failure in normal brain development, then this is bad news. A developmental disorder will result. This is because the information that the faulty module was designed to process cannot be dealt with in an automatic way. The information now has to be processed by the all-purpose basic processing mechanism. Acquiring knowledge in the particular domain of the module is bound to be slower and more cumbersome.

In Anderson's model the cognitive system works like a small company with dedicated specialists and a responsible head office. When one of the specialists is ill, one of the company directors steps in but, having no special talent or training, will do the job less well. Taking the analogy further, some companies work better because they have more energetic directors. They are also more resilient if they lose a specialist employee.

The analogy suggests that poor IQ test performance can arise for two quite different reasons: a problem in the operation of the basic processor (an inefficient head office), or lack of a module (a missing specialist employee). Brain pathology in the first case would be expected to be widespread, but in the second case, circumscribed. Still, even if only one single module is faulty, then this might have wider repercussions.

High intelligence – low measured IQ

In an attempt to assess the limits of perceptual information processing and its relationship to IQ in autism, Kristina Scheuffgen used Mike Anderson's test of inspection time.[7] This test has no special requirements of prior knowledge, involves no burden on memory, and does not require fast motor responses. The test estimates how long you need to inspect a display to say whether two vertical lines are equal or different in length. The shorter the time you need, the better. It means that you are "on the ball" and that a brief window of opportunity is sufficient for you to take in the display. It means you are processing information efficiently. Short inspection times are typical of people who score highly on tests of fluid intelligence; long duration thresholds are typical of those who score poorly. This correlation is interesting because the test is nothing like a standard IQ test. It does not involve elaborate problem-solving strategies or memory, and it does not rely on fast speed of responding. It seems to tap the efficiency of the basic information processor.

The task was presented in the form of a computer game that was sufficiently motivating to engage the children for hundreds of trials to establish the briefest possible inspection-time window. It turned out to be 40 msec on average, exactly the same as in normally developing children, whose average Wechsler Full Scale IQ was 118, and 35 points higher than the average IQ of the autism group. This difference is equivalent to two standard deviations.

When we compared those autistic children who had the lowest Full Scale IQ, 68 on average, with a group of learning-disabled nonautistic children whose average IQ was 62, the autistic children's inspection time was significantly shorter (42 vs 60 msec). This study proved that basic information-processing capacity is not necessarily reduced in autism.

The two different reasons for obtaining a low IQ score – reduced basic efficiency and a missing cognitive module – could explain the difference between the nonautistic and the autistic children. In autism we assume that the ToM module is missing. In the group with nonspecific learning disability we assume that general processing capacity is low. But why was measured IQ so low in the autism group? In the preceding chapters we have already considered some of the repercussions of the missing ToM module on social interaction, on language learning, and on the ability to learn informally from others.

Let us consider informal learning, because it is particularly relevant in this context. To recap, informal learning simply happens by being around other people, and by being interested in what they are talking about. This leads to incidental learning and shared background knowledge between a group of people. The acquisition of such shared knowledge is facilitated by the ability to attribute thoughts and beliefs to others. Incidental knowledge about IQ tests and attitudes to taking tests are part of the shared background knowledge in our culture. It is plausible that informal learning contributes to the motivation to perform well in face-to-face situations. It is also plausible that it contributes to the ability to interpret the point of the questions that testers ask. Incidental knowledge can also be helpful in answering some of the questions. If this argument is correct, then mentalizing difficulties alone can result in lower than expected IQ scores on some tests.

Inspection time, a sufficiently novel test, does not seem to be affected by cultural knowledge gathered through informal learning. It is, therefore, a more neutral measure of basic information-processing capacity in the case of autism. Another example is Raven's Matrices. This test dates from the middle of the twentieth century and is much used as a test of so-called fluid intelligence, independent of crystallized knowledge. The Raven test uses abstract shapes arranged in rows and columns, where the last position of the matrix has to be completed. Yet another example is the Seguin Formboard test, a classic test dating from the beginning of the twentieth century and designed to be independent of taught knowledge. This test employs cut-out geometric shapes that have to be fitted into exact spaces. The materials are abstract and the tasks are self-contained in their goals. Individuals with autism can perform well on all these tests, provided their basic processing capacity is unimpaired. However, we should expect less good performance on IQ tests that depend on informally acquired knowledge.

IQ Test Peaks and Troughs

The Wechsler Scales of Intelligence (WISC for children, WAIS for adults) consist of a number of different well-tried subtests. They have provided an abundance of information on the characteristic pattern of test performance in children and adults with autism. It is worth dwelling on these findings, if only because most individuals with autism will be tested on the WISC or WAIS in the course of their assessment.

Because of the way the scales are constructed, and because we assume that there is such a thing as general intelligence or basic processing efficiency, the "normal" child shows an even level of performance on a large variety of subtests, exactly average for each age group. Children who are below or above average intelligence are also expected to achieve scores of roughly the same level on all subtests. If one draws a graph representing scores on the various tests, normally a more or less horizontal line is obtained. A wildly uneven line, like geological turbulence recorded by a seismograph, is characteristic of the performance pattern of children with autism. Their test profile seems to be different from that found in any other clinical group.

Not every child with autism shows exactly the same profile, but group data show a remarkably clear pattern. This pattern is recognizable by having two opposite poles of performance. The two poles can be discerned despite differences in intelligence level and cultural environment. Even those individuals with average or superior intelligence show this pattern.[8]

The pole of worst performance lies on those subtests that demand a high degree of communicative competence and commonsense social reasoning. The most typical of these is the Comprehension subtest. This test, illustrated in figure 8.2, requires commonsense answers to seemingly ordinary, but novel, hypothetical questions. It is not sufficient to give a "correct" answer, as in the example; the answer needs to be relevant to the question. This relevance is automatically provided by incidental learning of shared cultural knowledge. As argued already, we would expect children with autism to be impaired in this respect. Yet it is not the case that people with autism are poor at understanding and answering *any* sort of questions. Questions that request precise information on a topic that is of particular interest to the autistic child are answered readily. It is likely that this knowledge has been acquired

Figure 8.2   Example of Comprehension subtest

Figure 8.3   Example of Block Design subtest

explicitly and from their own experience, rather than incidentally and from other people. Thus, on the Information and Vocabulary subtests of the WISC, children with autism almost always perform better than on the Comprehension subtest.

The pole of best performance lies on subtests of which Block Design is the most typical. This test of spatial ability requires copying an abstract pattern with little cubes within a time limit, as illustrated in figure 8.3. Many autistic individuals can obtain a score on this test that is as good as or better than that of a normal child of the same age. On the other hand, this test remains difficult for most children with general learning disability, however hard they try. It is perhaps not surprising that this test is comparatively easy for children with autism, since it shares critical similarities with Inspection time, Raven's Matrices, and Seguin Formboard tests. All these tests aim to be independent of shared cultural knowledge, and they are all likely to tap basic processing efficiency independent of mentalizing ability.

School Intelligence and World Intelligence

How far can we go in assuming that shared cultural knowledge influences test-taking ability? Anomalies in estimating intelligence by standard tests in different cultural groups have often been commented on. A person who can solve a problem in real life may not be able to solve it in the test situation. In the case of autism we often find the reverse. A fascinating study of well-adapted and normal child street vendors in the town of Recife in Brazil illustrates the contrast.[9] The young street vendors, who had never been to school, were extremely adept at calculating prices and change when selling fruit or vegetables to their customers. However, these same children were unable to do similar calculations when the problems were taken out of context and given as a test in the psychological laboratory. For success in a test situation, it is necessary to be accustomed to the idea of solving problems outside their real-life context. This idea is vigorously promoted by schooling. Schooling normally provides the opportunity to work on problems for their own sake and to acquire seemingly useless knowledge. The result is what we might call school intelligence, the opposite of world intelligence. The case of the Brazilian children shows a sharp contrast of world intelligence and school intelligence and highlights the importance of context to world intelligence.

People who have never been to school find the neutrality and detachment of solving abstract problems strange. They have learned through their own experience and from others what is useful and important for their lives. Their world intelligence in fact prevents them from revealing the abilities they have in a test that is geared toward school intelligence. Ironically, it is precisely on the supposedly culture-free tests (Block Design, Seguin Formboard, Raven's Matrices) that people who have not had the benefit of schooling are at a disadvantage. This contrasts with the case of autism, where – as long as there is no additional intellectual impairment – performance on precisely these tests can be excellent. In the normal case, excellence on these tests appears to be facilitated by formal education. I assume that formal education, like autism, enables people to disregard context and to solve problems in their own right. Presumably, explicit teaching fosters the latent abilities of abstraction in the human brain. In contrast, the harsh "school of life" may suppress these latent abilities and foster the situation-dependent solution of practical problems.

Normal children everywhere do well when they understand and take account of context. This is not the case in autism. Here we have some evidence of an unusual ability to disregard context. The ability to entertain a thought out of context (disembedded thought) is also typical of school learning. Consider the acquisition of literacy. When becoming literate the child must learn to free language from its embeddedness in everyday situations so as to achieve the ability to look at the sound of speech and its relationship to letters. Aspects of words such as their sound structure are quite separate from their meaning but must be attended to in their own right when learning the rudiments of spelling. Another example of the advantage of disembedded thought is that it facilitates looking at information, untainted by a particular context or bias. For example, a good judge can put aside prior knowledge of the accused person's previous convictions, and dispassionately regard the current evidence.

Perhaps people with autism have no need to free thought from its embeddedness in everyday situations, as it is never embedded in the first place. Some have excellent reading and spelling ability, ahead of their ability to understand the meaning of what they are reading. Some autistic children show remarkable abilities for abstract mathematics, for instance knowledge of prime numbers, but do not actually put this knowledge to use. Some are capable of a neutral analysis of an otherwise loaded situation, but do not put their knowledge into action. All this would suggest that they have good school intelligence, but poor world intelligence. Even with superior numeric ability, children with autism would fail to make a living as street vendors.

If a tendency to disregard context is a characteristic of autistic intelligence, then we would have a possible explanation for the unusual skills and talents of autistic children.

Rote memory skills, and what lies behind them

It is easier to explain failure than it is to explain success in children whom we presume to be "entitled" to impaired performance by virtue of their impaired brain development. Nevertheless, the psychological investigation of autistic peak performance has been a fruitful area of discovery. Indeed, it is peaks rather than troughs in performance that give us the main clues to subtle differences in cognitive processes. The "islets" of abilities may not be the tranquil oases they seem, but rather volcanoes of unusual activity.

Feats of rote memory are a typical example of "islets" of ability in children with autism. Beyond the mere observation of verbatim recall of speech or songs, we can draw on experimental studies. Beate Hermelin and Neil O'Connor in London were the first to carry out systematic experiments on the abilities of children with autism in an innovative series of investigations between 1964 and 1970. During this period, ideas about information-processing models first entered into the arena of psychological theories. This meant that models could be constructed where input could be separated from output, and both were separated from central processes where messages are received and stored, and actions initiated. This marked the revolution of cognitive psychology over behaviorism. I had the great good fortune to be taught by these pioneering investigators, and their innovative studies on verbal recall inspired my own work, as well as that of many others. Their experiments were summarized in a monograph that appeared in 1970,[10] and here I will highlight just a few of their findings.

Hermelin and O'Connor introduced the method of comparing children with autism with much younger normal children and also with nonautistic mentally retarded children. The important requirement was that the children in the three groups should perform similarly on certain tests that have norms based on mental age. This is known as the mental age matching procedure. It ensures that any differences in performance found on experimental tasks are not due to one group being generally more impaired, or simply less developmentally mature. This method enabled a breakthrough in what previously was an impasse. We learn little from repeatedly demonstrating inferior performance in a clinically abnormal group. For instance, to find that mentally retarded children cannot do well on tasks that correlate with IQ tells us nothing that we did not know already.

What is of interest is whether, over and above any general depression of performance, there is some specific problem or perhaps some specific talent. By equating groups in terms of their performance on a relevant task one can overcome the impasse. Because of the almost inevitably poorer performance of handicapped children, a normal comparison group will consist of younger children. Younger children almost inevitably perform less well than older children. Even more relevant is a comparison group of children who have suffered neurological impairment that resulted in intellectual impairment, but not in autism. A difference between such a group and an autism group should pinpoint deficits that are specific to autism. This procedure was also used in the experiments on mental state attribution described in chapter 5.

Let us return to the question of rote memory skills. If children with autism and other children were matched for their capacity to recall a list of digits, then it would be interesting if differences were found on other recall tasks. Such significant differences were indeed found. The task was to try to recall as much as possible of a string of words that was deliberately longer than the previously tested span of recall, the so-called digit span. Children with autism – and we are here talking of children with moderate or severe learning disabilities – did something highly consistent on these tests: they always remembered the end of the string, regardless of what kind of string it was. The normal children only did this when the word string was entirely random, for instance: "what–see–where–leaf–is–ship–we." Then all children repeated something like "is–ship–we." This is exactly what one would expect when memory capacity is exceeded: more recent material pushes out older material. However, this general rule does not hold when the string to be remembered is not random. In one condition, half of the string was in fact a short sentence, for example, "where–is–the–ship–what–see–was–leaf." In this case the normal children repeated the sentence part, wherever it was in the sequence, and lost the rest. The children with autism repeated "see–was–leaf," the last part of the message, just as everyone else does when sequences are random – and lost the sentence. Of course, when the sentence was at the end of the string, they repeated it perfectly.

In another experiment, the string was a superlong sentence: for example, "On–Sunday–the–children–went–to–the–park–to–feed–the–ducks."[11] If treated as a string of 12 separate words, this would be way beyond the memory span of the children taking part in the experiments. However, young normal children often managed to repeat perfectly 12-word sentences and longer ones, even though they could repeat no more than about three random digits. Presumably, the sentence structure and the meaning acted as a stimulus to pack the words in such a way that they made one single meaningful unit, and thus the children's "span" capacity was not exceeded. The children must have oriented automatically toward the meaning of the sentence. This aided their recall.

The children with autism who took part in the experiment, especially the ones with greater intellectual impairment, were not able to do this mental trick. They were better at recalling sentences than jumbled words, but significantly less so than normal children. The children with autism were also less inclined than the normal children to reorder scrambled sentences into something more grammatical. Unlike the normal children, they did not feel compelled to organize stimuli into coherent patterns. This really is a compulsion in normal people and it can be observed easily: if people are asked to repeat a long but ungrammatical sentence, they usually cannot help correcting it. For instance, when hearing "The fox was chase by a large flock of white geese" you would probably automatically say "chased" rather than "chase" as given in the sentence. Indeed the tendency to correct deviant patterns and to re-organize jumbled material is not unique to language.[12]

In another experiment, I attempted to find out if children with and without autism might use different strategies to remember a sequence of red and green counters. The type of error made during learning revealed whether the sequence was learned counter by counter or as a whole rule-governed pattern.[13] Normal children quickly picked up the relevant rule for the pattern. Moreover, they exaggerated it. Their errors could be predicted by the rule. If the pattern included mostly red–green alternations, then the child produced even more such alternations. If there were mostly long runs of one color, the child produced even longer runs. Somehow, the children gathered the essence of each pattern even before they had properly learned it. This too might be explained by an automatic orientation toward overall meaning. Children with autism did not show this strategy. They were not influenced by the overall rule, but instead they were influenced by the last single element. This they either repeated or alternated, and hence the errors they made could be entirely predicted on the basis of a small fragment of the pattern. In this sense, children with autism showed a diminished interest in overall pattern structure.

A person with autism may remember all the details of a train timetable without being a train enthusiast and without wanting to make use of the information for traveling. The key word is *rote* as opposed to meaningful. Kanner talked of the "truly phenomenal memory that enables the autistic child to recall and reproduce complex nonsense patterns, no matter how disorganized they are, in exactly the same form as originally construed."[14] To praise this as an achievement is odd. Normally it is not nonsense that one wants to recall, and the ability to do so is far less useful than the ability to recall sense. This we so much take for granted that it fails to impress us. Good performance in recalling rote material would normally be paired with even better performance on memory for meaning. However, astounding isolated feats of rote memory in children with autism are usually accompanied by poor ability to extract meaning, and may therefore signal a peculiarity of their cognitive processing style.

Although this work dates back several decades, results in recent studies of memory in autism still resonate with these conclusions. In 2001, Minshew and Goldstein investigated auditory and visual memory in 52 high-functioning young adults with autism and 40 normal controls.[15] They found that performance between the groups was equal on simple memory tasks and on letter span, but a significant impairment in the autism group was found when task complexity was increased. This was true regardless of sensory modality. The authors explain the progressive degree of impairment with increasing complexity as a result of a failure to initiate organizing strategies and as a result of poor use of contextual cues.

Bright Splinters of the Mind

This is the title that Beate Hermelin gave her recent book in which she describes her research on one of the most fascinating topics in autism research, the savant phenomenon.[16] The label *savant* has replaced the old label *idiot savant*, where the juxtaposition of two opposites expressed the paradox of outstanding performance in one field, against a background of generally poor performance in almost all other fields. Beate Hermelin analyzed individuals who have generally low intelligence but have special talents in writing poetry, learning foreign languages, performing music, drawing and painting, calculating, and knowing the day of the week for any date in the calendar. These are the areas of excellence found in about 10 percent of people with autism, and this is not counting unusual rote memory skills. Savant skills are a delight to the individual and to others, no matter whether they result in enduring artistic productions, or simply in joyful but ephemeral activity.

Who are the savants? There is the stunning example of Nadia.[17] Between the ages of four and seven, Nadia produced drawings admired by professionals and compared with the beauty of cave paintings from 30,000 years ago.[18] Nadia is an interesting example that demonstrates that a precocious talent can vanish as quickly as it appeared. Her artistic productivity stopped when she made developmental progress in other areas, such as language. Other cases, however, show sustained productivity, and even reveal additional outstanding talents. Stephen Wiltshire is an example. By the age of 12 years Stephen's artistic drawings had attracted the attention of a president of the Royal Academy of Arts. Sir Hugh Casson said of him:

Stephen Wiltshire draws exactly what he sees – no more, no less. He stands before the object – usually a building – for, say, 15 minutes, seeming to watch rather than to observe it. Later he will draw it, quickly, confidently, and with an accuracy all the more uncanny because it is done entirely from memory and without notes. He misses no detail – nothing. The only inaccuracy is that the object in his drawing is "mirrored." His preferred subject is always architecture and the pricklier and more complicated the better.[19]

Since his early success, Stephen has gone on to become even more famous. Oliver Sacks accompanied Stephen on several of his drawing expeditions and vividly documented his methods of working. Stephen benefited from the art lessons he received and was able to extend his repertoire from line drawings to color. He also developed a talent for music and can improvise and perform with gusto. In an enthralling essay Oliver Sacks reflects on the nature of Stephen's talent and on what it means to be a prodigy.[20] Just as with Beate Hermelin's book, it does not shirk the paradoxes in the condition and brings the reader as close to the mystery of savant talent as it is possible to get at present.

There are many thriving original artists who are also autistic, too many to mention. In some cases, their work can be seen on autism websites. However, it would be very difficult to give an aesthetic judgment of this work. No one has yet tried to find out whether art critics could readily spot savant art, but I suspect that under the right conditions this might not be too difficult. The range of talent is astounding and includes the painterly as well as the graphic, architectural themes as well as portraits. For instance, the exquisitely detailed drawings of Gilles Trehin, which can be seen on his website, show the complex architecture of a vast imaginary city that he named Urville. A young woman called Claudia is another accomplished artist with sustained productivity, who uses bold and often simple designs. She is one of the cases analyzed in detail in Beate Hermelin's book. She drew my portrait, shown in figure 8.4, in about 15 minutes when she was 22 years old.

Examples of musical talent are also plentiful. For instance, Nigel, who has very low measured intelligence and is quite unable to look after himself, is a sought-after pianist. He has a vast repertoire of classical music and can learn a new piece by hearing it played only once. Kate, diagnosed with Asperger syndrome, who is now middle-aged, has written poetry from the age of 20. However, just as Stephen is not interested in other people's art, she is indifferent to other people's poetry. She has many difficulties typical of autistic people and lives in a sheltered community. Savant individuals, such as Stephen, can put their talent to professional use, but it appears that for them it is the activity that counts, not the end product. Stephen, for instance, hardly cares what happens to his drawings and whether they get lost or

Figure 8.4 Portrait of Uta Frith by Claudia (1989)

damaged. He needs sympathetic helpers to look after his interests and to act as interface to the marketplace.

Explaining the savant talent

Despite the ingenious efforts of researchers, savant skills remain an enigma. We do not know why or how a child becomes a savant. The outstanding ability often appears to arise out of the blue and without significant teaching or practice. Nor does it necessarily have to be only a single skill. People often wonder whether obsession and single-mindedness are necessary to develop outstanding talents. If so, then autism would provide ideal conditions. This still does not explain the creativity and originality of savant art, music, and poetry.

It is possible that savant abilities are a unique feature of autism and a sign of a different intelligence. The Australian researcher Ted Nettlebeck, who also pioneered the test of inspection time in mentally handicapped populations, points out the inadequacy of current theories of intelligence to account for the phenomenon.[21] He suggests that savant skills demonstrate the brain's capacity to develop new cognitive modules in certain domains that create a hotline to knowledge stored in long-term memory, and operate independently of basic information-processing capacity. The linguists Neil Smith and Ianthe Tsimpli, who studied Christopher, a multilingual savant, make a similar suggestion.[22] This savant has developed procedures for rapid mapping of words in any language to words in English, his native language. While his acquisition of words in new languages is phenomenal, he does not in fact acquire new syntactic forms. While he can translate texts in many languages word by word into English, he cannot converse in these languages.

If savant individuals can set up modules for new specialist procedures in different domains, how do these modules get started in the first place? The start of a savant skill, which might lead to the creation of a new self-contained cognitive module, could be quite accidental. Beate Hermelin points out that in those few cases where the first appearance of calendar ability has been pinpointed, the beginning is an intense interest in an isolated calendar date, perhaps a birthday. More dates are added, perhaps other birthdays, and each of them is remembered perfectly by date and day. Steadily, more knowledge about the calendar and its repetitive structure is added like a growing crystal. It is likely that the knowledge is built up first in units of a week, and then in units of months and finally years. The internal knowledge base continues to expand and will incorporate leap years. Access to the knowledge in long-term memory involves a quick "look-up" procedure for days and, because of the repetitive structure of the calendar, it works equally well for the distant past and future. However, the further away from the present, the longer this "look-up" takes. What day will it be on October 14, 2020? D., a 30-year-old man with autism, and an IQ of 52, could tell you in two seconds.

Why only some individuals gain expert knowledge, and most people do not, is a mystery, but it is surprisingly easy to construct a model for a computer program to acquire calendar knowledge, going from small units to larger ones.[23] Knowledge of explicit rules is not necessary. Simple principles of associative learning between small units of information are sufficient. A cognitive style with a preference for focusing on small elements of information might provide the building blocks from which the calendar savant can create increasingly impressive structures in memory.

This cognitive style of focusing on separate elements has also been considered in relation to drawing skills. Laurent Mottron, a researcher working in Canada, made careful observations of a draughtsman savant and showed that his drawings always started from a single, and unimportant, detail.[24] He would gradually build up the whole picture piece by piece, and in contrast to professional draughtsmen, who usually started with a rough outline of the overall design.

The ability to start with a focus on small units may also apply to musical skill. The ability to remember absolute pitch might be an example of an unusual focus on the elements of a melody. All musical savants possess absolute pitch, but many individuals with autism who are not musically trained do as well. Autism researcher Pam Heaton studied this hitherto unsuspected talent.[25] She was able to teach autistic children to remember absolute tones even though they did not know their names, by providing animal pictures to go with specific sounds. In this way the children could point to the correct animal when they heard a particular note, a skill that far exceeded that of a control group of nonautistic children. Furthermore, when listening to a chord, children with autism were better able to discern a single target tone than other children.

We shall see in the next chapter that a detail-focused cognitive style may be the basis for many of the characteristics of autistic intelligence.

chapter 9

A Fragmented World

Fragments mend
make for
genius
fragmentation
when normal thinking
would give up.
The pieces find the resource within

bits of the whole
puzzled jigsaw,
my self.

This is one of the poems by Kate, a woman with autism whose poetry has been analyzed by Beate Hermelin in her book *Bright Splinters of the Mind.*[1] Nothing could be more apt to introduce the theme of this chapter.

The Puzzle of the Jigsaw Puzzle

An extraordinary facility with jigsaw puzzles is common in autism. However, the way children with autism prefer to construct a puzzle may be quite different from the way a normal child does it. To investigate this Beate Hermelin and I once carried out an experiment where we contrasted performance with two types of jigsaw.[2] In one type there were rectangular puzzle pieces with straight edges with a picture, and in another, there were typically jagged pieces but without a picture. With the second type of jigsaw, the children with autism performed much better than young normal children of the same mental age. They enjoyed fitting piece together with piece, even when there was no picture emerging in the end.

In most commercially available jigsaw puzzles there is a picture. The picture is broken up regardless of its natural shape or content boundaries. When I do a jigsaw puzzle I am continually amazed at how different a fragment of a visual detail looks when the puzzle piece is in place compared to when I just see the piece alone. I look for a piece with a dog's ear, for instance. At first it always looks as if there is no such piece, but once found and fitted, the detail is perfectly clear.

Georges Perec, in his novel *Life, a User's Manual*, writes about this experience and how a single piece changes character:

> The pieces are readable, take on a sense, only when assembled; in isolation, a puzzle piece means nothing – just an impossible question, an opaque challenge. But as soon as you have succeeded . . . in fitting it into one of its neighbours, the piece disappears, ceases to exist as a piece. The intense difficulty preceding this link-up – which the English word *puzzle* indicates so well – not only loses its *raison d'être*, it seems never to have any reason, so obvious does the solution appear.[3]

Perhaps the child with autism can still see the individual puzzle pieces in the completed puzzle. Perhaps completing the puzzle is very much a piece-meal exercise starting from small sections and almost incidentally resulting in a large picture at the end. If this were the case, doing puzzles without a picture would be just as easy. As a metaphor, the jigsaw puzzle persisting as fragments, even when put together, symbolizes the effect of autistic detachment. In contrast, for the nonautistic person, fragments, once assembled into a single picture, lose their meaning as fragments and are only meaningful as part of the greater unit they belong to, the whole picture. This represents an effect of context on meaning, or what I have termed strong central coherence. The lack of an effect of context, and by implication, the lack of a drive for meaning, can be termed weak central coherence.

Hidden Figures

The difficulty of finding jigsaw pieces is reminiscent of the pastime "find the hidden figure." Amitta Shah, then a PhD student at the MRC Cognitive Development Unit in London, had the idea of investigating how well autistic children could locate such hidden figures.[4] She was able to use a standardized test, the Children's Embedded Figures Test,[5] and found that autistic children

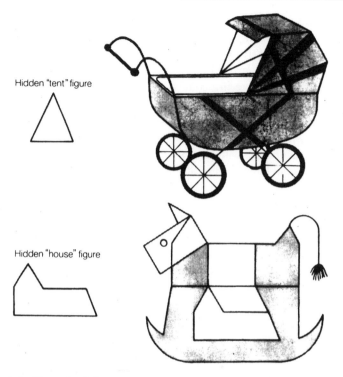

Hidden "tent" figure

Hidden "house" figure

Figure 9.1 Examples from the Children's Embedded Figures Test (Witkin, Oltman, Raskin and Karp, 1971)

By kind permission from Consulting Psychologist Press, Inc., Palo Alto, CA

scored above average for their mental age. They were faster and more accurate than normal children of the same mental age. Examples of embedded figures used in this test are shown on figure 9.1. A small target shape has to be located in a drawing of a larger shape made up of confusing lines.

When one looks at these figures it seems as if the larger shapes created by criss-crossing lines are so compelling that one simply cannot see the small, embedded target shape. It is swallowed up by the bigger figure, and is now an intrinsic part of this object. Witkin and others maintained, on the basis of unjustly forgotten studies, that people who are good at finding embedded figures are also good at other tasks purporting to measure "field independence," a lack of influence of context both in visual perception and in social interaction.[6] These authors suggested that field-dependent people are easily swayed by others' opinion and tend to take on the prevailing views of their group; field-independent people are unaffected by current crazes and don't care so much about other people's opinion. People with a high degree of social detachment tend to be good at spotting embedded figures. The terms strong and weak central coherence map closely onto the terms field dependence and independence.

One way of describing field independence or weak central coherence is the unusual ability to disregard context. For example, the detached detective sees a clue to the murder in a pair of shoes, which were unnoticed by others because they were placed in a wardrobe with other shoes. The detective, however, can spot some fresh dirt on them and knows that the valet would not have put them there without first cleaning them properly. Undoubtedly, the detective would have excelled at finding embedded figures, and moreover is likely to show social detachment, even a touch of autism. The Sherlock Holmes type of detective needs to be aloof from the emotional machinations of the group of suspects that he or she investigates.

Many children and adults have difficulties when trying to find embedded figures, taking many seconds to spot them. It seems strangely effortful to detach the hidden figure from its surrounding context. It is as if there was a strong force pulling all the information in the picture together. It certainly feels like a force, because in order to pull apart the whole figure, one has to resist a natural tendency to see a thing as a whole, or a *gestalt*.

Central coherence, then, can be seen as a force (imagine a flowing river) that pulls together large amounts of information (many tributaries). If it is strong, this force could be responsible for the difficulty in disembedding figures. Weak central coherence, on the other hand, could explain facility with this task. Judging by the large individual differences in embedded figures test performance, some people have a bias toward strong, and some toward weak, central coherence. People with autism who excel at doing jigsaw puzzles and finding embedded figures seem to have weak coherence.

In the extreme, weak coherence means not seeing the wood for the trees; strong coherence means not seeing the trees for the wood. It is one thing to talk about trees and woods, but what about trees and branches, branches and twigs, twigs and leaves, and so on? Would there always be a preference for piecemeal, local information, however low the level? There must be a limit. Small amounts of information that eventually contribute to the larger picture too must be pulled together in their turn from even smaller amounts by some locally acting cohesive force (imagine little streams). Otherwise perception would be hopelessly fragmented (imagine small trickles).

But there must be a limit to strong coherence too. Otherwise some people could never see any hidden figures, or find a misprint in a book, and would never notice a dent on their car. Central cohesive forces may have their own dynamics and change over time within individuals and may differ over different domains of interest. I say this because people can be inconsistent in their views and can easily hold contradictory beliefs, if they have derived them from different information sources (imagine different large rivers, each in its own landscape). It may be that only very exceptional individuals can create true global consistency (all rivers flowing into one ocean).

Block Design

As we have seen in the last chapter, one of the best-documented strengths in autism is excellence on the Block Design test. The critical feature that links Block Design to Embedded Figures is that a big geometric shape, a gestalt, has to be broken up into small shapes. The big shape has to be copied with little building blocks. The design elements that correspond to the blocks are in fact analogous to hidden figures. They have to be "found" before the design can be reconstructed. Hence, the first problem for the person tested is to separate the given design into appropriate segments. This component of the task has little to do with what is generally thought of as spatial ability. However, it could have a lot to do with the postulated central coherence in high-level central thought processes. If children with autism show weak coherence, they should show less of a tendency to perceive the design as a whole, and the initial step of mental segmentation should be easy for them.

Young normal children might find the Block Design task difficult for the same reason that they find the Embedded Figures task difficult. Their cognitive systems are predisposed from the start to operate with a strong drive for central coherence. It may take them several years before they learn to control the high-level central cohesive force. This may be true too for nonautistic children with general intellectual impairment. In contrast, children with autism seem to lack this central cohesive force and may never obtain it.

If this is so, then it should be possible to improve the performance of young normal and retarded children on the Block Design task simply by making sure that the job of segmentation is done for them. A strong central cohesive force can be resisted just by pulling apart those components in the pattern that correspond to the blocks (fig. 9.2). Amitta Shah introduced such a manipulation experimentally with new designs that had to be copied by children with autism and those without.[7]

The results supported the prediction. Prior segmentation massively improved the performance of nonautistic children, whether normal or learning-disabled. Conversely, it had little effect on the performance of able children with autism, who were extremely fast even with the unsegmented designs.

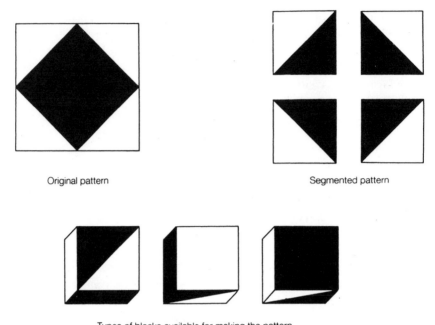

Original pattern   Segmented pattern

Types of blocks available for making the pattern

Figure 9.2   Presegmented Block Design example

In contrast, the young normal and the mentally retarded children were sometimes hard-pressed to perform the unsegmented condition at all within a given time limit. However, when the design was segmented for them, they were almost as fast as the children with autism.

Rote Memory

As we saw in the previous chapter, people with autism have superior rote memory. But what they remember seems to be curiously fragmented. The great writer Jorge Luis Borges has provided a powerful metaphor for the relationship between detailed memory and piecemeal experience. His story, "Funes the Memorius," is a fictional account of a boy with a phenomenal memory, the consequence of brain damage.[8] In the story this boy relabeled every number of the number system with some arbitrary name. He saw entirely different events at successive moments in time which he had to represent. One sentence may suffice to show how the story brings out the pain of this condition: "It bothered him that a dog at 3.14 (seen from the side) should have the same name as the dog at 3.15 (seen from the front)." Funes had the capacity and the burden to represent and store all these minutely different experiences.

A real-life mnemonist, "S," analyzed and described by the great Russian neuropsychologist, Alexander Luria,[9] showed uncanny resemblances to Borges's fictitious case. "S" had the capacity to remember long and seemingly random sequences of events. So extraordinary was his ability that he performed in public. When Luria once presented him with a string of numbers on a piece of paper, arranged in perfectly ascending order of counting, he still remembered the numbers as if they had appeared in random order. When asked afterwards, he said that at the time he had not realized that the numbers were arranged in a simple sequence.

The example reminds us that more limited memory capacity creates a need to chunk single elements into larger coherent units. The single elements can even be recovered later if necessary. For example, the computer manager requests that for security reasons you must choose a password made up of a random string of symbols. You are told that you should avoid memorable dates or names, as such a password could very easily be broken. This demand brings a high risk of forgetting, and one trick to overcome this problem is to create memorable phrases or images from the random sequence of symbols. You could use a phrase, and then take the first letter of each word. "Take the A-train at 8 and change" becomes "TtAta8ac." The random sequence is remembered better as a phrase because the phrase is a more coherent meaningful piece of information. Without such high-level cohesion, pieces of information would remain as pieces and would risk getting lost in memory.

Superior rote memory that is based on small elements, and ordinary memory that is based on large coherent units, give an inkling of how both strategies, the piecemeal and the global, can lead to advantages and disadvantages. When trying to find the correct key in a bunch of similar keys, and when trying to identify a street in a city map, the piecemeal strategy is helpful. On the other hand, when trying to extract the gist from a long lecture, or when trying to understand an ambiguous message, the global strategy is helpful.

Elements and their Context

An example related by the British psychiatrist Digby Tantam also illustrates weak central coherence, or lack of influence from context. A patient exhibiting autistic symptoms from early childhood obsessively collected information about the addresses of juvenile courts. It is unknown how this extremely odd interest arose. However it came about, it would be less odd if it emerged from a general interest in courts, buildings, or town plans. In this case it would not be just a fragment, however well studied, but part of the bigger picture. But this was definitely not the case for this patient. When asked why he did not want to know about the addresses of nonjuvenile courts, he replied, "They bore me to tears." This was not a joke on his part. The remark showed a total lack of understanding that interests are expected to be justified as part of a coherent pattern of likes and dislikes, and not arbitrary. Sometimes, scientists can get absorbed in one extremely narrow and minute aspect of a problem. The difference between good science and abstruse curiosity lies in keeping in mind the relationship between detail and the greater pattern of knowledge into which this detail will have to fit.

A drive for coherence and the ability to make use of context are one and the same thing. There are many tasks where overall context influences our perception of individual elements, and where a tendency for strong central coherence is advantageous. We are often not even aware of the powerful effect of context on one and the same stimulus. The color of a patch in a painting changes hue according to what colors surround it. In social life, a remark quoted out of context can be devastating. On the other hand, a transgression of the law can be overlooked if context is taken into account.

The vagaries of English spelling provide a nice example for the unconscious effect of context. In English, you can have words that are spelled identically, yet sound different and have different meanings. Read aloud the following sentences without thinking: (1) She took the dog for a walk on a long lead; (2) The box was as heavy as lead. Presumably the sentences were meaningful and you noticed nothing peculiar. If so, then strong coherence has been at work. Without being aware of it, you used context to sound out the word "lead" with a different outcome in the two sentences. Because the word is integrated into the sentence, there is no confusion between the two possible meanings of "lead." Individuals with autism cannot so readily modify the pronunciation according to context. Yet when their attention is drawn to the ambiguous words, they are able to change pronunciation appropriately.[10]

Normally, the sentence context is an unconscious backdrop for word pronunciation. If this backdrop is missing, reading comprehension may suffer. This, then, is a downside to weak central coherence. A passage taken from Gunilla Gerland's autobiography refers to an undesirable effect of piecemeal experience: "I always felt there was something I didn't really understand . . . Even when I understood quite a lot, there was always something left – the actual way it all hung together. I made a huge effort . . . The world was an ever-changing mystery, things happened suddenly. How? Why?" Gunilla, a highly intelligent woman, who was diagnosed as autistic in adulthood, goes on to say that she had to make a conscious effort to see relationships between objects: "I suddenly realised that the kitchen and the bathroom had something to do with each other, so I could begin to find other similarities such as that there was water in both rooms."[11]

This example poses the question of categorization and generalization. Human beings constantly classify things and events and generalize from one event to another. In categories that are useful in real life, bathroom and kitchen count as similar. Clearly many differences in detail have to be discounted to see the similarity in the global sense. It seems that in Gunilla's case, her ability to classify things into broad categories that resembled those used by other people was hard won.

In the previous chapter we considered the effect of context on test performance of people who never went to school. Tasks that are embedded in context, for instance, doing subtraction in your head while giving change, contrast with doing subtraction during a written exam. One and the same person can perform very differently in these contrasting situations even if the numerical problems are identical. The unschooled person seems to be influenced more strongly by context. Raven's Matrices, Block Design tests, and the Embedded Figures Test, are all testing abilities taken out of real-life context. Performance on these tests is enhanced in people who have had the benefit of formal education. Schools foster the acquisition of abstract knowledge, knowledge that is not dependent on specific context. In this sense, school fosters weak central coherence.

Detachment and Coherence: The Grand View

In the first edition of this book I was encouraged by John Morton, then director of the MRC Cognitive Development Unit in London, to express my ideas on central coherence in the manner of a "grown-up" theory. Having led by example in putting forward novel theoretical ideas that were fruitful in generating new research, John Morton was surely responsible for the prominence of this section in the book, which did indeed generate new empirical data. As a tribute to the new research, which challenged the theory, I have left the following section describing my original hypothesis (almost) unchanged.

We have now enough evidence to formulate a hypothesis about the nature of the intellectual dysfunction in autism. In the normal cognitive system there is a built-in propensity to form coherence over as wide a range of stimuli as possible, and to generalize over as wide a range of contexts as possible. It is this drive that results in grand systems of thought, and it is this capacity for coherence that is diminished in children with autism. As a result, their information-processing systems, like their very beings, are characterized by detachment.

Detachment, as a technical term, refers to a quality of thought. It could be due either to a lack of global coherence or to a resistance to such coherence. The autistic kind of detachment is not the same as the deliberate detachment that is fostered by formal education and goes with scientific objectivity. Deliberate detachment presupposes coherence and results from reflection on coherence. In everyday language, detachment implies a lack of bias and a lack of impressionability as well as a certain social aloofness. This connection is not mere coincidence. Nevertheless, autistic detachment has different causes. It is unreflected, and it results from a lack of coherence.

The theory of impaired central coherence can well account for excellence on Block Design and Embedded Figures tests. It can also account for the excellent rote memory performance of children with autism. It remains to be seen how well it explains specific failure on the Comprehension test. Poor performance on Block Design and Embedded Figures in young children and in unschooled individuals, on the other hand, can be explained by a natural propensity of the mind toward central coherence, which they have not, as yet, learned to control. Ordinary conversation and the understanding and answering of questions as intended by the questioner implies striving for high-level global, not merely local, coherence of information.

The normal operation of central coherence compels human beings to give priority to the understanding of meaning. Hence we can easily single out meaningful from meaningless material. Indeed it goes against the grain to deal with anything meaningless. Despite the processing effort that it involves, we remember the gist of a message, not the message verbatim. Furthermore, the gist is remembered better if it can be slotted into a larger context. The need to slot information into a larger and larger context is another way to look at the effect of high-level central cohesion. Much work will be needed to specify what kind of job it does.

The ability to make sense, and to see meaning and structure in everything, is very useful. On the other hand, it is something we cannot help doing. From this point of view it is an extension as well as a limitation of our information-processing capacity. It must not be overlooked that as far as the internal inconsistencies of one's beliefs are concerned, there are great limitations. Total coherence is only a dream; in reality it is as much outside the normal individual variation as is lack of coherence.

As evidence for our ability to make sense of what we attend to, I put forward experiments that manipulate sequence meaning and sequence structure. These experiments use different materials. However, all have a common denominator, that is, the contrast between stimuli that are detached and stimuli that are strongly held together. In one type of experiment unconnected and connected words (connected by virtue of underlying meaning) were compared; in another, nonsense sounds in unpredictable and in predictable order (predictable by virtue of underlying sequence structure) were compared. The third type of experiment employs isolated and embedded shapes (connected by overall design). The thread running through all the results is the high performance of children with autism on tasks requiring isolation of stimuli and favoring detachment, and their low performance on tasks requiring connection of stimuli and favoring coherence. In contrast, for young normal children, retarded children, and also unschooled older children from a different cultural background, the balance goes entirely in the opposite direction. Therefore, I assume that a central cohesive force is a natural and useful characteristic of the cognitive system. I also assume that it is significantly weaker in autism.

When looking back over the evidence presented, we find that it is possible to explain the pattern of abilities in autism by a relatively simple and strong hypothesis: a tendency to weak central coherence. This hypothesis goes further than merely restating that there are some peaks and some troughs in test performance. The whole pattern of abilities makes sense when seen as deriving from the particular preferences of a dynamic operating characteristic of very high-level central thought processes.

New Ideas

A cognitive style

The grand view of 1989 is still visible to some extent. However, new work has enriched this view and has begun to change it. The work of Francesca Happé in particular has led to revisions. Happé showed that the effects of central coherence can be seen not just in higher-level tasks, such as extracting meaning from sentences, but also in low-level visual tasks.[12] She demonstrated the type of central coherence acting on immediate visual context that creates optical illusions. An example is the Ebbinghaus illusion (previously incorrectly attributed to Titchener) illustrated in figure 9.3. Here, the middle circles in the two drawings are really identical in size. However, one is seen as larger

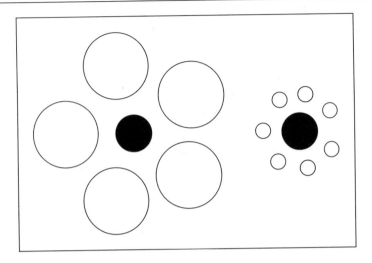

Figure 9.3 The Ebbinghaus illusion

than the other. This is because the context of the surrounding circles influences the perceived size of the middle circles. If the surrounding circles are small, the middle one appears relatively larger and vice versa. This type of illusion, which is determined by context, is more readily resisted by individuals with autism than by control groups.

Happé's work has been crucial in redirecting research interest away from the focus on deficits and toward the strengths in autism.[13] She collected evidence for detail-focused processing in autism in three quite different domains: visual perception, auditory perception, and verbal semantics. She formulated the hypothesis that central coherence is a cognitive style that varies from weak to strong in the normal population and is reflected in a normal bell-shaped distribution of scores on relevant tests. The population of individuals with autism would also be expected to show such a bell-shaped distribution, but with the mean shifted toward the weak extreme. This interpretation has the potential to explain inconsistencies in findings, since there is clearly overlap between the two populations that can result in negative findings when small groups are compared.

Recently, strong support for Happé's view has been obtained in the clinically normal relatives of boys with autism.[14] In this study, around half of the fathers and a third of the mothers of boys with autistic disorder showed signs of a weak coherence style of processing on both visual and verbal tasks. This was shown in their superior task performance. In this respect they differed from the parents of boys with dyslexia and parents of ordinary boys. Moreover, a weak processing style, as identified by high scores on the laboratory tasks, related to certain everyday behaviors in the normal relatives of autistic children. These included the presence of special interests, attention to detail, insistence on routines, and intolerance to change. These features are reminiscent of Kanner's description of "insistence on sameness" in autistic children. Among the general population too there are those who stand out from the crowd by their unusual interests and analytical skills. Such individuals, who nowadays have the advantage of being able to talk to each other on dedicated websites, are discovering affinities with each other and with autism. Nicknames such as "anoraks," "nerds" and "geeks" have often been affectionately applied to such people in the age of the Internet and video games.

"Systemizing"

Simon Baron-Cohen and his group in Cambridge reported similar findings for the relatives of individuals with autism, starting from slightly different premises.[15] He identifies an information-processing style that he calls "systemizing," which is based on an intuitive understanding of how mechanical things work, and a preference for information about the physical as opposed to the psychological world. In this way, Baron-Cohen is looking at a particular information-processing style, combined with a particular information content. Style and content not only fit individuals with autism but also many normal people, and definitely modern-day "geeks." The kind of information that "geeks" might systemize could, for example, be about digital cameras, their specification, their availability, and their cost.

Baron-Cohen contrasts systemizing with empathizing, which refers to the attribution of mental states, and is the same as mentalizing. Using experimental tasks that tapped either of these abilities, he found that, as expected, individuals with autism show excellent systemizing but poor empathizing. The two cognitive styles map onto traditionally held differences between males and females, and also between sciences and humanities. Indeed, Baron-Cohen found that there is a preponderance of fathers of people with autism in engineering, computing, and scientific professions. He is now actively looking for biological markers that distinguish systemizers.[16]

Is there a contradiction between weak central coherence, a piecemeal processing style, and systemizing? The term systemizing implies that it is concerned with structure. However, systemizing is highly compatible with weak central coherence: systemizers typically collect information in self-limiting taxonomies that do not link up with each other. An example of a self-limiting and self-contained taxonomy is the structure that the calendar savant builds up piecemeal, starting with single days, going on to weeks, then months, then years. Just like crystals, small units of information can grow into systems from a single seed in self-replicating structures to large and beautiful patterns. In this way they automatically produce a rule-governed and coherent system.

The fascinating example of Elly Park illustrates the coexistence of weak central and strong local coherence.[17] Elly paid close attention to shadows because they were important and meaningful to her, and very relevant to her moods. When Elly traveled to a different time zone, she was alarmed that her shadow at 6 p.m. was not where it would have been at home. She could not relax until her mother had explained to her that 6 p.m. on her watch meant it was only 5 p.m. at the new place. This example suggests that Elly's scheme that linked shadows with time of day was rule-governed and coherent. It really mattered to her when there were unexpected discrepancies. Nevertheless, her scheme was narrow and self-contained. For instance, the length of shadows of others was not part of the scheme and of no concern to her. Elly's scheme was not only limited in scope, but difficult for others to share. Elly was not able to see her scheme for what it was: a small fragment in a wider pattern of realities, in need of enlargement and modification. This insight would depend on having strong central coherence across large amounts of information.

Enhanced perceptual processing

The ability to discriminate fine detail by ear and by eye has often been credited to autistic children. Is this a consequence of weak central coherence, or is it a phenomenon in its own right? Is it a result of superefficient low-level perceptual processing, as suggested by researchers Mottron and Burack?[18] What would superefficiency entail? Autistic children might not be prepared to see similarities at a more abstract level, and hence would fail to place stimuli into the same category, even when they only differ in the tiniest detail.

Some evidence for this possibility exists. Kate Plaisted and Michelle O'Riordan conducted innovative studies that demonstrated that superior discrimination was detrimental to category learning and to generalization. Children with autism learned a specific pattern of dots very well, but then failed to generalize to another set of dots, which were displayed in a slightly different layout.[19] On the other hand, children with autism performed brilliantly on difficult visual search tasks where the target stimuli differed from distracter stimuli by one small feature only.[20] This work is exciting as it promises to get to a very basic characteristic of perceptual processing.

One such basic characteristic may be an inefficiently working visual system, known as the magnocellular system (named after the big size of the nerve cells that make up this system). Inefficiency in this system leads to a reduced ability to perceive the direction of fast-moving stimuli. This has indeed been found in several studies in different groups of children with developmental disorders, including autism. Elizabeth Milne with John Swettenham and colleagues proposed that the magnocellular system processes patterns in terms of their overall gestalt, while a different visual system, the parvocellular system (named after the small size of its cells) processes stimuli in terms of their individual features. If there was only a magno-system, then the world would look soft and fuzzy without lines or contours. If there were only a parvo-system, then contours and details would stand out in sharp relief. It is possible that these two systems are unbalanced in autism. This would indeed lead to a different way of seeing things.[21]

Difficulties in integration and generalization have also been documented by Laura Klinger and Geraldine Dawson at the University of Washington Autism Center. They found that children with autism had difficulty in applying a previously learned concept to a new situation where the concept would have been appropriate.[22] However, rather than assuming that this problem arose from superior low-level processing, they suggest that the problem is a result of impaired high-level processing. This impairment prevents the formation of abstract categories. Using two types of tasks, they showed that children with autism were not able to abstract an implicit prototype, but could form categories if it was possible to do so by memorizing rules.

While many studies have focused on vision, Laurent Mottron and his colleagues, working in Montreal, have focused on hearing, and also found evidence for enhanced low-level processing. In one musical experiment they set up an ingenious situation producing a conflict between global and local processing.[23] The transposition of a melody can be thought of as a gestalt, and involves global processing, while the recognition of a single erroneous note involves local processing. Individuals with autism were perfectly able to transpose a melody into a different key, showing good global processes. But they were also superior to controls in spotting a single erroneous note when this error was very subtle, showing good local processing. Given that many individuals with autism have the ability to remember the absolute pitch of individual notes, Mottron and his colleagues propose that individuals with autism show enhanced processing of the elementary physical properties of sounds.

The theory of weak central coherence is highly amenable to being explored by the technique known as neural network modeling. So far, only some beginnings exist.[24] Experiments demonstrating enhanced visual and auditory processing argue for change in the original formulation of the theory of central coherence. However, other experiments argue against such a change. This unresolved question reminds us that information processing happens in a vast dynamic system. It is driven both from top down (i.e., controlled by prior knowledge) and bottom up (i.e., controlled by incoming data). The pervasive problem for the autistic brain may be to join up these two information streams. If so, the old and new hypotheses can be reconciled by assuming that bottom-up processing is prolific, precisely because there are problems with top-down processing.

Relationships between mind reading and central coherence

What do the new ideas say about mentalizing failure and processing style in autism? Happé considers a variety of possible relationships, and suggests that the ability to develop sophisticated mentalizing strategies is facilitated by the ability to make use of context.[25] According to Baron-Cohen, there is a trade-off between empathizing and systemizing, suggesting that systemizing as a strategy is inappropriate for interpreting social relationships. Ideas about enhanced discrimination have little to say about mentalizing.

In the first edition of this book I suggested that weak central coherence was a deeper underlying problem that might also explain the mentalizing difficulties in autism. This was because I believed that understanding subtle social interactions required massive integration of multimodal information. The need for high-level integration of information would thus be a stumbling block to acquiring a theory of mind. However, this cannot be right. Many able people with autism manage to acquire a theory of mind, even without the facilitating effects of a mechanism that allows intuitive mentalizing. I also believed that by attributing states of mind, people can create larger chunks and better coherence of the information available and thus reduce memory load. For example, we can make sense of the painting on the cover of this book, showing a rich young man being cheated at cards, without having to remember all the different clues to the meaning that the painter provided. Again, this may be wrong, and what matters is only a detail, perhaps the ability to understand the language of the eyes. But now two interesting alternatives open up. First, mentalizing may not require massive amounts of information integration. Second, and also contrary to what I assumed previously, some people with autism may actually have a preference for strong rather than weak central coherence. If so, then Happé's suggestion implies that those with stronger coherence are better able to acquire social understanding and can more readily compensate for their mentalizing deficit. These are testable hypotheses.

"MEN ARE FROM MARS AND WOMEN ARE FROM VENUS"

The popular prejudice about the typical male and the typical female has found much fuel from autism. "Aren't all men autistic?" is now a common facetious remark. We all know that prejudices are wrong in the individual case, and yet we can often recognize a grain of truth in them. Hans Asperger was the first to remark that autistic intelligence represents an extreme of male intelligence, an idea that has been revived by Simon Baron-Cohen.

Intriguingly, as awareness of autism has increased, so has the awareness that some people have more than a dash of autism. In some places it is considered cool for a young man to be a geek, to wear thick-rimmed glasses, and to have narrow technical and academic interests. Geeks and would-be geeks have their own Internet groups. Like individuals with autism, they seem to be prone to collect facts and objects, and to learn absolutely everything about a certain field of specialization. They are often teased for their lack of interest in the human element. As yet, no one has given tests of central coherence to this interesting group. Would they show excellent performance on the Embedded Figures task? Would they show "field independence" and all that it entails for thought detachment and social detachment?

Many open questions remain in the search for a characteristic processing style in autism and the broader autism phenotype. What might be the relevant neural property of a brain that integrates information to a high degree? There might well be a vast interconnecting network that depends on strong long-range connections between widely dispersed regions. Happé points out that right-hemisphere lesions often lead to diminished global perception. A piecemeal style has also been identified in children with Williams syndrome, and this may give clues to its basis in the brain. The main goal for future research on cognitive processing in autism, whether this is labeled weak central coherence, enhanced perceptual processing, or systemizing, must be to find a neurological basis.

POSTSCRIPT

When rereading Kanner's 1943 paper, I was astonished to find that his interpretations of autistic children's repetitive behavior anticipate weak central coherence:

> A situation, a performance, a sentence is not regarded as complete if it is not made up of exactly the same elements that were present at the time the child was first confronted with it. If the slightest ingredient is altered or removed, the total situation is no longer the same and therefore is not accepted as such. . . . *The inability to experience wholes without full attention to the constituent parts* [my italics] is somewhat reminiscent of the plight of children with specific reading disability who do not respond to the modern system of configurational reading instruction but must be taught to build up words from their alphabetic elements. This is perhaps one of the reasons why those children of our group who were old enough to be instructed in reading immediately became excessively preoccupied with the "spelling" of words.[26]

chapter 10

Sensations and Repetitions

At the age of five Jerry had been diagnosed as autistic by Leo Kanner. At the age of 31 he talked about his childhood to the psychiatrist J. R. Bemporad.

> According to Jerry, his childhood experience could be summarized as consisting of two predominant experiential states: confusion and terror. The recurrent theme that ran through all of Jerry's recollections was that of living in a frightening world presenting painful stimuli that could not be mastered. Noises were unbearably loud, smells overpowering. Nothing seemed constant; everything was unpredictable and strange. Animate beings were a particular problem. Dogs were remembered as eerie and terrifying. . . . He was also frightened of other children, fearing that they might hurt him in some way. He could never predict or understand their behavior. Elementary school was remembered as a horrifying experience. The classroom was total confusion and he always felt he "would go to pieces." There were also enjoyable experiences. He liked going to the grocery stores with his mother so he could look at the labels of canned goods as well as the prices of objects. He also remembered liking to spin objects but could not describe the pleasure this activity gave him. His life seemed to have markedly changed when he discovered multiplication tables at around age 8. He denied that arithmetic helped give his world a sense of order; he said he simply liked working with numbers. Similarly, he could give no reason for his need for sameness or rituals beyond stating that that was how things should be.[1]

Jerry's recollections give us a glimpse of the importance of sensations and feelings in the life of the autistic person. It is not that Jerry had sensory impairments – if anything, he was hypersensitive – but that his perceptions remained fragmented. "Everything was unpredictable and strange" means that stimuli were always different and unexpected, as if they were not embedded in a large coherent pattern. Repetitions, on the other hand, such as spinning objects, studying labels, and doing arithmetic problems, were connected with enjoyable emotional reactions. As far as Jerry was concerned, there was no other reason for indulging in repetitive behavior.

Gunilla Gerland's recollections of her own childhood could be similarly described:

> To the world around me, my behaviour was utterly incomprehensible. I kept touching things all the time – poking my fingers into or under bottles, sofa arms and door-handles, rubbing my palm against turned bannisters. I simply had to touch all these things that had the curve I needed.

> I didn't find it dull eating the same thing all the time, though should it start to become so, that was nothing compared with the mortal danger of risking unknown food . . . The chewing surface of my teeth was occasionally incredibly sensitive to touch – almost electric . . . I wanted to put my teeth into someone, an arm . . . I liked biting people, and on the odd occasion I was allowed to bite my big sister.[2]

Phenomena of heightened or sometimes lowered sensitivity to sensations are often associated with autism and are easily recognizable signs, but we know very little about them. Many other reports exist of hypersensitivity to noises, and the picture of the autistic child who cowers with both ears covered provides a symbol of the acute suffering that hypersensitivity can bring. The narrow preferences for certain food and clothes shown by many children with autism may not only signal an insistence on sameness, but may originate in part from hypersensitivity to taste and texture.

The Five Senses

Seeing, hearing, touching, tasting, and smelling are the means by which we receive information from the outside world. It is a logical first step to investigate if any of the senses are used less efficiently in autistic children, but experiments ruled this out quickly. Children with autism can have impaired hearing, but most do not. Some have impaired vision, but again, most do not. One of the earliest attempts to explain the cognitive problems of children with autism was the following idea: what if they preferred to use the senses closest to the body – touch, taste, and smell – at the cost of those senses that deal with information from distant sources – vision and hearing? This might explain why young children with autism tend to touch, taste, and smell objects and people, often in a socially embarrassing way. Experimental evidence, however, soon showed that the excessive use of taste, touch, and smell was not specifically associated with autism, but was associated with low mental age. Normal babies also vigorously explore the world by means of these senses, but generally this phase does not last long. Looking and listening remain the most important activities for exploring the physical and social environment, even in handicapped children.

The next logical question was: what if complex information received by the senses was not processed in the same way by children with autism? Psychologists have long distinguished "bottom-up" and "top-down" processes in the complex handling of incoming stimuli. The former process is controlled by incoming data, the latter by previous experience. A few decades ago, many psychologists assumed that bottom-up processes had priority. Now, the general consensus is that top-down processes continuously modulate the bottom-up flow of incoming information. For instance, previous experience establishes whether incoming stimuli are expected or unexpected. If they are expected, then they are ignored. If they are unexpected, then they are automatically processed more thoroughly. In this way the onslaught of the mass of incoming stimuli can be controlled. In autism this type of control might be lacking.

Control of Attention

Autistic children have peculiar attention, not poor attention. The complaint is not that they are distractible, but rather that their attention is focused on odd things, and that they cannot be interrupted in their intense preoccupations. While powers of sustained attention appear to be great, the fine-tuned control of flexible attention is missing. But what is it that tunes attention? How do we know what is important so that we can attend to it? Some high-level, "executive" component in the mind has to decide what in the mass of incoming sensations is worth attending to. Problems can originate if this top-down command is not sufficiently clear and decisive. However, difficulties in the control of attention can also be caused by some hold-up in bottom-up processing, possibly because it is overloaded with too much detail.

It often seems that autistic children cannot attend well to simultaneously presented information and therefore select one narrow aspect of this information. The hypothesis of "stimulus overselectivity"[3] addresses this problem. It neatly explains why autistic children often fixate on minor features of the environment but ignore more important ones. For example, they might focus on an earring, while being oblivious to the person wearing it. This may be an example of information overload. However, the opposite could also hold.

Anybody can experience focusing on previously unnoticed cracks in a ceiling or marks on a surface through sheer boredom, that is, information "underload." A relevant example is that of an autistic boy whose fascination with drapery began when he had to watch stage productions in school. Being totally confused by the play or speeches, he would focus on the rippling curtains, which were especially fascinating under spotlights of changing color.

What is important to attend to?

What stimuli will capture the attention of a person who does not know what is worth attending to? What is the object of attention in a mind that has a problem in high-level control? Weeks and Hobson reported an experiment which showed that stimuli can have different importance for normal and autistic children.[4] They asked children to sort pictures of people, the same set on several occasions. It was possible to sort according to whether the expression of the face was happy or sad, and equally it was possible to sort according to whether a person did or did not wear a hat. At the first sort, autistic children tended to sort by hat, while nonautistic children tended to sort by facial expression. However, subsequent trials proved that both groups were able to sort by the other feature as well. Clearly, all children who took part in the experiment could discriminate and categorize by hat or by expression, but the relative importance of the two features was different for the two groups.

Why did different features grab their attention? Perhaps normally functioning minds are predisposed from interest and experience to give priority to social stimuli such as faces. Less priority would be given to hats, because they are only temporary attributes of people. However, for the immediate purpose of categorizing a small set of pictures, the autistic children might have found hats to be a salient feature that was easy to use. Faces of people do not seem to spontaneously capture an autistic child's attention. Evidence that young children with autism show a lack of attention specifically to social stimuli, such as people, but not to nonsocial stimuli, such as objects, comes from the lab of autism researcher Geraldine Dawson.[5]

One of the recurrent themes in biographical accounts of people with autism is that certain stimuli, that most people would find unremarkable, seem to hold inexplicable fascination for them. Other stimuli, which are interesting and salient to most other people, apparently leave them untouched. For instance, 12-year-old Elly (who has been referred to in previous chapters), showed an obsessive interest in color, light, and number.

In the evening, when Elly sets the table for dinner, she puts a tall glass by her plate. It is green, her preferred color, and it is divided into 8 equal levels by decorative ridges. Into this she pours her juice. It too is green. On most days, she will fill the glass exactly to the 6th or 7th level . . . the exact level is determined by the type of day with respect to weather and phase of moon. [6]

Temple Grandin, in her autobiographical account of an autistic childhood, mentions being preoccupied with things other people would hardly pay attention to:

I also liked to sit for hours humming to myself and twirling objects or dribbling sand through my hands at the beach. I remember studying the sand intently as if I was a scientist looking at a specimen under the microscope. I remember minutely observing how the sand flowed, or how long a jar lid would spin when propelled at different speeds. My mind was actively engaged in these activities. I was fixated on them and ignored everything else. [7]

The observations from these very different individuals demonstrate that incidental features of the environment can become the main focus of attention for a person with autism. They also hint at some link between sensation, restriction, and repetition.

Explanations of Stereotypic Actions and Thoughts

Repetitive actions are one of the main diagnostic criteria of autism. However, they are not uniquely associated with autism. Repetitive actions have long been recognized as a common component of mental disturbance. Kraepelin in 1899 listed stereotypies as one of the characteristic symptoms of what he called dementia praecox, later known as schizophrenia. Stereotyped movements are common in patients with severe brain disorders and in particular those that involve the brain system that connects frontal lobes with a structure deeper in the brain, which because of its stripy appearance is known as striatum.

Stereotypies are not just present in movements, but also in thoughts, and hence can be invisible. The definition and classification of repetitive phenomena remains unsatisfactory, and such labels as stereotypies, mannerisms, perseverations, obsessions, and compulsions are often used interchangeably. Indeed, there may be no sound theoretical basis for making a distinction. Whether or not a repetitive act is a compulsion, and the individual tries to resist it, is only known by introspection.

Many ordinary people too exhibit repetitive movements and ruminations. However, a study showed that the mere presence of other people significantly decreased the amount of repetitive movement that undergraduate students displayed while nervously waiting to take a test.[8] In normal people, stereotyped behavior is socially undesirable probably because it signals boredom or inattentiveness. In the case of people with autism the presence of others may not have an inhibiting effect on stereotypies.

Why do repetitive acts occur at all? A living machine such as the human brain never stands still. It constantly responds to stimuli. Even when it does not respond, it runs, just as an engine continues to run in neutral gear. Brain impairment often means that the organism cannot respond flexibly and quickly. Still, the mental engine runs. Often the activity is quite undirectional and appears as endlessly repeated loops of behavior. Such loops also occur in perfectly normal people. Pacing up and down, tapping, humming, swaying, rocking, scratching, nail biting, ruminations, are all stereotypies of a useless but nonpathological type in the repertoire of all human beings. The list is long and includes any variety of action fragments one cares to think of, including thoughts. The presence of stereotypies in stressful situations has led to the hypothesis that movement repetitions and thought repetitions are part of some homeostatic mechanism that controls level of arousal. However, stereotypies do not necessarily decrease arousal.[9] If anything, they often increase it. As regulators of internal states, repetitions seem to be extremely inefficient. Instead, they seem to be consequences of some general readiness to spring into action.

Repetitions can be observed in neurological patients and in laboratory animals and can therefore be related to brain mechanisms. For this reason this area of research has been fruitful in establishing links between autistic symptoms and brain abnormality.[10] Cambridge-based neuroscientist Ros Ridley relates stereotypic to perseverative behaviors, as both imply stimulus-bound behavior with a restriction of behavioral choices.[11] She concludes that stereotyped behavior can be due to an excess of dopamine in the basal ganglia, while perseverative behavior can be due to inadequate levels of dopamine, which can be caused by lesions in the frontal lobes. These conclusions fit remarkably well with Damasio and Maurer's theory of dopamine dysfunction, the first neurological theory of autism, which they proposed as early as 1978.[12] Intriguingly, a number of different disorders, including attention deficit disorder, Tourette's syndrome, and schizophrenia, all implicate the dopamine system in some way.[13] Dopamine deficiency may also be responsible for the frequently observed difficulty in initiating actions and occasional freezing of actions midway, phenomena that are also shown by patients with Parkinsons's disease.[14]

People with frontal lobe damage show perseverative actions that are reminiscent of those of people with autism. Furthermore, they also share other impairments of higher-level control of attention, such as an inability to carry out complex actions without prompting. Some anecdotes that are told of frontal patients are similar to those told of autistic people. For instance, a patient who performed extremely well on IQ tests had difficulties in looking after herself. When shopping she continued loading her basket with the same favorite food even though she already had stocks of it at home. When cooking, she could not do two things at once, even just bringing water to the boil while peeling potatoes. She was fine, however, with a shopping list in her hand, or when following a recipe book with step-by-step instructions.

Routines and Rigidity

More uniquely characteristic of autism than simple motor and thought stereotypies are the so-called elaborate routines of behavior. They involve larger units of action and consist of more than simple mouthing, rocking, or pacing. Precise definitions are lacking, so clinical judgment is at present the only basis for deciding what counts as "elaborate." It is generally agreed that an elaborate routine must be more than a short fragment of action and must include long and possibly complex sequences of thoughts or fixations. A typical list of examples is given in this extract from a mother's letter:

> I don't quite know when John's obsessions began but I suppose he was about three when he started to post anything he could find into our letter box, anyone else's letter box – or even the pillar box. This was shortly followed by a passion for ringing doorbells. The great interest from four to seven years was "wog lights" – street lamps. He would stand at the window watching them all go on at night. In his fourth year he developed a great interest in reflections as seen in the windows, in shiny surfaces and loved carrying round a lens or binoculars. Putting little coloured pegs into their holes was an absorbing occupation, and also into any similar holes he could find. Then, when he was about six, came his interest in buses. Of course he had his collection of buses, but unless I initiated some play they were just handled. The other thing was distinguishing buses which passed by; one kind had stairs in the middle and a white roof and he became quite upset if the stairs appeared in front and the roof was yellow.

Neither the content nor the quality of special interests and routines in autistic individuals has been systematically investigated. Such aspects as rigidity, perseveration, and resistance to change are still quite unexplored, but there are a few pointers. In an early experiment that I carried out in order to study pattern making in young children,[15] I gave them either two or four stamps with different ink colors. These could be pressed down to make marks in a row of boxes any way they liked. I also encouraged children to play freely with a xylophone, which had either two or four bars in place. Nowadays such experiments would lend themselves ideally to a computer game format, an idea that would have seemed like science fiction in the 1960s, when I did the studies.

The colored patterns and tunes that the autistic children produced were not playful and free, but extraordinarily rigid. For example, the whole row of boxes was filled with red ink only, or the bars of the xylophone were tapped only in alternating fashion. There was one other odd feature that I observed in these studies. When given a xylophone with four bars the children with autism hardly ever used all four. Exactly the same restrictive behavior was found with the color patterns: some children with autism only ever used one color, some only two. This was not the case for the intellectually impaired nonautistic children, nor for the young normal preschoolers who took part in the experiment, who were trying out all the available materials in an exploratory way. What these studies suggest is that spontaneous behavior in autism is not random, but has a limited structure of its own. Of course, people with autism are often reported to behave in a rigid and restricted way in everyday life. For instance, they are known to insist on putting each object in their room in its particular place every day, and rituals cannot be interrupted without a serious tantrum. One boy was reported to have eaten only white bread sandwiches, another only dried pasta, for several years.

Fragments of sensations and actions

In the previous chapter we considered the theory of weak central coherence. Can this theory also explain the varieties of sensory phenomena in autism? Sensations in a fragmented mind may remain pieces of information not integrated into a meaningful pattern of perceptions. But why are there so many reports of hypersensitivity? Perhaps sensations retain an absolute value (e.g., absolute pitch) and are not modified by context. Perhaps top-down control does not modulate the incoming flood of data, so that every stimulus is treated as unexpected.

Can weak central coherence account for repetitions of actions? Actions can be segmented into small units, just like perceptions. The smaller and more separate they are, the more accurate copies they can be in a repetition, and the more glaring the repetition would be to the observer. With larger action sequences, repetitions would tend to vary in detail. Therefore, they would not appear stereotyped in the sense that small action fragments do. Consider repetitive preoccupation with multiplication. Multiplying numbers is stereotyped activity, but doing math homework every day is not. It seems possible that repetitions and odd sensations are both effects of a fragmented world and two sides of the same coin.

Two difficult questions are raised by this hypothesis. First, why are fragments of behavior, if they are such, repeated endlessly; and secondly, why is repetition so rigid, even automaton-like? My guess is that repetition is the natural setting for input and output systems, and that they are normally stopped when they are acknowledged by a high-level controller. Such acknowledgement could be the signal for an input device to start processing new information and for an output device to change to new action. In other words, it is switching off rather than switching on that needs special action by a central controller. This assumption would readily allow one to think of the brain as a constantly running engine. The impaired brain in autism could show disengagement between top-down and bottom-up processing streams, because the top-down control processes are too weak to function appropriately.

What of rigidity? It seems to me that flexibility is a quality particularly appropriate for a higher-level context-using mechanism, but not appropriate for lower-level processing devices where reliability would be more important. It may well be that higher-level thought processes pay for flexibility by loss of automaticity. From an evolutionary perspective it is obvious that the behavior of neurologically primitive organisms is rigidly programmed. Even if neurologically sophisticated organisms suffer from specific damage to top-down control processes, then the mode of operation of bottom-up processes could remain perfectly intact and appear repetitive.

Executive Functions

The control of actions through executive systems has been a flourishing area of cognitive neuroscience.[16] Executive abilities are not needed for routine actions, for instance, well-practiced skills such as walking and eating. They are needed, however, when a change of plan occurs, and more generally, whenever routine behavior no longer suffices. Executive abilities are crucial for keeping several tasks going at the same time and switching between them. They are vital for high-level decisions to resolve conflicting responses, for overriding automatic behavior, and for inhibiting inappropriate impulsive actions. Impairments in all these situations, but not in routine tasks, can be observed in patients who suffer from frontal lobe damage. Hence the frontal lobes are plausible candidates for a high-level supervisory system. Most patients who show signs of executive dysfunction retain good perception, language, and other automatic intellectual functions.

One way of imagining what it would be like to have executive problems is to think of caricatures of old age. Older people sometimes show a mild form of what is otherwise a cruelly severe type of dementia that primarily attacks the frontal lobes. From middle age onward most of us will have sufficient personal experience of these phenomena and, if we are lucky, we can laugh about them. This is not about the common memory loss for names, but a particular type of forgetfulness that is really about ongoing tasks and future plans. Old people are forgetful in the way that they can't keep in mind two tasks at once. They may be in the middle of addressing an envelope, when the sound of the postman catches their attention; they put their glasses down to go to the door; at the door, they look inside the letter box, even though the postman went right past; the door handle feels sticky. They look for the cleaning stuff. There are too many bottles and pots to choose from and they get out the same ones again and again. They give up, not being sure any more what they wanted. Of course, they have forgotten where they put their glasses. They can't complete one thing and are constantly distracted by another.

Sounds familiar? Far worse is frank dementia, including the increasing rigidity of habits, and lack of inhibition, which can lead to socially inappropriate actions. All these are signs of weakening executive functions. At the same time, routine functions are fine. The list of executive disorder is long and includes the following problems in neuropsychologists' jargon: impaired working memory; inability to switch tasks, to plan ahead, and to search methodically; inability to generate novel ideas and initiate actions; excessively stimulus-driven behavior; impulsivity and lack of inhibition of predominant responses.

Neuropsychologists did not take long to notice that autistic people, even those with high intellectual ability, show executive problems.[17] Tests designed to address different executive functions show that not every patient with frontal lobe damage is impaired on all of them, and this is true for people with autism also. Since it is plausible that different parts of the executive or supervisory system are located in different parts of the frontal lobe, these findings may give hints as to where to look for anatomical abnormalities. However, the mapping of the frontal lobes and understanding of their function is still at an early stage.

Repetitive actions can be seen as a natural consequence of a lack of higher-level executive control. Imagine a virtual reality computer game without a player. There are some well-powered, smart fighter modules that are triggered by the sight of an equally smart enemy, and they carry on doing their specialized fighting jobs over and over again. This is inevitable when no player commands them to stop. If the brain has such smart specialized modules, then clearly it cannot do without a supervisor.

In this scenario repetitive actions are the output of smart modules that are not stopped, but are easily started by some trigger stimulus. Preoccupations, likewise, are thoughts that are triggered by some accidental stimulus, and cannot be stopped. The source of perseveration may be a lack of supervisor with the power to override the modules. To compound the problem there is no supervisor to initiate a novel program. Michelle Turner found that children with autism, regardless of their intellectual level, were impaired in their ability to generate new ideas when asked to do so.[18] This fits with the clinical observation that repetitive behavior is at its most intense when the child with autism is asked to think of new things to say or do, or when no one is available to prompt different actions.

The effects of executive function failure extend beyond repetitive actions. Difficulties in switching tasks and shifting one's mindset from doing one thing to doing another are features that are not unique to autism, but they are strongly associated with autism. This has been demonstrated by using tests of executive function, for instance, the Wisconsin card sorting test, which consists of a set of cards that can be sorted according to different features, such as color, shape, or number. First the experimenter encourages sorting according to the dimension spontaneously chosen by the patient. But suddenly the experimenter no longer rewards sorting by this dimension, but by another secretly chosen dimension. This change will produce perseverative errors. People with an efficient supervisory system do not perseverate for long but will switch almost instantly to the newly rewarded dimension. An even more taxing task for the supervisory system is to change set, that is, to drop an overlearned rule and adopt its opposite. Think of the children's game "Simon says." Here you trick the other player by giving the familiar command for an action, and thereby trigger the action, but the rule is that you should not carry out the action unless it is preceded by the phrase "Simon says."

In all these tasks the behavior of individuals with autism is marked by perseveration and by an inability to switch flexibly from one action to another or one rule to another. The common problem seems to be an inability to regulate behavior top-down. Parts of the frontal lobes of the normal human brain confer these flexible powers that are critical to adaptation in everyday life. People with autism may lack such a highly adaptive mechanism. In this case, a critical control system of the brain must be malfunctioning.

Links between executive dysfunction and other theories of autism

Could autistic weakness in central coherence be another facet of impaired executive functions? The possibility is worth pursuing. The brain basis of the ability to achieve meaning from context is as yet unknown. It would not seem far-fetched to link this ability with a component of the supervisory system. For example, to make good decisions, the supervisory system needs to integrate information from many sources. Hence, one component of executive function may well be concerned with multimodal integration.

At first glance, it is not easy to see how the lack of top-down control of attention might relate to mentalizing and to weak central coherence. Perhaps stimulus overload is common due to enhanced processing of elementary stimuli. Small differences in the quality and quantity of sensory information might remain salient and impossible to ignore. On the other hand, if you cannot impose meaning on sensations in terms of some overarching categories, you are at the mercy of fleeting and constantly varying impressions. Mentalizing failure may result in a lack of overarching categories in social situations and this may again contribute to overload.

As we have already seen, two mechanisms of attention – focusing on a target and sustaining this focus – appear to be working well in autism, while problems are associated with a lack of control of attention. This lack of control is difficult to pin down. Attention should ideally be a flexible instrument serving a drive for meaning. For instance, after focusing on some detail, this instrument should automatically return to the service of the bigger picture. Imagine going on a walk and using binoculars from time to time to look at birds, but resting your eyes on the landscape and sharing this view with your hiking companion. Using the same image, an autistic person uses binoculars all the time, and will not be interested in sharing the bigger view with a companion. It may be only in the bigger view or greater pattern that we share something of what others consider to have significant meaning. By contrast, it is in the looks through the binoculars that one might expect idiosyncratic interests not shared by others.

Links to mentalizing abilities are less clear. Brain lesions in the frontal lobes may cause patients to fail executive function tests and theory of mind tests, but the performance on these tasks is unrelated. This suggests that these tasks rely on independent brain systems.[19] One patient with a lesion in the left amygdala (see next chapter) that existed from birth resoundingly failed on theory of mind tasks, but performed well on a large battery of tasks challenging his executive functions.[20] Links between mentalizing and executive functions may however exist in the case of normal development. Josef Perner and Birgit Lang reviewed different ideas about possible connections and highlight the intriguing possibility that the conscious awareness of mental states is a prerequisite for the emergence of self-control in normal four year olds. They make the plausible suggestion that understanding one's own mind provides better insights into how to exert self-control.[21]

At present, it is difficult to decide whether or not (at least) three separate primary deficits are present in autism and affect different brain systems. All three may be necessary to explain the full picture of the autistic spectrum. Ultimately, however, it may be possible to link these theories together. In the last chapter we will return to this question.

chapter 11
Seeing the Brain
Through a Scanner

The evidence that autism is a disorder of the brain is overwhelming. It is now hard to believe that at one time clinicians held the view that autism was a disorder of the mind and not the brain. This idea drew support from the fact that there was at first no direct evidence of brain abnormality, but it was only lack of tools that made it impossible to see the evidence. Now we are much better equipped with the increasingly sophisticated neuroimaging techniques. These can produce high-quality photographic pictures of the brain, and can show what happens in the brain while the living human being is engaged in looking, listening, thinking, feeling, and remembering.

In this chapter I will attempt to review current knowledge in this fast-moving field. Because the results are new and mostly not yet replicated, only original sources rather than reviews must be referenced. There are far more references in this chapter than in the other chapters in this book, which makes the chapter more like a journal article. This may be taxing for readers who are not used to this style, but at this stage it is simply not possible to make summary statements with confidence. Instead it is necessary to emphasize the preliminary nature of the evidence.

Long before neuroimaging technology emerged, indications of brain abnormalities in autism were abundant and shattered the belief that autism was a "psychological" rather than an "organic" condition.[1] Epilepsy is one of these signs and may well be a sign of abnormality in brain structure. Intellectual retardation can also be taken as a sign of early brain abnormality. However, even individuals with good performance on intelligence tests can show obvious neurological signs, for instance poor motor coordination.[2]

Such evidence only establishes that brain abnormality is present, but does not reveal its nature. We are presented with a tricky problem. If there is a whole scatter of neurological abnormalities, which of these will be a cause of autism – and which will be merely a correlate? Identifying the neurological basis of autism must not be confounded with identifying the basis of developmental disorders in general, of mental retardation, of hyperactivity, or of language disorder. After all, autism can exist without any of these added complications, and there are a variety of developmental disorders, each with its own causal story. This makes investigations of cases of autism without additional symptoms particularly important.

What is Wrong with the Brain?

The challenge of the search for the brain basis of autism has been accepted enthusiastically. However, the range of factors to be considered is huge. Where would one expect to find the abnormality? At the level of the single neuron? At the level of a dedicated brain system, such as exists for movement, vision, hearing, or language? Or should we look at the interconnections between such systems rather than at the systems themselves? Should we focus on particular neurochemical transmitter systems?

Looking at the postmortem brain under the microscope was for a long time the only way to obtain information about brain abnormalities. The pioneering work in the field was done by Margaret Bauman and Thomas Kemper at Harvard Medical School. However, the number of postmortem brains available is small, and among these the number of cases unconfounded by other problems, such as epilepsy and severe mental retardation, is minute. At the same time, each brain is a continent to explore under the microscope, an almost impossible task when not guided by prior knowledge and hypotheses about where to look. Nevertheless, detailed observations of cell structure have shown abnormalities in particular regions. The most striking abnormalities were related to increased cell packing density.[3] These abnormalities can be dated according to their time of origin and their consequences for development. In this way Margaret Bauman dated brain abnormalities in autism to a stage of gestation as early as five weeks. If there is some deviation in the early stage of a developing system, there are bound to be downstream effects. Such effects may be invisible even under the microscope.

Since autism is a developmental disorder, we may presume that underlying it is not some sudden damage, but an abnormality of brain development, which may become manifest only gradually. Hence the normal development of the brain must be taken into account when hypothesizing what kind of abnormality could cause autism. Nerve cells follow growth instructions laid down in the genes, so that abnormalities appear if a gene program is faulty.

Obviously, faults can arise for many reasons. The immature brain has more densely packed cells and more synapses per cell than the mature brain. In this sense, the autistic brain resembles a more immature brain. Developmental problems may be caused by a failure to switch off, rather than to switch on, growth of connections. If so, this could explain the puzzling finding that people with autism have bigger brains.

Bigger Brains

Increased head circumference and increased brain weight are among the most robust recent findings on brain abnormalities in autism to date.[4] An increase in overall volume has been consistently found, and about 30 percent of cases have abnormally big brains. Why have we not known about the bigger brains before? This fact was obscured by another subgroup of people with autism who had abnormally small brains (microcephaly). Microcephaly is known to be associated with certain medical conditions and severe mental retardation. If this group, which suffers from severe problems in addition to autism, is put to one side, then the average brain size for people with autism is seen to be well above the normal average.[5]

What are the implications of bigger brain size for autism? An important clue is given by the fact that the greater size is not evident at birth, but is evident in early or middle childhood.[6] Bigger brains could therefore very well be due to overabundant growth of connections between nerve cells and a lack of pruning.

The normal brain in childhood and through to adolescence undergoes waves of growth and subsequent cutback resulting in reorganization. This process is controlled by genes, but environmental influences also play a role. At first, connections between brain cells – synapses – proliferate. Then large numbers of the connections that have just been formed are eliminated.[7] This two-phase reorganization conjures up the image of a well-tended garden where, after accelerated growth, plants need to be vigorously pruned. Just as in the garden where rapid growth occurs at different times in different plants, so the time course for growth and cutback is different for different brain regions.[8] It is possible, therefore, that a failure to eliminate overproduction affects only selected brain systems, and other systems may not be affected.

What might lack of pruning entail?

Since we have no direct evidence of a failure in pruning in autism, all we can do is speculate about this possibility and its implications. It is plausible that cognitive processes that are subserved by brain regions that contain too many synapses would be inefficient. One possible scenario is that in autistic brains, a lack of pruning affects mainly top-down processing systems, which depend on efficiently organized neural feedback connections. Bottom-up processing systems rely on neural feedforward connections, and these are probably laid down earlier and remain more stable during development.[9] Neural feedback connections, on the other hand, may have several phases of reorganization, each involving growth followed by pruning. It is plausible that each reorganization in which overproduction of cells is not followed by elimination makes matters worse. Epilepsy, which is due to an increased electrical discharge of nerve cells, might conceivably be a consequence of overabundant nerve connections.

As indicated in previous chapters, an inefficient top-down system of control would result in poor ability to modulate bottom-up systems. This could be a possible cause of many of the social and nonsocial features of autism. One of the major phases of growth and subsequent cutback of synapses may well coincide with the 18 months revolution, which signals the end of infancy. It may also signal the beginning of new ways of learning through gathering information from other people. As discussed earlier, this form of learning is based on the ability to track intentions in others and is particularly obvious in the way children learn the meaning of words. It is also obvious in the way they communicate with their peers in social play. The 18 months revolution appears to be absent or delayed in autism, and this could be due to a failure of reorganization of specific brain regions that support the ability to "mind read."

Given that phases of reorganization may affect other brain regions at other times during development, there are some further speculations. The prefrontal cortex is one of the last brain regions to mature. This may involve gradual loss rather than formation of new synapses with strengthening of the remaining synaptic connections.[10] This process of maturation might well be delayed or disturbed in autism. If so, this would account for executive function deficits, which are now known to be more evident at later rather than at earlier ages. Having previously contributed much of the important evidence for executive dysfunction in autism, Bruce Pennington and his colleagues found no special signs of such dysfunction in four-year-old children.[11] This finding has been confirmed by Geraldine Dawson and colleagues.[12] It may well be that top-down control becomes deficient only after the lack of pruning of feedback connections that have their origin in the frontal lobes. These studies suggest that developmental abnormality needs to be traced in the same individuals over time. In the future we may be able to see the developing brain in dazzling motion, as we can now see the waxing and waning of plants in vivid film sequences. Such a technique would be useful to test the so far speculative ideas about growth and lack of cutback of synapses in autism.

New Insights from Brain-imaging Techniques

The ability to watch the living brain while it thinks has revolutionized the study of mind and brain. The crucial breakthrough was an achievement in engineering. The revolution is similar to the revolution created by X-rays, when it was possible to see the bones and organs of the body through the skin. In order to see the brain, scanners had to be developed that use cameras placed around the head, which take pictures through the skull. What do these cameras take pictures of?

Positron emission tomography, or PET, uses radioactive tracers. When tiny amounts of radioactive substances, for instance oxygen 15 in water, are injected into the bloodstream, using an intravenous method, you can follow the tracer in the blood and watch where the blood flows in the brain by detecting the highly energetic radioactivity. The whole brain is scanned continuously until the radioactivity has disappeared after about two minutes. Each time a new scan is taken, the head has to be properly realigned. A special headrest is often used. How can you see activity in the brain? The idea is that whenever neurons in some part of the brain are working they require replenishment of energy. The blood brings this energy to wherever it is needed in the form of oxygen and glucose. By detecting where the blood flow is greatest we can find out which part of the brain is working hardest. A session may include a dozen such scanning periods during which a volunteer may be presented with visual or auditory stimuli, and may be asked to respond verbally or by pressing a button.

Magnetic resonance imaging, or MRI, is a more recent method with certain advantages. It also makes blood flow visible, but over shorter time periods, and it manages without radioactivity. However, there are drawbacks too. The head is placed inside a powerful magnetic coil, which produces such noisy booms that earplugs are necessary. Furthermore, the person scanned has to lie very still in an enclosed space for several minutes up to one hour, and some people find this uncomfortable. Stimuli may be displayed on a monitor, and volunteers may be asked just to look at them or press a button. Because of very small changes in its magnetic properties, blood that is carrying oxygen can be detected and it is possible to see which parts of the brain the oxygen-rich blood flows to and therefore deduce which regions are working hardest. MRI can also be used to give photographic quality 3-D images of the structure of the brain at rest. It is possible to see the shape of the folds of the cortex, the sulci (valleys), and gyri (ridges) as well as all the structures underneath the cortex.

Because of the considerable practical difficulties in both PET and MRI the numbers of individuals scanned in most studies are small. The radioactivity in PET scanning prohibits it from being used freely, while the magnetism in MRI scanning is safe but is associated with loud noise. In all scanning experiments subjects are required to remain in the same position for an appreciable time. In the case of children this has meant that they are usually scanned when they are asleep, which makes it difficult to observe brain activity during a particular task.

The development of scanners is only part of the technical revolution that has made it possible to see the living brain. The next step was to make sense of the thousands of pictures that the scanners took. This is a problem of statistical analysis of such magnitude that it is still being worked on. The smallest unit is called a voxel and makes up a tiny cube of a few millimeters. Not only does the analysis need to cover the whole brain, it must take account of the fact that people's brains, just like their bodies, have different sizes and shapes, but still have roughly the same structure. One approach is to look only at preselected regions of interest. Another approach is to look at the whole brain, which obviously involves far more extensive data analysis.

In the analysis of whole brains, where each brain has been statistically transformed in such a way that it fits a standard template, one can obtain average activations from a whole group of subjects. In the same way one can envisage transforming the whole body into a standard shape, which would leave the positions of the organs relative to each other unchanged, but would get rid of gross differences in size. Structural or functional abnormalities can be revealed if a suitable comparison group is available, which of course must also be statistically processed to fit the standard template. When applied to measures of blood flow this technique is called statistical parametric mapping. In the technique known as voxel-based morphometry, an average brain, consisting of thousands of these tiny picture cubes, is made up for a group of people, which can then be compared to another. Any anatomical differences obtained are independent of brain size.[13]

Over and above these technical and practical difficulties, the results from brain-imaging studies are difficult to interpret. This is because we still know very little about the function of most parts of the brain. One major limitation is that the visible blood flow increases occur in large areas in the brain and concern millions of neurons. Ideally we would like to know what small groups of neurons do, and what happens within a single neuron. Studying the activity of single

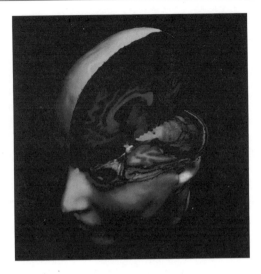

Figure 11.1   Schematic picture of the whole brain
With thanks to Chiara Portas

neurons with special probes can usually be done only in animals and provides vital information about how the cells in the brain actually work.

Despite these difficulties, the use of brain imaging has led to new insights about cognitive processes. For instance, it has been possible to confirm that executive functions in the brain are distributed over the frontal cortex. It has been possible to identify certain areas of the brain that process specific information, such as faces. Most of this knowledge is still preliminary, but already the techniques have been applied to autism.

The Brain at Rest

The anatomy of the brain is obviously complex, and because of its three-dimensional structure it is hard to visualize specific regions. Figure 11.1 gives an impression. Good sources of anatomical pictures are available on the Internet and I myself have used the following websites, which I gratefully acknowledge:

http://www.uni-ulm.de/uni/fak/medizin/auz/hirn.htm
http://www9.biostr.washington.edu/
http://medstat.med.utah.edu/kw/brain_atlas/mri/
http://ric.uthscsa.edu/projects/talairachdaemon.html

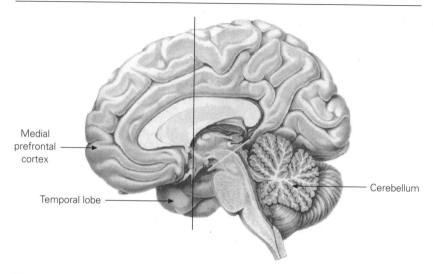

Medial prefrontal cortex

Temporal lobe

Cerebellum

Figure 11.2   Slice through the middle of a schematic brain

The cerebellum

The cerebellum is an ancient and important structure at the back of the brain, and of vital importance for many different motor and cognitive functions. Figure 11.2 shows a schematic view using an imaginary cut through the middle of the brain. Margaret Bauman found abnormalities of the posterior inferior regions in both cerebellar hemispheres, with a significant reduction of cells.[14] Eric Courchesne at the University of California, San Diego, using structural scans that allowed a direct measurement of shape and volume, reported that the middle part, the vermis, was reduced in size in autism.[15] Since Courchesne's original report there has been considerable controversy about this finding, and in different studies the vermis of the cerebellum has been found to be either abnormally small or abnormally large.[16] More recent studies have not clarified the situation. For instance, a larger cerebellum may be part and parcel of the increased overall brain size in autism.[17] However, two independent studies using voxel-based morphometry, which controls for brain size, both found evidence of increased grey matter density bilaterally in the posterior lobes of the cerebellum.[18] An important role of the cerebellum, in conjunction with the frontal lobes, is the control of attention, especially shifts of attention. It is possible, therefore, that cerebellar abnormalities are linked to the peculiarities of attention in autism.[19]

The temporal lobes

There are several reasons that make the temporal lobes regions of special interest in autism. For instance, a proportion of people with autism have epilepsy, which often originates in the temporal lobes. Embedded in the temporal lobes are the amygdaloid structures, and these as well as other structures of the temporal lobes have been highlighted in animal studies as a part of the social and emotional brain. Patients with damage in these regions have social difficulties that are reminiscent of autism. Another reason for the particular interest of the temporal region of the brain comes from tuberous sclerosis, a rare disorder where small tubers tend to grow in the brain. Some of the children afflicted with this condition have also been diagnosed as autistic. In all these cases the tubers were lying in the temporal lobes.[20]

Using the scanner, researchers have measured blood flow in autism when the brain is at rest because this can reveal areas of persistently abnormal perfusion. This in turn may relate to abnormal anatomical structures. Without any particular expectation of which, if any, brain region would show abnormal perfusion, two recent, well-controlled studies have revealed consistent abnormalities in the temporal cortex.[21] Both these studies investigated school-age children who were mentally retarded as well as autistic, and used control groups matched for age and IQ. The children were sedated during the scanning procedure in order to minimize head movements. The data were analyzed using statistical parametric mapping. In both studies reductions of blood flow were observed in the autism group, in the temporal lobes of both sides of the brain, the superior temporal gyrus. Figure 11.3 illustrates the findings of the study by Zilbovicius and at the same time shows the position of the temporal lobe. The meaning of this finding is still obscure, and it remains to be seen whether the same pattern of temporal lobe hypoperfusion occurs in autistic individuals with IQs in the normal range.

The amygdala

The amygdala is part of the ancient social brain that humans share with many animals.[22] Figure 11.4 illustrates the site of the left amygdala in a so-called axial section of a postmortem brain. This slice is taken at the point indicated by a vertical line in figure 11.2. The amygdala is connected with

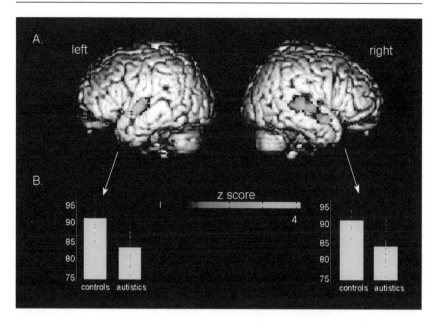

Figure 11.3 Figure from Zilbovicius et al. (2000) in *American Journal of Psychiatry*, 157, 2000, p.1990

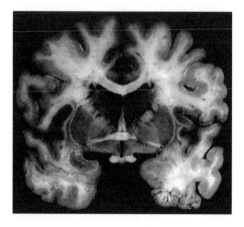

Figure 11.4 Site of the amygdala in axial section in postmortem brain outlined in white. Here the folds of cortex can be seen clearly. The outer layers of the cortex are colored gray and contain only neurons, the layer beneath is white and contains only axons, the connecting fibers between neurons.

other parts of this system, such as the superior temporal cortex (STS) and frontal cortex (in particular, orbitofrontal regions). Postmortem examination of this part of an autistic brain has shown cellular abnormalities. For these reasons, dysfunction of the amygdala in autism, or of the connections between amygdala and other parts of the brain, is a strong possibility.[23]

The evidence for the role of the amygdala in autism is not as strong and not as consistent as one would suppose, given its interest to many researchers. Studies by Jocelyn Bachevalier and Mort Mishkin on the function of the amygdala region are often cited as an animal model of autism.[24] A surgical lesion in the temporal lobe to remove the amygdala and adjacent portions of the brain in very young rhesus monkeys showed interestingly different behavioral consequences to such lesions in adults. Here the resection resulted in young monkeys showing a lack of social interest, a lack of initiation of social contact, and expressionless faces, while in adults loss of memory was the most prominent consequence. A more recent study by Prather, Amaral, and colleagues reported that early lesions of the amygdala in monkeys led to increased fear of other animals.[25] At the same time the operated monkeys showed less fear of objects that other monkeys are normally afraid of, for instance, a toy snake. This study reminds us that the functions of the amygdala in regulating fear and other emotional responses are complex, and different subregions within the amygdala need to be distinguished.

While the phenomena described in these studies are reminiscent of autism, they are only vaguely reminiscent. It may be that animal models for autism will always be unsatisfactory because they depend on the identification of analogous behavioral symptoms. The core symptoms of autism seem to affect very human-specific aspects of social and nonsocial behavior, such as language and communication.

Studies concerning the shape and volume of the amygdala in autism, as seen in MRI scans, are as inconsistent as the studies of the cerebellum. Two studies[26] have observed reduced amygdala volume, one has observed no difference,[27] and one reports an increase in volume.[28] The two voxel-based morphometry studies, which are independent of overall brain size, both observed increased gray matter density in the general region of the amygdala.[29]

Of these studies I can describe one in more detail, because I was involved in it.[30] In this study 15 volunteers with high-functioning autism or Asperger syndrome and 15 nonautistic adults of the same age and intellectual level were compared. MRI scans of the individuals in the two groups were averaged to obtain a picture of the density of gray and white matter throughout the whole brain.

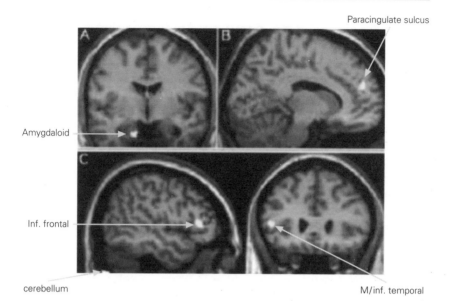

Figure 11.5   Based on figures in Abell et al. (1999) study in *Neuroreport*, 10, 1647–51

We had no specific hypothesis as to which, if any, areas might show group differences, especially as the group of autistic adults included many people who were extremely well compensated and had university degrees. Figure 11.5 shows the maximum differences between the brains of the two groups. These differences in gray matter density are small but highly significant. There might be additional differences that we did not see because the statistical cut-off points used are very strict. On the other hand this means that the differences we found are likely to be robust. In hindsight, the regions that showed statistical differences were all quite plausible. They highlight the temporal lobes, the cerebellum, and the frontal lobes, regions that are heavily interconnected and hence can be thought of as representing a system. This system seems to be centered on the amygdala. The regions around the amygdaloid structures and posterior to them at the back of the brain were enlarged, while the regions anterior to them in the front of the brain were reduced in size. Perhaps there is a bottleneck in this system, where too much is coming in and too little going out.

We considered these admittedly preliminary results exciting, because they hint at a link between structural and functional abnormalities. We will come back to this in the next section.

The Brain in Action

How do functional imaging studies identify which pattern of brain activity is associated with a particular cognitive process? After all, the brain is active all the time. It is done by comparing activity during the performance of two tasks, which are identical in every way except for one: the presence of the cognitive process of interest in the experimental task, and the absence of that process in the comparison task. Sometimes an additional baseline task is used, which can be set against both experimental and comparison tasks. An example is provided on p.195. This material was first used in a study by Fletcher et al. to identify the mentalizing system,[31] and includes Happé's Strange Stories.[32] During scanning the task is to read and understand a story to answer a question. However, only one of the two stories demands "mind-reading" ability. The baseline task presents unconnected sentences. These too have to be read so that a question about one of the sentences can be answered. Subtracting brain activity resulting from the experimental and the comparison and/or baseline task from activity resulting from the experimental task leaves you with brain activity associated with the cognitive process of interest. In each of the three conditions volunteers silently read text appearing on a monitor while they were lying in a PET scanner and answered questions. Each condition was represented by four different stories read during 12 scanning episodes. Only stories that provoked "mind reading" should engage the critical cognitive process we were interested in. We reasoned that you could not answer the question properly unless you had been engaged in mental state attribution. There was no such requirement for the other types of stories and the unlinked sentences.

When brain imaging is used to study autism, what we hope to find is a difference during the critical task, but not during the other task or during the baseline task. In other words, the pattern of activity associated with some cognitive process (manifest in the brain as the difference between the experimental task and the control task) will be different in the autistic group compared to the control group.

There are essentially two approaches for choosing tasks relevant for functional imaging studies of autism. One approach is to identify a brain region of interest (e.g., the amygdala) and then select a task that is known to elicit activity in this region in normal volunteers (e.g., looking at fearful faces). The other approach is to identify a cognitive process of interest (e.g., mentalizing) and then select tasks (e.g., "theory of mind" tasks) that have successfully related this process with activity in circumscribed brain regions.

STORY INVOLVING MENTAL STATE ATTRIBUTION

Helen waited all year for Christmas, because she knew at Christmas she could ask her parents for a rabbit. Helen wanted a rabbit more than anything in the world. At last Christmas Day arrived, and Helen ran to unwrap the big box her parents had given her. She felt sure it would contain a little rabbit in a cage. But when she opened it, with all the family standing round, she found her present was just a boring old set of encyclopedias, which Helen did not want at all! Still, when Helen's parents asked her how she liked her Christmas present, she said, "It's lovely, thank you. It's just what I wanted." (The question afterwards was: Why did she say this?)

STORY NOT INVOLVING MENTAL STATE ATTRIBUTION

Mrs Simpson, the librarian, receives a special book which she has to catalog and find an appropriate place for. She has to decide which section to file it under. The library is very big, and has different sections on many different subjects. The new book is about plants and their medical uses, and is heavily illustrated. However, Mrs Simpson does not put it on the shelf with the rest of the books on botany. Neither does she put it with the books on medicine. Instead, she carefully takes it into a separate room. In this room all the books are kept in special cases, and the temperature is kept constant. (The question afterwards was: Why did she do this?)

UNLINKED SENTENCES

She is always saying that someone will eventually find the treasure. Everyone is allowed two visits and no more. At the psychiatry department they were interviewing the new nurses. Jim will win the first race of the meeting. She has taken all the children to visit the zoo today. Simon's uncle is wearing a new suit. The same phrase of twenty-three notes recurred throughout. (The question afterwards was: Will Jim lose the first race?)

However, there is one other difficult problem in comparing results between clinical groups and normal volunteers. It is obviously problematic to interpret results of scanning studies when some subjects were not performing the tasks very well. The differences found might simply be a correlate of performance level and say nothing that we did not know already. It is difficult to distinguish cause and effect when one group is impaired at performing the task. The resulting activation could either cause or simply reflect their poor performance. This problem was avoided in the studies discussed below by using easy tasks and autistic individuals with IQs in the normal to high range. Therefore, we do not as yet know what brain activations would be found in individuals with more severe forms of autism. Yet another unanswered question is in which way children would differ from adults. The search for the neurophysiological effects of development on cognitive functions has hardly begun.

Testing the mentalizing system

Even though the concept of mentalizing is still relatively new, there have been several studies in which normal volunteers have been scanned while solving problems that require thinking about the mental states of others. A wide range of different paradigms has been used varying from reading stories to watching animated films.

So far there are only a handful of studies with autistic volunteers and these volunteers are all exceptionally well-compensated adults with Asperger syndrome or high-functioning autism. They all can attribute mental states to others, at least in simple scenarios. Nevertheless, they take longer than normal adults and make errors during these tasks that normal adults hardly ever make. So far, there have been three studies in which autistic individuals were scanned while thinking about the mental states of others. In one early study the volunteers read the stories and unlinked sentences shown on p.195.[33]

As the example illustrates, the mentalizing stories hinge on the ability of the reader to attribute mental states to the protagonists, and this was hard for the autistic volunteers. For instance, they had to infer that Helen must have been disappointed with her present, but did not want to hurt her parents' feelings. On the other hand, they found it easy to infer that the book that the librarian was cataloguing must be precious. Typically, they performed with total accuracy when answering the question after reading the unconnected sentences.

In another study volunteers had to match the expression of a pair of eyes with a complex mental state term (e.g., suspicious), a task that was developed by Simon Baron-Cohen. The contrast (baseline) condition was to judge the gender of the person whose eyes you saw.[34]

Fulvia Castelli, then a PhD student at the UCL Institute of Cognitive Neuroscience, conducted the third study with the help of Francesca Happé, Chris Frith, and myself.[35] In this study, which had a long history of development, volunteers watched animated cartoons in which two triangles moved around in such a way as to elicit attributions of mental states, for instance one triangle surprising or teasing another. In comparison conditions the triangles moved randomly or they moved purposefully without eliciting more than simple descriptions of their actions, for example, fighting, following, or chasing each other. Examples of the animations and details of the study are available at the website indicated in the paper. While watching those animations that were scripted to compel viewers to attribute all sorts of mental states to the little triangles, a network of brain regions became highly active – over and above any activity seen when watching the other types of animations. This is shown in figure 11.6.

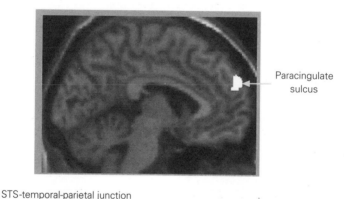

Figure 11.6 Components of the mentalizing system, using pictures based on Castelli et al. (2002) in *Brain*, 125, 1–11

The network contains the same three regions of the mentalizing system that have been obtained in previous studies with normal volunteers. In addition it shows two visual regions, which is presumably to do with the fact that the sequences that compelled people to mentalize were visually more complex.

Rudiments of a mentalizing system

The three regions that have been consistently activated by the requirement to consider the mental states of others, in all studies done so far, are the rudiments of a mentalizing system in the brain. They are situated in the medial prefrontal cortex, in the posterior superior temporal sulcus (STS), and in the temporal pole in the vicinity of the amygdala. We should probably imagine the three regions to be merely tips of an iceberg, that are just visible but hint at others beneath the surface.

What do the findings actually mean? It would be disappointing if all we could say is: "In these three regions – who would have thought it? – the brain is active when we are thinking about our own and other minds." We need to know why. But this is still far from clear. Fortunately, we have some help from other studies that have also activated these critical regions. What are the common factors? Figures 11.7, 11.8, and 11.9, delineated by Chris Frith, can give some clues. The relevant studies have been summarized in reviews.[36]

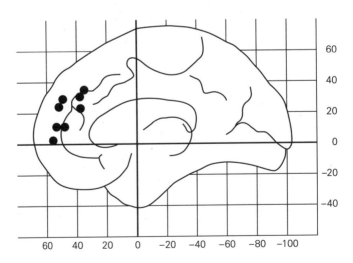

Figure 11.7 Paracingulate sulcus (medial prefrontal cortex)

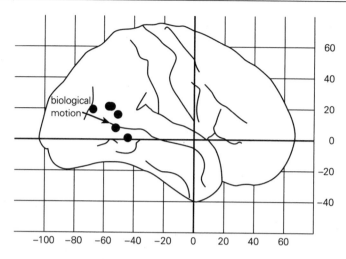

Figure 11.8 Temporoparietal junction (superior temporal sulcus)

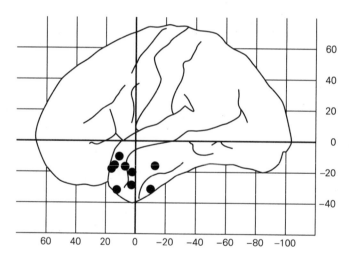

Figure 11.9 Amygdaloid region (temporal poles)

The medial prefrontal region (shown in figure 11.7) of the mentalizing system appears to be active whenever people look into their own thoughts or feelings. This was shown, for instance, when people had to report whether they felt pain at a particular moment. The same region is also active when another person addresses you, either by looking at you intently or by calling your name.[37] It is also active when people are asked simply to rest, and to pursue their own thoughts, identified by Marcus Raichle as "self-referential thought."[38] It is highly plausible that a component to do with monitoring one's own mental states and feelings should also be a component of mentalizing.

The temporoparietal region shown in figure 11.8 appears to be active whenever a person observes movements of other agents. Typically, movements of other agents are biological, for example, a mouth moving or a limb reaching, rather than mechanical, such as a pendulum swinging or a weight falling. Thus, movements of eyes, hands, and mouths are of particular interest to this region. This again makes sense as a component of the mentalizing system: the proper focus of such a system should be on agents like ourselves and their actions.

The amygdaloid region shown in figure 11.9 is known from many studies, including those outside the scanner, to be particularly concerned with emotional states of other people, especially sadness and fear. It is active even when people are not explicitly aware of the emotion. This would also make it an important component when intuitively attributing mental states to others.

All these clues are plausible, but they are preliminary suggestions, mainly because we are ignorant of the neural connections between the three regions, even though we know that they are connected. For the full story we need to know how the monitoring of one's own inner states, the observation of other agents, and the recognition of emotional values, can be linked up together to form a cognitive mechanism that is more than the sum of these parts. It may well be that after technical improvements additional components will emerge in future studies, and that the neural connections will become clear.

Reduced activation of the mentalizing system in autism

In all three studies of mentalizing in individuals with autism or Asperger syndrome done so far, the three regions of the "mind-reading" network were less active. Why a reduction? Perhaps the neurons themselves are different and work less efficiently, but so far no one has looked for direct evidence for this. Perhaps the structures themselves are sound, but the connections between them are weak. This possibility is amenable to study with improved techniques that allow the investigation of functional connectivity between brain regions. Looking for anatomical connectivity is another matter and needs different techniques that have not yet been tried.

One suggestive coincidence is that one of the three mentalizing components, the one located in the medial prefrontal cortex, the so-called paracingulate sulcus, showed abnormally reduced grey matter density in the structural MRI study described on p.193. As can be seen in the figure (11.5), as a second component, the amygdaloid region was also pinpointed as abnormal, showing increased gray matter density in the autism group.

IS THERE A BOTTLENECK IN THE MENTALIZING SYSTEM IN AUTISM?

The study using animations provided one possible clue as to why "mind reading" is impaired in autism. This new clue was one of the two additional visual regions, which was highly active in all people while they watched sequences that provoked mental state attributions. This region was in the extrastriate visual cortex. In this region, known to be associated with very early phases of (bottom-up) perceptual processing, the autism group showed an entirely normal pattern of increased activation for the critical conditions. This was in sharp contrast to the other regions of the mentalizing network (probably involved in top-down processing), which showed reduced activation. In other words, relevant visual information was failing to get through to regions that might be able to extract its social significance. This bottleneck was confirmed in another way. Correlational measures showed significantly less connectivity between the extrastriate visual regions and superior temporal sulcus (STS), one of the three main components of the mentalizing system, in the autistic group. Thus, there is less information link-up between these regions than in the normal brain – in other words, a bottleneck.

How is information link-up regulated in the normal case? As discussed in the previous chapter, the classic psychological account of information processing was bottom-up. For example, a visual scene would be first analyzed in terms of visual features, and these would be combined into objects. Recent evidence from anatomy, neurophysiology, and neural network modeling suggests that this is not how the brain works. In addition to neural feedforward (corresponding to bottom-up) there are also feedback (corresponding to top-down) connections between neurons, and these are in the majority.[39] Incoming information is modified by these feedback connections.[40] This requires strong and possibly long-range connections between neurons, across different brain regions. Through these connecting pathways signals can be sent that modify neurons in distant areas. For instance, when people deliberately attend to a moving stimulus, neural connectivity is enhanced between two areas of visual cortex, one concerning basic visual processing (V2), and one concerning motion processing (V5). This enhanced connectivity is generated by top-down signals from an attentional system located in the parietal and prefrontal cortex.[41]

Testing executive functions

Although brain-imaging studies of top-down control of attention (i.e., voluntary attention, the opposite of mere capture by salient stimuli) in normal volunteers have been productive, nobody so far has used these paradigms for people with autism. Clearly, given the discussion in chapter 10, which highlights executive function impairments in autism, we would expect to see a different pattern of activation, and probably again reduced activation. As discussed in this chapter, disorders of executive function are likely to be responsible for the repetitive behavior and difficulties in the control of attention of autistic individuals. Executive functions select and control low-level processing routines especially in novel situations. They are required for successful performance of working memory tasks, for tasks involving planning, and for tasks in which prepotent responses have to be suppressed. There have been many brain-imaging studies of normal volunteers while they perform executive function tasks. These studies confirm the involvement of the prefrontal cortex in such tasks.

Testing central coherence

Weak central coherence, as discussed in chapter 9, may be the source of the superior performance of autistic individuals on certain perceptual tasks such as finding hidden figures. People who adopt the style of strong central coherence cannot find the hidden figures, and are susceptible to visual illusions, but are good at extracting the gist.

A series of imaging studies with normal volunteers investigated the ability to attend to the global or the local aspect of complex visual figures.[42] As in the studies of selective attention, attention to global or local aspects was associated with modulation in specific regions of the extrastriate visual cortex. Again, the source of the signals that sustained attention to either the local or the global level seemed to lie in a frontoparietal network of regions.

There is so far just one study scanning autistic individuals and control subjects while they performed a task in which embedded figures have to be found.[43] The control task required subjects to view a blank screen passively. From such a comparison it is difficult to isolate the cognitive processes that are specifically involved in finding hidden figures. This is because looking at a blank screen is very different from looking at a complex pattern, so that other areas of the brain, which are not part of the critical processes, are bound to be active during the experimental condition. Nevertheless, interesting differences were observed between the autistic individuals and the controls. The autistic people showed relatively greater activation in extrastriate regions of the visual cortex, while the controls showed relatively greater activation in the prefrontal cortex. The observation would be consistent with the idea that the early stages of sensory processing (emphasizing local features) are intact in autism, while the top-down modulation of these early processing stages (required to extract global features) is not functioning properly.

Here, for once, the task chosen for imaging was one in which the autistic people's performance was excellent rather than impaired, and this is important for the argument that the reduced brain activation seen is not just a side effect of poorer performance. Given this result, weak central coherence, which is thought to lead to superior ability to detect hidden figures, could thus be seen as a function of the frontal lobes. If top-down control is weak, then bottom-up perceptual processes could outweigh it. In this case the two streams of information might not join up properly, and a bottleneck could be created, in the perhaps limited number of working junctures. In the animation study, for instance, visual areas showed normal activation in autistic brains, but other mentalizing areas showed reduced activation. This bottleneck was associated with lack of connectivity.

Testing face recognition

Apart from studies of mentalizing failure, the identification of brain abnormalities in social cognition has also been approached from another point of view. As discussed in chapter 6, individuals with autism may have specific problems in the perception of social stimuli such as faces. Faces are important stimuli in social interactions since they provide clues as to who people are and what they are thinking and feeling. Autistic individuals are poor at recognizing faces from memory compared to their excellent memory for buildings and other objects.[44]

In normal volunteers the presentation of faces, in contrast to objects such as houses or furniture, robustly activates a region of the fusiform gyrus in the inferior temporal lobe that has become known as the fusiform face area (FFA).[45] Reading the emotional expressions on faces activates a variety of areas determined by the nature of the expression. In particular, fearful faces activate the amygdala.[46]

There have so far been three studies in which autistic individuals were scanned while looking at faces, two of face recognition,[47] and one of the recognition of emotional expressions in faces.[48] In all three studies the fusiform face area was robustly activated in the control subjects, but not in the autistic individuals. In the studies of Pierce and of Critchley the autistic individuals also showed reduced activation of the amygdala. In the study by Schultz the autistic individuals showed greater activity in an area of the inferior temporal cortex when processing faces. This area was activated by the control subjects when processing objects. Schultz and his colleagues interpret this as evidence that the autistic individuals were using low-level feature-based strategies for processing faces. Perhaps here too there is a suggestion of a bottleneck. Perhaps in autism top-down signals that normally cause enhanced processing in specialized face areas fail to detect "faceness." This would result in a failure to modulate the information processed by visual systems of the brain. As a result objects and faces would be processed similarly to each other.

What can we conclude so far?

The few studies that involved people with autism performing certain tasks in the scanner have all shown reduced activation in whatever brain area was most relevant to the normal performance of the task. One way of explaining the reduced activation was to consider a bottleneck, a failure in connectivity between feedback and feedforward neural connections.

A strong possibility, which has been running through many of the other chapters in this book, is that lower-level perceptual processes are working well in autism, but are not modulated by higher-level processes. Perhaps the bottleneck in information processing can be speculatively linked to bigger brains in autism. The increase in brain size might be caused by an over-abundance of synapses that normally receive vigorous pruning. If so, feedback connections might be more affected by such a failure than feedforward connections, which develop earlier and are more stable. A failure of pruning would cause abnormalities in the flow of information. This then could be associated with an inadequate top-down control system.

The possibility of important discoveries about the brains of autistic people is tantalizing, but we need more knowledge on how to use the new techniques and interpret the results. Everything up until now has been done on the edge of the possible. So it was when astronomers first looked at the stars through poor telescopes. They were seeing new things, but some of them were only barely visible, and these were often misinterpreted. It is therefore possible that the data I have presented in this chapter will be overturned when better techniques become available in the future.

chapter 12
A Different Brain –
A Different Mind

"Explaining the enigma" is the somewhat reckless subtitle of this book. My aim, when the first edition appeared in 1989, was to separate fact from fiction. Now the job is to separate important facts from the background noise created by the mass of possibly unreliable and definitely confusing data. As before, my approach is to be guided by theory rather than to accept data indiscriminately. After first simplifying the questions to make them amenable to at least preliminary answers, in the last five years the facts about autism have become more complex again. This had to be so, with the massive increase in publications from hundreds of authors all over the world. It is time for another attempt at simplifying.

Sound and Unsound Theories of Autism

As with all disorders where the etiology is largely unknown, weird and wonderful speculation will flourish. The riddle of the beautiful child with autism locked in his or her own world is an irresistible challenge to amateur psychologists. They are tempted to base their answers on a few facts and observations. Any sensible theory of autism must be compatible with what we know about brain development. Theories that consider autism as emotional maladjustment, or as a form of adult mental illness, are obsolete. Autism is due to abnormalities of brain development. I have tried to show that these abnormalities are subtle and limited to some mental functions only, and again only to some aspects of these. Most aspects of the ability to handle objects and to perceive the world through the senses are normal; and so are the capacities to form abstract concepts, categorize events, understand spatial relationships, know about cause and effect, and make logical inferences. Such is the riddle of autism that the missing ingredient is so subtle that even in the core symptoms of social interaction and communication a great deal of competence exists. This subtle and often elusive ingredient is what a good theory of autism needs to identify and explain.

However, autism is a common developmental disorder and it can occur in combination with other developmental disorders and in the context of extensive brain abnormality. Every clinician knows that there are many children with autism who do not have a normal physical appearance, cannot move well, are clumsy when handling objects, have problems with their sensory perception, do not speak, or have considerable problems in abstract thinking. For the theorist, however, all of these impairments, striking, significant, and handi- capping as they are, have to be stripped away because they are not part of the core of autism. They are therefore not part of a specific theory of autism.

Autism is a disorder with a bewildering variety of manifestations. Hence the notion of a spectrum of autistic disorders. In this book I have assumed that despite the variety there is still a common denominator. This concept of autism is distilled from the variety of signs and symptoms and has proved to be amenable to explanation at biological, cognitive, and behavior levels. Nevertheless, what we now call autism may well be broken up into smaller entities or more specific phenotypes in the future. It is only too easy to think up reasons for subgroups on the basis of just one level of explanation, for instance, all children who start to speak late might form one group, or all children who show an excess of a particular mineral in their hair. To establish valid subgroups, the critical test will be to carry through the distinction at each of the three levels of explanation. We will have to wait and see.

Three Theories

In this book I have discussed three theories, each of which can account for some aspect of autistic disorder. The mind-blindness hypothesis is the first of the three theories. As discussed in chapters 5 to 7, it tries to account for the social and communication impairments in autism that are the hallmark of the disorder. The impairments can range from severe to mild, but are present in every individual diagnosed as autistic, regardless of age and ability. According to the theory, the intuitive and automatic attribution of mental states to others is lacking. In the most severe cases there is no understanding of mental states at all. In the mildest cases, compensatory learning has led to the acqui- sition of a conscious theory of mind, and such individuals are capable of attributing and manipulating mental states. As this conscious theory of mind is neither intuitive nor automatic, its use in everyday life is slow and hence not quite sufficient for normal social communication. Compensatory learning accounts for the remarkable improvements that occur in understanding mental states after long periods of learning.

The second theory is about the strengths of the autistic mind. We cannot ignore the fact that 10 percent of autistic people have special talents, a conservative estimate as this does not include rote memory skills. Robust evidence from intelligence tests, as discussed in chapter 8, points to certain peaks in performance in all autistic individuals regardless of age and ability. A reason for the peaks and for the talents is suggested by the theory of weak central coherence, the topic of chapter 9. This theory proposes that individuals with autism have a preference for a style of information processing that is focused on detail. This style can also be present in nonautistic people and confers advantages in the superior processing of perceptual detail.

The third theory addresses the absence of higher-level control of action and attention in many people with autism. Chapter10 is concerned with these problems. The absence of top-down control implies a handicap in the self-organization of any behavior that is not routine. Impaired executive functions are the cause of stereotyped behavior and narrow interests. Successful educational programs show that weak control can be strengthened by external prompts. Structure imposed from outside, that itself becomes routine, leads to improvements over time.

The three theories each address important symptoms. The mind-blindness theory is appealing, because many problems in social interaction and in communication can be understood as a consequence of the inability to realize fully what it means to have a mind and to think, know, believe, and feel differently from others. The central coherence hypothesis makes it possible to understand a broader cognitive phenotype that is not characterized by a deficit. The executive function hypothesis is helpful in understanding repetitive behavior and suggests ways of managing the everyday problems of people with autism. The three theories complement each other, and together they seem to cover most of the important features of autism.

A Unified Account

Do the three theories address quite independent dimensions of mental life that just happen to coincide in autism? No one has yet carried out a study of all the features of autism, in the tradition of Lorna Wing's and Judith Gould's Camberwell study, which identified the triad of impairments. This triad of impairments of social and communicative impairments can be explained by the mind-blindness theory, but we do not know to what extent impairments in mentalizing, impairments in executive functions, and a preference for detail run together. A population study would be needed.

However, I do not think that it is premature to speculate about a link between the three theories. Can it really be coincidence that we see mind blindness, weak central coherence, and a failure in executive mechanisms? To stimulate debate I will offer some musings on possible connections. This is meant as a fresh start in a search for better theories. I propose that there is an intersection between the critical cognitive components in all three theories, and that this intersection is an "absent self."

The absent self

I believe that all three theories have one common feature. They implicate high-level cognitive processes that have something to do with self-consciousness. A common theme between central coherence and executive function theories is a lack of a balance between top-down control, which is weak, and bottom-up processing of information, which is strong. The mind-blindness theory suggests that a single module is malfunctioning, again perhaps because of a mismatch between bottom-up processing and top-down strengthening of social signals.

Mentalizing in the normal case inexorably leads to awareness of yourself as agent. Perhaps without such awareness, a high-level mechanism for top-down control cannot be established. What is this mechanism that has this control? Is there is an embodiment of self "where the buck stops"? To help us think about this question, I wish to revive a naive image that has been rejected by philosophers and psychologists alike. This is the homunculus, a little man who resides in the brain. The problem with this idea has always been that you will soon find you have to place another homunculus inside the first homunculus and so on. The buck never stops. But suppose there is one homunculus where the buck does stop. Imagine one such homunculus that is the last one in a set of nested Russian dolls, the special one that does not come apart.

The idea of the homunculus, despite being reviled as unworkable, has in fact never died. Neuroscientists take it for granted that there are top-down control mechanisms of attention, presumably requiring some agent that has the control. Most philosophers and psychologists assume that there are many kinds of self, all situated in the brain and all functioning for specific purposes.[1] For instance, there is the self here and now, the bodily self, the narrative self, and so forth. Imagine now that only the homunculus has self-awareness.

In honor of Russell Hoban's classic children's book *The Mouse and his Child*, I would like to call this homunculus "the last visible self." Here is how Hoban introduced the idea of the "last visible":

> An empty tin can . . . stood near the mouse and his child. BONZO dog food said the white letters on the orange label, and below the name was a picture of a little black-and-white spotted dog, walking on his hind legs and wearing a chef's cap and an apron. The dog carried a tray on which there was another can of BONZO dog food, on the label of which another little black-and-white spotted dog, exactly the same but much smaller, was walking on his hind legs and carrying a tray on which there was another can of BONZO dog food, and so on until the dogs became too small for the eye to follow.[2]

How does the last visible self represent an intersection between the three theories? How does it link attribution of mental states, central coherence, and executive functions? Because there is a mentalizing mechanism in the brain, the homunculus can become consciously aware of itself. Because there is a drive for central coherence in the brain, the homunculus can have access to integrated information, a useful resource. Because there are executive functions, this homunculus can exercise and delegate control. Given these three components, the last visible self can rise above the other selves. This flying power metaphorically speaking allows a bird's eye view where the self is only one among many others. For this reason this self can readily connect with other people's last visible self-aware selves. The last visible self is a trick and a grand illusion, but it works. Perhaps individuals with autism do not have this trick.

This is not such a strange proposition. You can do without this last visible self, but paradoxically this would mean high egocentrism. Only this self is aware that other people too have self-aware selves. This necessarily includes a realization that there is such a thing as egocentrism. The pure egocentric does not realize this. I propose that pure egocentrism has a type of self in the center that is not ultimately aware of itself and the selves of others.

An absent self-aware self is not a calamity. I speculate that it only gradually emerges in older children and adolescents. It is there when children can see themselves from a metaphorical bird's eye view. Adults too don't normally think about it. However, by having such a self we can, if we want, consider our position in society, our relationship to others in the context of our personal history, in the context of the history of humankind, of "Life, the Universe, and Everything."

The last visible self may often be asleep. This does not matter as long as there are other hard-working executive selves. For instance, there could be a hard-working self-disciplined self that also matures late, and that is responsible for inhibiting impulsive behavior of the kind that leads to short-term gain only but to long-term pain. There is no reason to suppose that in autism this type of self cannot work well. There could also be problems because the meaning of information received is not sufficiently integrated with other meaning, and this means that executive selves do not have the proper overview to make good decisions. In autism it may well be that if executive selves are in conflict, bottom-up processes have the balance of power. This could have the unexpected benefit in the creation of a special talent. Another consequence would be pure egocentrism. This too is not a calamity, as it induces others to help. In my experience the egocentrism in the autistic individual is so transparent that one simply does not treat it the same way as egocentricity in normal people. In the case of autism a natural response is to wonder why. In the case of normal people, it is to be indignant.

SELF-KNOWLEDGE AND SELF-AWARENESS

Is there any evidence for a different kind of self-awareness in autism? Francesca Happé and I have argued that awareness of others and awareness of self tend to go together, and that is why self-awareness in autism is likely to be different from normal.[3] Here I would like to go a step further. Perhaps there is an awareness that is *all* self and does not include the reflection of the self in other selves. I would like to refer to this different kind of self-awareness as self-knowledge. Could it be that individuals with autism who acquire a conscious theory of mind, first and foremost attain knowledge of their own mind? This would mean that they can possess detailed knowledge about themselves, but not about others. If so, we could explain why the autobiographies of autistic people go into remarkable detail about their own inner states, far more so than most autobiographers, and why they hardly even speculate about how they may have affected people who play an important role in their lives.

What comes first: awareness of own mind or awareness of other minds? It is likely that normally both arise together. But this may not be the case in autism. The distinction between own and other people's mental states is not trivial. As mentioned in chapter 5, there are mirror cells in the brain that fire equally vigorously when a monkey grasps an object itself and when it watches another monkey or human grasping it. As far as the mirror cells are concerned, they respond to the actions of an agent, regardless of who this agent is. One theoretical possibility is that these cells are working well in the autistic brain, but are not influenced by those cells that normally distinguish the self from another agent. This would be a reason for unmitigated egocentrism, such as we see in small infants and in older autistic children who have not yet undergone the long process of socialization.

Autistic writers leave no doubt about the extensive self-knowledge of autistic people. They tell of inner feelings and bodily sensations of extraordinary vividness. They tell of childhood experiences with great detail. However, when they were children, they had never told anyone. It is possible that they simply did not know that their inner experiences were different from the inner experiences of other people. Normal children get this fundamental insight early and for free, by virtue of their intuitive mentalizing ability. With a late-acquired conscious theory of mind, this insight is hard won. Perhaps this is why individuals with Asperger syndrome realize that they had unusual experiences only when looking back. In a most intriguing and informative book, Clare Sainsbury collected together recollections of 25 people with Asperger syndrome about events that puzzled them when they were at school. The examples provide evidence of much suffering that was caused by not telling others about their experiences. This is aggravated by the fact that the experiences themselves were often unusual and could not have been guessed.[4]

It would be wrong to think only of the exceptional people who write about themselves, when we talk of self-knowledge in autism. Autistic adolescents with low IQs and language ability far below the level of Asperger syndrome people are also able to talk about themselves. This was demonstrated in a study by Lee and Hobson, who used an interview technique designed to elicit statements about the self. One cannot doubt that these adolescents had appropriate representations of the physical, psychological, and narrative self. Nevertheless, what these authors call the interpersonal self, which represents relationships with others, was poorly represented in autistic self-concepts.[5]

LOOKING INWARD

Autobiographies and interviews about concepts of oneself are one way to learn about self-knowledge and self-awareness of people with autism. Another way is to study the ability to report inner feelings about ongoing events. This was done in an experiment with Russell Hurlburt,[6] who had developed a method for eliciting "what was on your mind at a particular moment – frozen in time." Hurlburt had already collected data from many people, including patients with various psychiatric disorders, using this technique. He tried his technique with Francesca Happé and myself and convinced us that it was worth trying.

This is how it works. You carry around with you a small device, a beeper that is programmed to beep at random intervals while you go about your daily business. As it beeps you are to "freeze the moment." To help you remember you write down a few notes with date and time and what you were actually doing, as well as something about your thought. You might in this way collect a dozen or more events, and each of these would then be analyzed at length in a clinical interview. In this interview Russell Hurlburt asked questions that probe form and content of people's thought as they remembered it. Was there a visual form to it? If so, what about color and size, perspective view, detail? Was it abstract? Did it contain words? Was there a feeling? Where was it located?

From his studies of normal people's introspections Hurlburt was able to conclude that they all had a variety of forms, ranging from visual to verbal and abstract, and this was true even of people who considered themselves as strong visualizers. There was of course also a great variety of content, and whatever some people said of themselves before the experiment, they did not think about only one thing after all. The probing questions in the interview made sense to people. For example, I reported that at one moment when the beeper went, I happened to touch a piece of paper. The feeling was located in my fingertips. It was intense. I also reported a feeling of pleasure and happiness, which according to my notes directly emanated from the fingertip that had touched the paper. This introspection contained no visual imagery, no abstract thoughts and no words, but these were present in some of my other introspective reports.

We were eager to know what people with autism would report. Would they be able to tell us about their inner experiences and would these be different experiences? We found three men of high verbal ability but with different degrees of mentalizing ability. These degrees perfectly correlated with the ability to engage in introspection. The first was able to attribute second order beliefs and needed only brief training on the introspection task. The second could also attribute second order beliefs (John believes that Mary believes . . .) but made errors and needed a large amount of training to do the task. The third was only able to attribute simple beliefs and even after lengthy training could hardly do the task at all. We obtained sufficient material from these cooperative subjects to conclude that the form of their introspections was the same in all cases – it was always visual and concrete. Often their reports of the inner state at the frozen moment were only barely different from their reports of what actually happened at the moment of the beep. This suggests that they did not fully realize that reports of mental states are supposed to be different from physical states. Normal people in these interviews give very distinct descriptions of what actually happened and what went on in their minds. In terms of content as well as lack of variety, autistic introspections were remarkably different.

One other thing struck us, namely that none of these subjects expressed any interest in what kind of mental states other people reported. In contrast, normally the first thing that anyone asks at an interview with Russell Hurlburt is: "Do other people report similar things or are they completely different?" More than anything, this lack of natural curiosity in our subjects suggested to us that their awareness of own and other minds was fundamentally limited.

Knowing how one knows

There is still much to be learned about the development of self-knowledge and self-awareness in normal children as well as children with autism.[7] Imagine that a young child has seen something that another child has not seen. Does the child realize that this means he or she now has knowledge that the other child does not have? To explore this deceptively simple scenario, Josef Perner carried out an experiment of the utmost simplicity.[8] Josef took a trinket from a whole box of things by lucky dip and put it in a cup. He then ostentatiously let the child look inside, making clear all the time that I (who sat at the other end of the table) was not allowed to look inside. He verified that this was understood by asking: "Did you *see* what is in the cup?" and "Did Uta *see* what was in the cup?" Now the critical questions were: "Do you *know* what is in the cup?" and "Does Uta *know*?" Astonishingly half of the autistic children who were tested, said, "Yes, Uta knows [what is in the cup]," when I had not seen the object and could not have known. All were of a mental age above that at which normal children could easily give the right answer.

There are obvious implications of such a striking finding. In many children with autism we cannot take it for granted (as we would in a normal three year old) that they realize that "to see is to know" and that if someone has not seen or heard something, he or she does not know and needs to be told. For instance, Clare Sainsbury wrote:

> My mother recalls that often, when she dropped me off at primary school, I would turn to her in a panic and demand, for example, "Where is the frying pan?" This would invariably be the first she'd heard of it and it would take lengthy interrogation of me to establish that everyone in the class had been told to bring a frying pan in; it had never occurred to me that she needed to be told this in order to provide it.[9]

There is a further consequence of the failure to know where knowledge comes from. The child does not understand the difference between justified knowledge and a mere guess. For instance, in our experiment one child insisted there was a panda in the cup (even though he had not seen it and said he had not seen it). When he was shown what it actually was, a rose, he did not react with surprise. Could it be that he often experiences wrong expectations of this type? Could it be that for a child without the ability to make sense of other people's knowledge and beliefs, "anything could happen"?

Improbable ideas

Milton is an intelligent autistic boy of 12 who took part in our experiments on reading. He read – fluently – selected passages of text and we asked various questions to test his text comprehension and general knowledge. After he had given a particularly good answer we asked quite casually, "Oh, how did you know that?" His matter-of-fact reply was, "By telepathy." We repeated the question on several other occasions, and he always answered in the same way. He never said, "I just read about it," or "My teacher told me," or "It's obvious, isn't it?"

Milton had an explanation of how knowledge came to be in his head: it was put there by telepathy. We have not found an ordinary bright 12-year-old who would come up with such an idea. Nevertheless, it suggests a glimmer of understanding that there are such things as thoughts. Alas, a glimmer is not enough.

Milton did not reflect that this idea simply would not fit with other information he had about the world and could not understand why the experimenters laughed. Was the absent self to blame? Perhaps so. He did not use information from his own past experience, from general world knowledge, from the text that he had just read, nor from the intentions behind our questions. Instead he gave a stereotypic all-purpose answer. It is the sort of cause-and-effect explanation that would have been quite adequate for the question: "How does the iron stick attract the pins?" – answer: "By magnetism." Clearly, for everyday understanding the physical world is different from the mental world.

To be able to mentalize does not mean that we have fanciful ideas about what might be in the mind of someone else, but that we *know* for certain what one can surmise about another's thoughts and what one cannot surmise. Two anecdotes may illustrate this point.

The first anecdote is about an able young man who, despite suffering from autism, is very helpful with household chores and running errands. He often goes shopping and is trusted with money. One day, as his mother was mixing a fruit cake, she said to him: "I haven't got any cloves. Would you please go out and get me some." The son came back a while later with a carrier bag full of girlish clothes, including underwear, from a high street boutique.

Clearly, the boy had misheard the word "cloves" as "clothes," an understandable confusion, particularly as the word "cloves" is much more rarely used in everyday life than the word "clothes." This could be explained by the central coherence theory, which allows details to be interpreted in terms of their context. What normal young man would assume his mother had casually asked him to buy her clothes, just like that? The hypothesis is so outlandish that it should have been rejected immediately. "I *must* have misheard what she said" would be the expected response, followed by a request for clarification.

The second anecdote is reported by Gillberg and Coleman:

> A 10-year-old . . . autistic girl [with normal intelligence] showed catastrophic anxiety when the nurse, about to do a simple blood test, said "Give me your hand; it won't hurt." The girl calmed down immediately when another person said: "Stretch out your index finger." She had understood, at the first instruction, that she was to cut off her hand and give it to the nurse.[10]

As in the previous anecdote, this story gives an example of an error that is at once understandable, yet totally outlandish from one's experience and from cultural conventions.

In everyday life we cannot afford too many errors of literal interpretations; we seek interpretations that are coherent within a wider context that takes in social and cultural experiences. It is unlikely that the two individuals with autism in the anecdotes have so little life experience that they could not interpret the situations appropriately. Rather, they did not use experience in the same way as other children of the same age with the same IQ and background. It is interesting that the girl straight away abandoned her extraordinary interpretation of the nurse's request when an unambiguous instruction was given. This would not have been the case if she had a deep-seated suspicion of nurses. If only she had such a suspicion! It would make sense of her action in the normal way. For instance, it might fit into a pattern of hospital phobia, and would not simply be a bizarre reaction.

The self, communication, and context

When talking about improbable ideas, the specter of communication impairment in autism has loomed up again. In the end, communication impairment is what autism is all about. If we use the metaphor of the missing self, the most poignant consequence is an inability to communicate with other people's self-aware selves. We have previously considered the distinction between communication of bare messages and ordinary "ostensive" communication. It is this subtle difference that is difficult for individuals with autism and continues to create problems even for the well-compensated person with Asperger syndrome. Ostensive communication does not have to be in words, and does not even have to have a specific content. It can happen when you see someone looking at you intently and when you hear someone calling your name. This would seem to act as a wake-up call for the homunculus. Ostensive communication opens a wide, wild, inner world of relationships and meanings where constant gambles are being taken, and won, and lost. People with autism, impervious as they are to such gambles, cannot fully participate in such a world. It may fascinate them, or terrify them, but it will not readily admit them as players. In this world the game is played by self-aware selves that have enough flying power to allow them the necessary bird's eye view.

Context is at once the most essential ingredient in this game, and the one feature that distinguishes full intentional communication from bare message transmission. The hallmark of the latter is the piecemeal handling of information. Context can be seen at once by taking a bird's eye view. A piecemeal strategy is more like the experience of a pedestrian. In principle, there is nothing wrong with this. On the contrary, this mode of information processing guarantees stability: the same code always means the same thing. In everyday communication this guarantee does not apply. Here, the bird's eye view conveys an *obligation* to use context. This means often having to say "it depends." The meaning of any utterance in word or gesture can only be properly understood by *not* treating it piecemeal, but by placing it in context. Dan Sperber and Deirdre Wilson have this to say about context in communication:

> The set of premises used in interpreting an utterance constitutes what is generally known as the *context*. A context is a psychological construct, a subset of the hearer's assumptions about the world. It is these assumptions, of course, rather than the actual state of the world, that affect the interpretation of an utterance. A context in this sense is not limited to information about the immediate physical environment or the immediately preceding utterances: expectations about the future, scientific hypotheses or religious beliefs, anecdotal memories, general cultural assumptions, beliefs about the mental state of the speaker, may all play a role in the interpretation.[11]

Another e-mail message from A.C., the young woman with high-functioning autism or Asperger syndrome (she refers to it as HFA/AS) who explained her own view of the Georges de la Tour painting (pp.78–9), illustrates the importance of context in a game that critically depends on normal communication:

> I just thought of something else interesting: One time I played the game "Pictionary" with some people. Well, I thought I'd be really good because it's pictures, right? Well, it depends on speed in communication, and in my case I draw the exact picture of the thing, and that takes time, and it turns out to be slow. The other people draw these really quick things, and look at each other a lot when they do it. I theorize that they might be doing "eye language" with each other as they guess? Ugh! It's a very different version of doing Pictionary than my idea of it, and yet another example of how strange people who do not have HFA/AS are, in their way of thinking. I don't plan on playing Pictionary any time again soon ha ha!

A.C. uses plain communication of the kind that is really useful if you want to let another person know something by visual means only. However, this is just not in the spirit of the game. This springs from ostensive communication, which is inherently ambiguous and depends entirely on shared context. Hence the importance of meaningful eye contact, and hence the unimportance of the appearance of the drawings. The last visible self of normal players should be fully aware of this without any special explanation.

This example would fit well with the idea that there are deep links between making use of context (central coherence) and attributing mental states to others, an essential prerequisite of ostensive communication. There are also links to executive functions, if taking context into account also implies taking future events into account. For instance, cooking a meal in a hurry, even though it will be less than perfect, may allow a more important aim to be fulfilled, such as feeding a hungry child. This does not mean that cooking has to be done in a hurry every time, but that flexibility is required in judging the appropriateness of an action in context. Successful communication involves planning future moves and predicting the effect of one's actions on others in the long term. The Pictionary game, like many other games, is modeling a far bigger game beyond, and again – metaphorically speaking – it depends on the flying power of the last visible self.

Treatments that Work

It is all very well to theorize, to experiment, and to speculate, but what practical implications can be drawn from the ideas in this book? More and more books on methods of teaching and management in autism are appearing, each pleasing some people and antagonizing others. There are some general approaches that have proved themselves over time, and reviews exist that compare different psychological and pharmacological treatments and the theories behind them.[12] Educational treatments with structured content are generally agreed to be effective and have been widely put into practice.[13]

The treatments that work all have in common the belief that autism is not a condition that will go away. They also all suggest that there is much that can be done about it, and that improvements occur over a lifetime, not just in young children. There is no evidence that it is ever too late to start educational treatment, but common sense would hold that an early start would be best. Even though programs can be highly effective, the fact is that so far the underlying neurological condition has been untreatable.

Because of the tremendous individual differences between autistic individuals, and because of their inevitably changing needs during the course of life, specific advice has only limited application. However, some general ideas for the education and management of autistic children have come out of the theories discussed in this book. The evidence presented in this book has pointed to some underlying neurological dysfunction in autism. It has also pointed to the fact that it is possible to compensate for this dysfunction.

Acquiring knowledge of mental states the slow way

Regardless of whether the last visible self is asleep or absent in autism, it would seem important to promote knowledge of own and others' mental states. Such knowledge can be acquired even when the mechanisms that normally allow the intuitive and automatic attribution of mental states are missing. It can be done, for instance, by inserting conscious and explicit rules. This is made possible only with the full cooperation of others in the learning process. This is not learning by simply copying and being around another person. It is hard work, and requires patient repetition of events that have happened and what they mean. It seems to me that able Asperger children have discovered a method of self-teaching. They can use books, the Internet, words, and pictures, to glean information about the social world and the way it works in many different situations. They are often keen to please others and anxious to fit in with others. This in turn is a powerful motivation to learn.

There is every reason to believe that explicit learning works even when implicit learning fails. No matter that it is different from normal fast-track learning. No matter that the automatic attribution of mental states to others remains out of reach. To have the ability for nonautomatic attribution is a good enough accomplishment in most cases. An analogy might be seen in mathematics. Some people seem to have an intuitive grasp of mathematical concepts, which is often spatial, and as if they are seeing a picture of mathematical space. That is not to say that other people (perhaps most of us) who lack that intuitive grasp can never learn mathematics. However, mathematics learned without an intuitive sense is probably subject to more flaws and mistakes than mathematics learned with such a sense. The same may apply to music and art.

There are many examples of people with autism who learn what nonliteral remarks mean, how to tell from body language if someone is lying, how to tell when an apology is expected, and how to induce other people to be helpful. One bright boy with autism realized early on that he did not catch on to jokes, and it became an obsession with him to learn to get the point. After years of asking to have cartoons explained by his parents he became quite skilful at it, even if he seldom appreciated the joke. Obviously, children with impaired intellectual ability could not be expected to compensate to the degree that is sometimes possible in special cases.

In cases where inner resources might not be big enough for compensation, we need to give more external support. For example, if we systematically apply the reasoning that led to the various experiments on mentalizing ability, then perhaps we can make the social world more predictable for individuals who lack intuitive mind reading. It helps to adopt a literal and behaviorist mode as a partner of a person with autism, both as listener and speaker. Implications need to be spelled out, even if they seem redundant and self-evident in normal communication. For instance, it was necessary to tell a young man with autism not to stare at the girls in the office, because they might take offence. It was also necessary to explain to him that he should not emulate a colleague who had bought flowers for the boss, as he probably had his own ulterior motives.

Strengthening top-down control

Forward planning is perhaps the most important high-level executive job of the frontal lobes. It appears to be a job that is energy-consuming to the extent that you can't plan while you do some other demanding or novel task, which would involve the frontal lobes, at the same time. It is as if people with autism cannot muster this energy. Nor can young children and people with injury to their frontal lobes. In all these groups, dependence is a fact of life, and supervision is necessary in various degrees. This supervision has to come from the outside. This dependence is not to be decried, as it is a natural way of compensating for the lack of internal supervision. Supervision for semi-independent living in autism often leads to a highly acceptable way of living.

People with weak executive functions thrive on prompts and signals that help them initiate actions as well as finish them. A little trick like having a timer ticking away with the instruction "stop when the timer goes off" can work wonders. A reminder of the sequence of steps that are important in getting washed and dressed can be highly reassuring as well as instrumental in getting things done in the right order every time. Other strategies include explicit prompts and reminder notes, and a transparently structured environment. These are some of the most popular teaching methods used in schools for children with autism, and they have been evaluated experimentally.[14] Parents have been doing these things for ages. They intuitively know that they must strengthen the weak supervisory system of their children to lead them gradually to increasing independence. They rely on well-functioning routine behavior triggered by the appropriate stimuli. They can also set up semiautomatic reminders to initiate nonroutine actions. Of course, these aids and reminders still need to be checked and monitored.

Unlike the demands of compensatory learning, such techniques have relatively little cognitive cost for the patient, but they tax the ingenuity of the carer. In the case of autism, people sometimes worry about "making things too easy" and letting autistic individuals slide into a state of institutionalization. However, when the cognitive resources are limited, it would be cruel to demand constant effort and constant learning.

What about strengthening weak central coherence? I am not sure to what extent it is possible or even advisable to interfere with a preferred style of information processing. Weak central coherence is often an asset to people with autism. This asset can be turned to good effect in behavior modification schemes, where piece by piece a desired behavior is divided into a sequence of actions, each of which is reinforced by suitable reward. Of course, encouraging people to take into account context in everyday life, for example, when trying to work out what someone is doing or meaning, cannot be a bad thing. It might be possible to teach the difference between the literal meaning of a phrase and an ironical meaning by using the example of visual illusions where context changes perceptual detail.

Learning by association

In this book we have had many occasions to marvel at the excellent rote learning ability observed in children with autism. This is one of their strengths that educational programs have exploited with good success. There is no reason to think that this ability declines with age.

It has long been recognized that associative learning of a stimulus and a response is a useful technique that can benefit autistic children. The idea is that behavior can be changed if approached in the right way, gradually and with the appropriate management of reinforcements, designed individually for each child.[15] Of course there are limits. However, it is sometimes possible to teach a nonspeaking child to speak. For example, parents taught their little son to speak by first rewarding him for opening his mouth, then for producing a small and hardly audible vowel sound, then a louder sound, then an easy syllable, and so forth. The parents believed that the child was eager to learn to speak and had simply no idea how to control his mouth and his voice apparatus. Scientific evidence exists evaluating methods of behavior modification,[16] which comes in different forms.[17] Even critics who question the need for intensive application of the technique admit that there are situations when it is valuable.

The cost of compensation

There is no getting round the fact that there are costs associated with educational treatments of individuals with neurological conditions. I do not have material costs in mind. The costs I wish to highlight are cognitive costs to be contributed by the individual to allow compensatory learning. For example, when applying the effortfully learned rules of ordinary polite conversation, we should not expect that conversation will then be as easy as for any other person who has long internalized the rules through intuitive learning. Conversation may remain peculiarly stressful. To take another example, if a person with Asperger syndrome attends a party to please others and manages to mingle successfully with the crowd, this does not mean "he can do it if he only wants to," and that from now on he or she must be expected to conform every time. A simple setback, a preoccupation, a slight illness, a change of routine, can upset even well-rehearsed social interactions. This is especially upsetting to those individuals who have a strong desire to please and are often successful in their camouflage.

Compensatory learning is worth this cost, but a debt must be paid from somewhere else. The individual who does well with compensatory education is the individual who has large cognitive resources. With these resources costs can be paid and compensatory learning can proceed with speed and power. A poor start in brain development can then be made good and compensation then triumphs over adversity. The case of the successful person with Asperger syndrome shows us that there are ways of getting round missing brain mechanisms. It may take longer and it may be effortful, but it can be done.

There are cognitive costs also for people who care for an individual with autism. A lot of the effort involved in communication has to be shouldered by the nonautistic person. The nonautistic person has to emphasize what is relevant and has to elaborate topics carefully. Hints or raised eyebrows are unlikely to act as sufficient cues. In this respect people who are naturally inclined to be pedantic and rigid have a head start over those who are naturally inclined to flout the rules. Being pedantic, patient, and overemphasizing relevant points means working with people with autism, not against them.

Sometimes a pat on the back is needed. A person with autism with many compensatory skills tends to get less sympathy than the one who is totally mute and aloof. "Surely, he can't have autism – he makes eye contact and he speaks to me" is a familiar remark. Similarly one hears, "Surely, she can't be dyslexic – she's reading a book!" The common point here is that appearances can be deceptive. Compensatory learning does occur, but this does not mean that the underlying handicap has vanished. The pat on the back is usually well deserved. Imagine having to figure out consciously what another person might think, know, and believe as you are talking to them! The effort involved is considerable and means that there is no spare capacity to deal with sudden stress. The whole edifice of learned social rules can break down if something out of the ordinary happens.

It helps to understand the condition

Teachers and parents will find their own ways of applying the theories that I have discussed in this book if they find them useful to explain the very particular problems that children with autism experience. This hope is not idle. As an example of how she applied the idea that children with autism have difficulty in mentalizing, Margaret Dewey related the following incident:

> Donald came home from the autistic school, somewhat upset by a delayed start to the journey home. His parents sent him into the kitchen to get himself a drink. Soon his father followed to see whether Donald was all right. He arrived just in time to see Donald pouring milk down the kitchen drain. Of course, he reacted by shouting at Donald to stop, because the milk comes in gallon containers and is not cheap. He assumed this was some kind of weird expression of Donald's inner turmoil that day. Donald was greatly upset when reprimanded and immediately dropped to the floor and began to cry.

The interpretation based on the theory is that Donald did not like the taste of the milk, as it was old and might have started to go bad. He might have decided to pour it down the drain as he had seen his parents do with bad milk. What he did not do is defend his action when his father told him to stop. This is exactly what one would expect from a child who does not realize that someone else does not necessarily have the same knowledge as himself. Therefore the shouted order to stop was a totally unexpected reaction, a shocking turn of events that made no sense to him. His usually loving father should have praised him for throwing away the bad milk! This new interpretation greatly helped the parents when comforting Donald.

What I hope the three theories in this book will offer to those who are close to a person with autism is a better understanding of the real handicap that is caused by autism. This handicap is in its nature more similar to blindness or deafness than to, say, shyness. Imagine trying to bring up a blind child without realizing that he or she is blind. One might get quite impatient with the child bumping into things! A child cannot learn well from an impatient or angry teacher. Therefore it is important for all teachers, therapists, parents, and friends to have some knowledge of the nature of the handicap.

I have been deeply impressed by the skill and devotion of many parents, teachers, and therapists who get results without believing in miracles. I can also understand how desperate parents can get caught by the advertising "hypes" that are the scourge of rehabilitation. I hope that the information contained in this book will act as a sobering background when evaluating different schemes. There is still a long way to go before precise recommendations can be made that derive from a sound scientific basis. We are not expecting a magic pill or secret short cut to "normality."

The enigma of autism will continue to resist explanation. My attempt at simplification will have to face an onslaught of yet more complex facts. It may well be wrecked. But then, I would hope that there can again be a new synthesis. Parents, teachers, and clinicians, and individuals with autism themselves, just as they have done in the past, will all contribute rich new perspectives to the scientific understanding of autism. Autism is far too fascinating to be treated solely by scientists. It is, after all, one of the most powerful reflections of the human condition.

Notes

NOTES TO CHAPTER 1 WHAT IS AUTISM?

1. A large number of biographical accounts are available about individual cases, their first diagnosis, their development, and the impact of autism on the family. Among those that stand out as particularly vivid and informative are the following: Park, C. (1987) *The Siege: The First Eight Years of an Autistic Child*, 2nd edn. (Boston: Atlantic-Little, Brown); Hart, C. (1989) *Without Reason* (New York: Harper & Row); Fling, R. (2000) *Eating an Artichoke* (London: Jessica Kingsley).
2. Kanner, L. (1943) Autistic disturbances of affective contact, *Nervous Child*, 2, 217–50. Reprinted in L. Kanner, *Childhood Psychosis: Initial Studies and New Insights* (Washington, DC: V. H. Winston, pp.1–43).
3. Asperger, H. (1944) Die autistischen Psychopathen im Kindesalter, *Archiv für Psychiatrie und Nervenkrankheiten*, 117, 76–136. Translated by U. Frith in U. Frith (ed.), *Autism and Asperger Syndrome* (Cambridge, UK: Cambridge University Press, 1991, pp.37–92).
4. Bleuler, E. (1916) *Lehrbuch der Psychiatrie*. Translated by A. A. Brill as *Textbook of Psychiatry* (New York: Dover, 1951).
5. Kanner (1943), p.217.
6. Ibid., p.242.
7. Ibid.
8. Ibid., p.246.
9. Ibid., p.245.
10. Ibid., p.247.
11. Ibid., p.250.
12. Asperger, translation in Frith (1991), p.37.
13. Ibid., p.42.
14. Ibid.
15. Ibid., p.43.
16. Ibid., p.45.

17. Ibid., p.47.
18. American Psychiatric Association (2000) *Diagnostic and Statistical Manual of Mental Disorders*, 4th edn. DSM-IV-TR (text revision) (Washington, DC: American Psychiatric Association).
19. World Health Organization (1992) *The ICD-10 Classification of Mental and Behavioural Disorders: Clinical Descriptions and Diagnostic Guidelines* (Geneva: World Health Organization).
20. Kanner, L., and Eisenberg, L. (1956) Early infantile autism 1943–1955, *American Journal of Orthopsychiatry*, 26, 55–65.
21. Wing, L. (1991) The relationship between Asperger's syndrome and Kanner's autism. In U. Frith (ed.), *Autism and Asperger Syndrome* (Cambridge, UK: Cambridge University Press, pp.93–121).
22. Gilchrist, A., Green, J., Cox, A., Burton, D., Rutter, M., and Le Couteur, A. (2001) Development and current functioning in adolescents with Asperger syndrome: A comparative study, *Journal of Child Psychology and Psychiatry*, 42, 227–40.
23. Sainsbury, C. (2000) *Martian in the Playground: Understanding the Schoolchild with Asperger's Syndrome* (Bristol, UK: Lucky Duck Publishing).
24. Klin, A., Volkmar, F., and Sparrow, S. (eds.) (2000) *Asperger Syndrome* (New York: Guilford Press).
25. Werner, E., Dawson, G., Osterling, J., and Dinno, N. (2000) Brief report: Recognition of autism spectrum disorder before one year of age: A retrospective study based on home videotapes, *Journal of Autism and Developmental Disorders*, 30, 157–62.
26. Lovell, A. (1978) *In a Summer Garment: The Experience of an Autistic Child* (London: Secker & Warburg). Published in paperback as *Simple Simon* (London: Lion, 1983), p.1.
27. There is a variety of diagnostic checklists and interviews that are now available. The following instruments are widely used: Lord, C., Rutter, M., and Le Couteur, A. (1994) The Autism Diagnostic Interview – Revised: A revised version of a diagnostic interview for caregivers of individuals with possible pervasive developmental disorders, *Journal of Autism and Developmental Disorders*, 24, 659–85; Lord, C., Risi, S., Lambrecht, L., et al. (2000) The ADOS-G (Autism Diagnostic Observation Schedule-Generic): A standard measure of social and communication deficits associated with autism spectrum disorder, *Journal of Autism and Developmental Disorders*, 30, 205–23; Berument, S. K., Rutter, M., Lord, C. A., Pickles, A., and Bailey, A. (1999) Autism Screening Questionnaire: Diagnostic validity, *British Journal of Psychiatry*, 175, 444–51; Wing, L., Leekam, S. R., Libby, S. J., Gould, J., and Larcombe, M. (2002) The Diagnostic Interview for Social and Communication Disorders: Background, inter-rater reliability and clinical use, *Journal of Child Psychology and Psychiatry*, 43, 307–25.
28. Knobloch, H., and Pasamanick, B. (1975) Some etiological and prognostic factors in early infantile autism and psychosis, *Pediatrics*, 55, 182–91.

29. Davidovitch, M., Glick, L., Holtzman, G., Tirosh, E., and Safir, M. (2000) Developmental regression in autism: Maternal perception, *Journal of Autism and Developmental Disorders*, 30, 113–19.

30. Baird, G., Charman, T., Baron-Cohen, S. et al. (2000) A screening instrument for autism at 18 months of age: A 6-year follow-up study, *Journal of the American Academy of Child and Adolescent Psychiatry*, 39, 694–702.

31. A number of autobiographies of able individuals with autism spectrum disorder exist. Among the most informative as well as fascinating are: Grandin, T. (1995) How people with autism think. In E. Schopler and G. B. Mesibov (eds.), *Learning and Cognition in Autism* (Plenum Press: New York, pp.137–56) (Temple Grandin is a prolific writer and speaker and has published several autobiographical accounts); Gerland, G. (1997) *A Real Person – Life from the Outside*, translated from the Swedish by J. Tate (London: Souvenir Press) (This is a unique and perceptive account of inner experience from childhood and adolescence to adulthood).

NOTES TO CHAPTER 2 THE ENCHANTMENT OF AUTISM

1. Hudleston, Dom R. (1953) *The Little Flowers of St Francis of Assisi*, 1st English translation, revised and amended (London: Burns & Oates), pp.173–5.

2. Challice, N., and Dewey, H. W. (1971) The blessed fools of Old Russia, *Jarhrbücher für Geschichte Osteuropas*, NS 22, 1–11.

3. Hoffman, P. (1998) *The Man who Loved Only Numbers: The Story of Paul Erdös and the Search for Mathematical Truth* (New York: Hyperion Books; London: Fourth Estate, 1999).

4. Wyndham, J. (1957) *The Midwich Cuckoos* (Harmondsworth, UK: Penguin).

5. Hoffmann, E. T. A. (1967) *The Best Tales of Hoffmann* (New York: Dover).

6. Dick, P. K. (1972) *Do Androids Dream of Electric Sheep?* (London: Panther).

7. Weizenbaum, J. (1976) *Computer Power and Human Reason: From Judgement to Calculation* (San Francisco: Freeman), pp.3–4.

8. Pickles, A., Starr, E., Kazak, S., et al. (2000) Variable expression of the autism broader phenotype: Findings from extended pedigrees, *Journal of Child Psychology and Psychiatry*, 41, 491–502.

9. Mostert, M. P. (2001) Facilitated communication since 1995: A review of published studies, *Journal of Autism and Developmental Disorders*, 31, 287–313.

NOTES TO CHAPTER 3 LESSONS FROM HISTORY

1. Haslam, J. (1809) *Observations on Madness and Melancholy* (London: G. Hayden).

2. Lane, H. (1976) *The Wild Boy of Aveyron: A History of the Education of Retarded, Deaf, and Hearing Children* (Cambridge, MA: Harvard University Press; London: Allen & Unwin, 1978).

3. Ibid., p.39.

4. Ibid., p.43.

5. Ibid., p.42.
6. Ibid., p.39.
7. Ibid., p.43.
8. Ibid., p.45.
9. Ibid., pp.108–9.
10. Feuerbach, A. Ritter von (1833) *Kaspar Hauser: An Account of an Individual Kept in a Dungeon Separated from all Communication with the World from Early Childhood to About the Age of 17* (London: Simpkin & Marshall).
11. Rutter, M., Andersen-Wood, L., Beckett, C., et al. (1999) Quasi-autistic patterns following global privation, *Journal of Child Psychology and Psychiatry*, 40, 537–49.
12. Brown, R., Hobson, R. P., Lee, A., and Stevenson, J. (1997) Are there "autistic-like" features in congenitally blind children?, *Journal of Child Psychology and Psychiatry*, 38, 693–703.
13. Houston, R., and Frith, U. (2000) *Autism in History: The Case of Hugh Blair of Borgue* (Oxford: Blackwell).
14. Lucas, P. (2001) John Howard and Asperger's syndrome: Psychopathology and philanthropy, *History of Psychiatry*, 12, 73–101.

NOTES TO CHAPTER 4 IS THERE AN AUTISM EPIDEMIC?

1. Lotter, V. (1966) Epidemiology of autistic conditions in young children: I. Prevalence, *Social Psychiatry*, 1, 124–37.
2. Kanner, L., and Eisenberg, L. (1956) Early infantile autism 1943–1955, *American Journal of Orthopsychiatry*, 26, 55–65.
3. Wing, L., and Potter, D. (2002 in press) The epidemiology of autistic spectrum disorders: Is the prevalence rising?, *Mental Retardation and Developmental Disabilities Research Reviews*, 8.
4. Chakrabarti, S., and Fombonne, E. (2001) Pervasive developmental disorders in preschool children, *Journal of the American Medical Association*, 285, 3093–9; Baird, G., Charman, T., Baron-Cohen, S., et al. (2000) A screening instrument for autism at 18 months of age: A 6-year follow-up study, *Journal of the American Academy of Child and Adolescent Psychiatry*, 39, 694–702.
5. Kadesjö, B., Gillberg, C., and Hagberg, B. (1999) Brief report. Autism and Asperger syndrome in seven-year-old children, *Journal of Autism and Developmental Disorders*, 29, 327–32.
6. Wing, L., and Gould, J. (1979) Severe impairments of social interaction and associated abnormalities in children: Epidemiology and classification, *Journal of Autism and Developmental Disorders*, 9, 11–29.
7. Wing, L. (1996) *The Autistic Spectrum* (London: Constable). Reissued as *The Autistic Spectrum: A Parent's Guide to Understanding and Helping Your Child* (Berkeley, CA: Ulysses Press, 2001).
8. Wing and Gould (1979).

9. Lord, C., Schopler, E., and Revicki, D. (1982) Sex differences in autism, *Journal of Autism and Developmental Disorders*, 12, 317–30.
10. Volkmar, F. R., Szatmari, P., and Sparrow, S. S. (1993) Sex differences in pervasive developmental disorders, *Journal of Autism and Developmental Disorders*, 23, 579–91.
11. Shah, A., Holmes, N., and Wing, L. (1982) Prevalence of autism and related conditions in adults in a mental handicap hospital, *Applied Research on Mental Retardation*, 3, 303–17.
12. Croen, L. A., Grether, J. K., Hoogstrate, J., and Selvin, S. (2002) The changing prevalence of autism in California, *Journal of Autism and Developmental Disorders*, 32, 207–15.
13. Frith, U., and Happé, F. (1998) Why specific developmental disorders are not specific, *Developmental Science*, 1, 267–72.
14. Konstantareas, M. M., and Hewitt, T. (2001) Autistic disorder and schizophrenia: Diagnostic overlaps, *Journal of Autism and Developmental Disorders*, 31, 19–28.
15. Kolvin, I., Humphrey, M., and McNay, A. (1971) Studies in the childhood psychoses I to VI, *British Journal of Psychiatry*, 118, 381–419.
16. Green, W. H., Campbell, M., Hardesty, A. S., et al. (1984) A comparison of schizophrenic and autistic children, *Journal of the American Academy of Child Psychiatry*, 23, 399–409.
17. Elvevag, B., and Goldberg, T. E. (2000) Cognitive impairment in schizophrenia is the core of the disorder, *Critical Reviews in Neurobiology*, 14, 1–21.
18. Gillberg, C., and Coleman, M. (2000) *The Biology of the Autistic Syndromes* (London: MacKeith Press).
19. Rutter, M. (2000) Genetic studies of autism: From the 1970s into the millennium, *American Journal of Psychiatry*, 157, 2043–5.
20. Folstein, S., and Rutter, M. (1977) Infantile autism: A genetic study of 21 twin pairs, *Journal of Child Psychology and Psychiatry*, 18, 297–321.
21. Piven, J. (2001) The broad autism phenotype: A complementary strategy for molecular genetic studies of autism, *American Journal of Medical Genetics (Neuropsychiatric Genetics)*, 105, 34–5.
22. Happé, F., Briskman, J., and Frith, U. (2001) Exploring the cognitive phenotype of autism: Weak "central coherence" in parents and siblings of children with autism. I. Experimental tests, *Journal of Child Psychology and Psychiatry*, 42, 299–307; Baron-Cohen, S., Wheelwright, S., Skinner, R., et al. (2001) The autism-spectrum quotient (AQ): Evidence from Asperger Syndrome/high-functioning autism, males and females, scientists and mathematicians, *Journal of Autism and Developmental Disorders*, 31, 5–17.
23. Lamb, J. A., Moore, J., Bailey, A., and Monaco, A. P. (2000) Autism: Recent molecular genetic advances, *Human Molecular Genetics*, 9, 861–8.
24. Taylor, B., Miller, E., Farrington, C. P., et al. (1999) Autism and measles, mumps and rubella vaccine: No epidemiological evidence for a causal association, *Lancet*, 353, 2026–9.

NOTES TO CHAPTER 5 MIND READING AND MIND BLINDNESS

1. Nicolson, B., and Wright, C. (1974) *Georges de la Tour* (London: Phaidon).
2. Rutter, M. (1983) Cognitive deficits in the pathogenesis of autism, *Journal of Child Psychology and Psychiatry*, 24, 513–31, p.526.
3. Baron-Cohen, S., Tager-Flusberg, H., and Cohen, D. (1993) *Understanding Other Minds I: Perspectives from Autism* (Oxford: Oxford University Press); Baron-Cohen, S., Tager-Flusberg, H., and Cohen, D. (2000) *Understanding Other Minds II: Perspectives from Cognitive Neuroscience* (Oxford: Oxford University Press).
4. Baron-Cohen, S. (1995) *Mindblindness: An Essay on Autism and Theory of Mind* (Cambridge, MA: MIT Press).
5. Leslie, A. M. (1987) Pretense and representation: The origins of "theory of mind," *Psychological Review*, 94, 412–26.
6. Ibid., p.412.
7. Frith, U., Morton, J., and Leslie, A. M. (1991) The cognitive basis of a biological disorder: Autism, *Trends in Neurosciences*, 14, 433–8.
8. Wimmer, H., and Perner, J. (1983) Beliefs about beliefs: Representations and constraining function of wrong beliefs in young children's understanding of deception, *Cognition*, 13, 103–128.
9. Baron-Cohen, S., Leslie, A. M., and Frith, U. (1985) Does the autistic child have a "theory of mind"?, *Cognition*, 21, 37–46.
10. Leslie, A. M., and Frith, U. (1988) Autistic children's understanding of seeing, knowing and believing, *British Journal of Developmental Psychology*, 4, 315–24.
11. Perner, J., Frith, U., Leslie, A. M., and Leekam, S. R. (1989) Exploration of the autistic child's theory of mind: Knowledge, belief and communication, *Child Development*, 60, 688–700.
12. Baron-Cohen, S., Leslie, A. M., and Frith, U. (1984) Mechanical, behavioural and intentional understanding of picture stories in autistic children, *British Journal of Developmental Psychology*, 4, 113–25.
13. Leslie, A. M., and Thaiss, L. (1992) Domain specificity in conceptual development: Evidence from autism, *Cognition*, 43, 467–79.
14. First reproduced in Happé, F. (1994) *Autism: An Introduction to Psychological Theory* (London: UCL Press/Psychology Press; Cambridge, MA: Harvard University Press, 1995).
15. Charman, T., and Baron-Cohen, S. (1995) Understanding models, photos, and beliefs: A test of the modularity thesis of metarepresentation, *Cognitive Development*, 10, 287–98.
16. Sodian, B., and Frith, U. (1994) Deception and sabotage in autistic, retarded and normal children, *Journal of Child Psychology and Psychiatry*, 24, 591–605.
17. Happé, F. (1995) The role of age and verbal ability in the theory of mind task performance of subjects with autism, *Child Development*, 66, 843–55.

18. Happé, F. (1994) An advanced test of theory of mind: Understanding of story characters' thoughts and feelings in able autistic, mentally handicapped, and normal children and adults, *Journal of Autism and Developmental Disorders*, 24, 129–54.

19. Happé, F., Ehlers, S., Fletcher, P., et al. (1996) "Theory of mind" in the brain. Evidence from a PET scan study of Asperger syndrome, *Neuroreport*, 8, 197–201.

20. Frith, U. (2001) Mind blindness and the brain in autism, *Neuron*, 32, 969–79.

21. Yirmiya, N., Erel, O., Shaked, M., and Solomonica-Levi, D. (1998) Meta-analyses comparing theory of mind abilities of individuals with autism, individuals with mental retardation, and normally developing individuals, *Psychological Bulletin*, 124, 283–307.

22. Corcoran, R., Mercer, G., and Frith, C. D. (1995) Schizophrenia, symptomatology and social inference: Investigating "theory of mind" in people with schizophrenia, *Schizophrenia Research*, 17, 5–13.

23. Frith, C. D., and Frith, U. (1999) Interacting minds – a biological basis, *Science*, 286, 1692–5.

24. Gallese, V., Fadiga, L., Fogassi, L., and Rizzolatti, G. (1996) Action recognition in the prefrontal cortex, *Brain*, 119, 593–609.

NOTES TO CHAPTER 6 AUTISTIC ALONENESS

1. Volkmar, F., Sparrow, S., Goudereau, D., Cicchetti, D., Paul, R., and Cohen, D. J. (1987) Social deficits in autism: An operational approach using the Vineland Adaptive Behavior Scales, *Journal of the American Academy of Child Psychiatry*, 26, 156–61.

2. Frith, U., Siddons, F., and Happé, F. (1994) Autism and theory of mind in everyday life, *Social Development*, 2, 108–24.

3. Reddy, V., Hay, D., Murray, L., and Trevarthen, C. (1997) Communication in infancy: Mutual regulation of affect and attention. In: G. Bremner, A. Slater, and G. Butterworth (eds.), *Infant Development, Recent Advances* (Hove, UK: Psychology Press, pp. 247–73).

4. Carpenter, M., Nagell, K., and Tomasello, M. (1998) Social cognition, joint attention, and communicative competence from 9 to 15 months of age, *Monographs of the Society for Research in Child Development*, 63, no.176.

5. Tomasello, M. (1999) *The Cultural Origins of Human Cognition*. (Cambridge, MA: Harvard University Press).

6. Sigman, M., Mundy, P., Sherman, T., and Ungerer, J. (1986) Social interactions of autistic, mentally retarded, and normal children and their caregivers, *Journal of Child Psychology and Psychiatry*, 27, 657–69; Loveland, K. A., and Landry, S. H. (1986) Joint attention and language in autism and developmental language delay, *Journal of Child Psychology and Psychiatry*, 16, 335–49.

7. Sigman, M., and Capps, L. (1997) *Children with Autism: A Developmental Perspective* (Cambridge, MA: Harvard University Press).

8. Leekam, S. R., Lopez, B., Moore, C. (2000) Attention and joint attention in preschool children with autism, *Developmental Psychology*, 36, 261–73.

9. Blair, R. J. R., Frith, U., Smith, N., Abell, F., and Cipolotti, L. (2002) Fractionation of visual memory: Agency detection and its impairment in autism, *Neuropsychologia*, 40, 108–18.

10. Schultz, R. T., Gauthier, I., Klin, A., et al. (2000) Abnormal ventral temporal cortical activity during face discrimination among individuals with autism and Asperger's syndrome, *Archives of General Psychiatry*, 57, 331–40.

11. Bellugi, U., Lichtenberger, L., Mills, D., Galaburda, A., and Konerberg, J. (1999) Bridging cognition, the brain and molecular genetics: Evidence from Williams syndrome, *Trends in Neuroscience*, 22, 197–207.

12. Baron-Cohen, S. (1995) *Mindblindness. An Essay on Autism and Theory of Mind* (Cambridge, MA: MIT Press).

13. Baron-Cohen, S., Wheelwright, S., Hill, J., Raste, U., and Plumb, I. (2001) The "Reading the Mind in the Eyes" Test revised version: A study with normal adults and adults with Asperger syndrome or high-functioning autism, *Journal of Child Psychology and Psychiatry*, 42, 241–51.

14. Emery, N. J. (2000) The eyes have it: The neuroethology, function and evolution of social gaze, *Neuroscience and Biobehavioral-Reviews*, 24, 581–604.

15. Driver, J., Davis, G., Ricciardelli, P., Kidd, P., Maxwell, E., and Baron-Cohen, S. (1999) Gaze perception triggers reflexive visuospatial orienting, *Visual Cognition*, 6, 509–40.

16. Ruffman, T., Garnham, W., and Rideout, P. (2001) Social understanding in autism: Eye gaze as a measure of core insights, *Journal of Child Psychology and Psychiatry*, 42, 1083–94.

17. Lane, H. (1976) *The Wild Boy of Aveyron: A History of the Education of Retarded, Deaf, and Hearing Children* (Cambridge, MA: Harvard University Press; London: Allen & Unwin, 1978), p.8.

18. Attwood, A., Frith, U., and Hermelin, B. (1988) The understanding and use of interpersonal gestures by autistic and Down's syndrome children, *Journal of Autism and Developmental Disorders*, 18, 241–57.

19. Kanner, L. (1943) Autistic disturbances of affective contact, *Nervous Child*, 2, 217–50, p.250. Reprinted in L. Kanner, *Childhood Psychosis: Initial Studies and New Insights* (Washington, DC: V. H. Winston, pp.1–43), pp.42–3.

20. Dissanayake, C., and Crossley, S. A. (1996) Proximity and sociable behaviour in autism: Evidence for attachment, *Journal of Child Psychology and Psychiatry*, 37, 149–56.

21. Hobson, R. P. (1993) *Autism and the Development of Mind* (Hove, UK: Lawrence Erlbaum).

22. Park, C. (1987) *The Siege: The First Eight Years of an Autistic Child*, 2nd edn. (Boston: Atlantic-Little, Brown).

23. Kasari, C., Sigman, M., Baumgartner, P., and Stipek, D. J. (1993) Pride and mastery in children with autism, *Journal of Child Psychology and Psychiatry*, 34, 353–62.

24. Blair, R. J. R., Sellars, C., Strickland, I., et al. (1996) Theory of mind in the psychopath, *Journal of Forensic Psychiatry*, 7, 15–25.

25. Blair, R. J. R. (1999) Psychophysiological responsiveness to the distress of others in children with autism, *Personality and Individual Differences*, 26, 477–85.

26. Blair, R. J. R. (1996) Brief report: Morality in the autistic child, *Journal of Autism and Developmental Disorders*, 26, 571–9.

NOTES TO CHAPTER 7 THE DIFFICULTY OF TALKING TO OTHERS

1. Tager-Flusberg, H. (2000) Language and understanding minds: Connections in autism. In Baron-Cohen, S., Tager-Flusberg, H., and Cohen, D. J. (eds.), *Understanding Other Minds: Perspectives from Developmental Cognitive Neuroscience* (Oxford, Oxford University Press, pp.124–49).

2. Sabbagh, M. A. (1999) Communicative intentions and language: Evidence from right-hemisphere damage and autism, *Brain and Language*, 70, 29–69.

3. Lord, C., and Pickles, A. (1996) Language level and nonverbal social-communicative behaviors in autistic and language-delayed children, *Journal of the American Academy of Adolescent Psychiatry*, 35, 1542–50.

4. Tager-Flusberg, H., Calkins, S., Nolin, T., Baumberger, T., Anderson, M., and Chadwick-Dias, A. (1990) A longitudinal study of language acquisition in autistic and Down syndrome children, *Journal of Autism and Developmental Disorders*, 20, 1–21.

5. Bloom, P. (2000) *How Children Learn the Meanings of Words* (Cambridge, MA: MIT Press).

6. Baron-Cohen, S., Baldwin, D. A., and Crowson, M. (1997) Do children with autism use the speaker's direction of gaze strategy to crack the code of language? *Child Development*, 68, 48–57.

7. Kanner, L. (1946) Irrelevant and metaphorical language in early infantile autism, *American Journal of Psychiatry*, 103, 242–6.

8. Kanner, L. (1943) Autistic disturbances of affective contact, *Nervous Child*, 2, 217–50, p.227. Reprinted in L. Kanner, *Childhood Psychosis: Initial Studies and New Insights* (Washington, DC: V. H. Winston, pp.1–43), p.15.

9. Schuler, A., and Prizant, B. M. (1985) Echolalia. In E. Schopler and G. B. Mesibov (eds.), *Communication Problems in Autism* (New York: Plenum Press, pp.163–84).

10. Bartak, L., and Rutter, M. (1974) The use of personal pronouns by autistic children, *Journal of Autism and Childhood Schizophrenia*, 4, 217–22.

11. Snowling, M., and Frith, U. (1986) Comprehension in "hyperlexic" readers, *Journal of Experimental Child Psychology*, 42, 392–415.

12. Grandin, T., and Scariano, M. (1986) *Emergence Labelled Autistic* (Tunbridge Wells, UK: Costello), p.142.

13. Bishop, D. V., and Baird, G. (2001) Parent and teacher report of pragmatic aspects of communication: Use of the children's communication checklist in a clinical setting, *Developmental Medicine and Child Neurology*, 43, 809–18; Adams, C., Green, J., Gilchrist, A., and Cox, A. (2002) Conversational behaviour of children

with Asperger syndrome and conduct disorder, *Journal of Child Psychology and Psychiatry*, 43, 679–90.

14. Baltaxe, C. A. M. (1977) Pragmatic deficits in the language of autistic adolescents, *Journal of Pediatric Psychology*, 2, 176–80.
15. Baltaxe, C. A. M., and Simmons, J. Q. (1985) Prosodic development in normal and autistic children. In E. Schopler and G. B. Mesibov (eds.), *Communication Problems in Autism* (New York: Plenum Press, pp.95–125).
16. Shriberg, L. D., Paul, R., McSweeny, J. L., Klin, A. M., Cohen, D. J., and Volkmar, F. R. (2001) Speech and prosody characteristics of adolescents and adults with high-functioning autism and Asperger syndrome, *Journal of Speech Language and Hearing Research*, 44, 1097–1115.
17. Perner, J., Frith, U., Leslie, A., and Leekam, S. (1989) Explorations of the autistic child's theory of mind: Knowledge, belief and communication, *Child Development*, 60, 689–700.
18. Sperber, D., and Wilson, D. (1995) *Relevance, Communication and Cognition*, 2nd edn. (Oxford: Blackwell).

NOTES FOR CHAPTER 8 INTELLIGENCE AND SPECIAL TALENT

1. Roeleveld, N., Zielhuis, G. A., and Gabreels, F. (1997) The prevalence of mental retardation: A critical review of recent literature, *Developmental Medicine and Child Neurology*, 39, 125–32.
2. Zeaman, D., and House, B. (1963) The roles of attention in retardate discrimination learning. In N. R. Ellis (ed.), *Handbook of Mental Deficiency, Psychological Theory and Research* (New York: McGraw-Hill, pp.159–223).
3. Baird, G., Charman, T., Baron-Cohen, S., et al. (2000) A screening instrument for autism at 18 months of age: A 6-year follow-up study, *Journal of the American Academy of Child and Adolescent Psychiatry*, 39, 694–702.
4. Asperger, H. (1944) Die autistischen Psychopathen im Kindesalter, *Archiv für Psychiatrie und Nervenkrankheiten*, 117, 76–136. Translated by U. Frith in U. Frith (ed.), *Autism and Asperger Syndrome* (Cambridge, UK: Cambridge University Press, 1991, pp. 37–92).
5. Anderson, M. (1992) *Intelligence and Development: A Cognitive Theory* (Oxford: Blackwell); Anderson, M. (2001) Annotation: Conceptions of intelligence, *Journal of Child Psychology and Psychiatry*, 42, 287–98.
6. Fodor, J. A. (1983) *The Modularity of Mind* (Cambridge, MA: MIT Press).
7. Scheuffgen, K., Happé, F., Anderson, M., and Frith, U. (2000) High "intelligence," low "IQ"? Speed of processing and measured IQ in children with autism, *Developmental Psychopathology*, 12, 83–90.
8. Goldstein, G., Beers, S. R., Siegel, D. J., and Minshew, N. J. (2001) A comparison of WAIS-R profiles in adults with high-functioning autism or differing subtypes of learning disability, *Applied Neuropsychology*, 8, 148–54.

9. Nunes Carraher, T., Carraher, D. W., and Schliemann, A. D. (1985) Mathematics in the street and schools, *British Journal of Developmental Psychology*, 3, 21–9.

10. Hermelin, B., and O'Connor, N. (1970) *Psychological Experiments with Autistic Children* (Oxford: Pergamon).

11. Aurnhammer-Frith, U. (1969) Emphasis and meaning in recall in normal and autistic children, *Language and Speech*, 12, 29–38.

12. Frith, U. (1970) Studies in pattern detection in normal and autistic children: I. Immediate recall of auditory sequences, *Journal of Abnormal Psychology*, 76, 413–20.

13. Frith, U. (1970) Studies in pattern detection in normal and autistic children: II. Reproduction and production of colour sequence, *Journal of Experimental Child Psychology*, 10, 120–35.

14. Kanner, L. (1943) Autistic disturbances of affective contact, *Nervous Child*, 2, 217–50, p.249. Reprinted in L. Kanner, *Childhood Psychosis: Initial Studies and New Insights* (Washington, DC: V. H. Winston, pp.1–43), p.41.

15. Minshew, N. J., and Goldstein, G. (2001) The pattern of intact and impaired memory functions in autism, *Journal of Child Psychology and Psychiatry*, 42, 1095–1101.

16. Hermelin, B. (2001) *Bright Splinters of the Mind. A Personal Story of Research with Autistic Savants* (London: Jessica Kingsley).

17. Selfe, L. (1977) *Nadia: A Case of Extraordinary Drawing Ability in an Autistic Child* (London: Academic Press).

18. Humphrey, N. (1998) Cave art, autism, and the evolution of the human mind, *Cambridge Archaeological Journal*, 8, 165–91.

19. Wiltshire, S. (1987) *Drawings: Selected and with an Introduction by Sir Hugh Casson* (London: Dent), p.5.

20. Sacks, O. (1995) *An Anthropologist on Mars* (New York: Alfred Knopf; Toronto: Random House; London: Picador).

21. Nettlebeck, T. (1999) Savant skills – rhyme without reason. In M. Anderson (ed.), *The Development of Intelligence* (Hove, UK: Psychology Press, pp. 247–73).

22. Smith, N., and Tsimpli, I. M. (1995) *The Mind of a Savant: Language Learning and Modularity* (Oxford: Blackwell).

23. Norris, D. (1990) How to build a connectionist idiot (savant), *Cognition*, 35, 277–91.

24. Mottron, L., and Belleville, S. (1993) A study of perceptual analysis in a high-level autistic subject with exceptional graphic abilities, *Brain and Cognition*, 23, 279–309.

25. Heaton, P., Pring, L., and Hermelin, B. (1998) Autism and pitch processing: A precursor for savant musical ability, *Music Perception*, 15, 291–305.

NOTES TO CHAPTER 9 A FRAGMENTED WORLD

1. Hermelin, B. (2001) *Bright Splinters of the Mind. A Personal Story of Research with Autistic Savants* (London: Jessica Kingsley), p.49.

2. Frith, U., and Hermelin, B. (1969) The role of visual and motor cues for normal, subnormal and autistic children, *Journal of Child Psychology and Psychiatry*, 10, 153–63.

3. Perec, G. (1978) *Life, a User's Manual*, English translation by D. Bellos (London: Collins Harvill, 1987), p.189.

4. Shah, A., and Frith, U. (1983) An islet of ability in autistic children: A research note, *Journal of Child Psychology and Psychiatry*, 24, 613–20.

5. Witkin, H. A., Oltman, P. K., Raskin, E., and Karp, S. (1971) *Children's Embedded Figures Test* (Palo Alto, CA: Consulting Psychologists Press).

6. Witkin, H. A., and Goodenough, D. R. (1981) *Cognitive Styles: Essence and Origins* (New York: International University Press).

7. Shah, A., and Frith, U. (1993) Why do autistic children show superior performance on the block design task? *Journal of Child Psychology and Psychiatry*, 34, 1351–64.

8. Borges, J. L. (1956) Funes the Memorius, English translation in *Fictions* (New York: New Directions, 1962).

9. Luria, A. R. (1968) *The Mind of a Mnemonist: A Little Book About a Vast Memory*, transl. by L. Solotaroff (London: Jonathan Cape; Cambridge, MA.: Harvard University Press).

10. Snowling, M., and Frith, U. (1986) Comprehension in "hyperlexic" readers, *Journal of Experimental Child Psychology*, 42, 392–415; Happé, F. (1997) Central coherence and theory of mind in autism: Reading homographs in context, *British Journal of Developmental Psychology*, 15, 1–12.

11. Gerland, G. (1997) *A Real Person*, transl. from the Swedish by J. Tate (London: Souvenir Press), p.21.

12. Happé, F. (1996) Studying weak central coherence at low levels: Children with autism do not succumb to visual illusions, *Journal of Child Psychology and Psychiatry*, 37, 873–7.

13. Happé, F. (1999) Autism: Cognitive deficit or cognitive style, *Trends in Cognitive Science*, 3, 216–22.

14. Happé, F., Briskman, J., and Frith, U. (2001) Exploring the cognitive phenotype of autism: Weak "central coherence" in parents and siblings of children with autism. I. Experimental tests, *Journal of Child Psychology and Psychiatry*, 42, 299–307; Briskman, J., Happé, F., and Frith, U. (2001) Exploring the cognitive phenotype of autism: Weak "central coherence" in parents and siblings of children with autism. II Real-life skills and preferences, *Journal of Child Psychology and Psychiatry*, 42, 309–16.

15. Baron-Cohen, S. (2002) The extreme male brain theory of autism, *Trends in Cognitive Sciences*, 6 (6), 248–54.

16. Ibid.

17. Park, D., and Youderian, P. (1974) Light and number: Ordering principles in the world of an autistic child, *Journal of Autism and Childhood Schizophrenia*, 4, 313–23.

18. Mottron, L., and Burack, J. (2001) Enhanced perceptual functioning in the development of autism. In: J. A. Burack, T. Charman, N. Yirmiya, and P. R. Zelazo (eds.), *The Development of Autism: Perspectives from Theory and Research* (Mahwah, NJ: Erlbaum, pp. 131–48).

19. Plaisted, K. (2000) Aspects of autism that theory of mind cannot explain. In S. Baron-Cohen, H. Tager-Flusberg, and D. J. Cohen (eds.), *Understanding Other Minds: Perspectives from Developmental Cognitive Neuroscience* (Oxford: Oxford University Press, pp. 222–50).

20. O'Riordan, M. A., Plaisted, K. C., Driver, J., and Baron-Cohen, S. (2001) Superior visual search in autism, *Journal of Experimental Psychology–Human Perception and Performance*, 27, 719–30.

21. Milne, E., Swettenham, J., Hansen, P., Campbell, R., Jeffries, H., and Plaisted, K. (2002) High motion coherence thresholds in children with autism, *Journal of Child Psychology and Psychiatry*, 43, 255–64.

22. Klinger, L. G., and Dawson, G. (2000) Prototype formation in autism, *Development and Psychopathology*, 13, 111–24.

23. Mottron, L., Peretz, I., Ménard, E. (2000) Local and global processing of music in high-functioning persons with autism, *Journal of Child Psychology and Psychiatry*, 41(8), 1057–68.

24. Gustafsson, L. (1997) Inadequate cortical feature maps: A neural circuit theory of autism, *Biological Psychiatry*, 42,1138–47; McClelland, J. L. (2000) The basis of hyperspecificity in autism: A preliminary suggestion based on properties of neural nets, *Journal of Autism and Developmental Disorders*, 30(5), 497–502.

25. Happé, F. (2001) Social and non-social development in Autism: Where are the links? In: J. A. Burack, T. Charman, N. Yirmiya, and P. R. Zelazo (eds.), *The Development of Autism: Perspectives from Theory and Research* (Mahwah, NJ: Erlbaum, pp. 237–53).

26. Kanner, L. (1943) Autistic disturbances of affective contact, *Nervous Child*, 2, 217–50, p.246.

NOTES TO CHAPTER 10 SENSATIONS AND REPETITIONS

1. Bemporad, J. R. (1979) Adult recollections of a formerly autistic child, *Journal of Autism and Developmental Disorders*, 9, 179–98, p.192.

2. Gerland, G. (1997) *A Real Person – Life from the Outside*, translated from the Swedish by J. Tate (London: Souvenir Press), pp.11, 14–15.

3. Lovaas, O. I., Koegel, R. L., and Schreibman, L. (1979) Stimulus overselectivity in autism: A review of research, *Psychological Bulletin*, 86, 1236–54.

4. Weeks, S. J., and Hobson, R. P. (1987) The salience of facial expression for autistic children, *Journal of Child Psychology and Psychiatry*, 28, 137–52.

5. Dawson, G., Meltzoff, A., Osterling, J., Rinaldi, J., and Brown, E. (1998) Children with autism fail to orient to naturally-occurring social stimuli, *Child Development*, 68, 1276–85.

6. Park, D., and Youderian, P. (1974) Light and number: Ordering principles in the world of an autistic child, *Journal of Autism and Childhood Schizophrenia*, 4, 313–23, p.316.

7. Grandin, T. (1984) My experiences as an autistic child and review of selected literature, *Journal of Orthomolecular Psychiatry*, 13, 144–75, p.156.

8. Asendorpf, J. (1980) Nichtreaktive Stressmessung: Bewegungssteretypien als Aktivierungsindikatoren, *Zeitschrift für Experimentelle und Angewandte Psychologie*, 27, 44–58.

9. Frith, C. D., and Done, J. (1990) Stereotyped behaviour in madness and in health. In S. J. Cooper and C. T. Dourish (eds.), *The Neurobiology of Behavioural Stereotypy* (Oxford: Oxford University Press, pp. 232–59).

10. Turner, M. (1999) Annotation: Repetitive behaviour in autism: A review of psychological research, *Journal of Child Psychology and Psychiatry*, 40, 839–49.

11. Ridley, R. (1994) The psychology of perseverative and stereotyped behaviour, *Progress in Neurobiology*, 44, 221–31.

12. Damasio, A. R., and Maurer, R. G. (1978) A neurological model for childhood autism, *Archives of Neurology*, 35, 777–86.

13. Bradshaw, J. L., and Sheppard, D. M. (2000) The neurodevelopmental frontostriatal disorders: Evolutionary adaptiveness and anomalous lateralisation, *Brain and Language*, 73, 297–320.

14. Wing, L., and Shah, A. (2000) Catatonia in autistic spectrum disorders, *British Journal of Psychiatry*, 176, 357–62.

15. Frith, U. (1972) Cognitive mechanisms in autism: Experiments with colour and tone sequence production, *Journal of Autism and Childhood Schizophrenia*, 2, 160–73.

16. Shallice, T. (1988) *From Neuropsychology to Mental Structure* (Cambridge, UK: Cambridge University Press).

17. Russell, J. (ed.) (1997) *Autism as an Executive Disorder* (Oxford: Oxford University Press).

18. Turner, M. (1997) Towards an executive dysfunction account of repetitive behaviour in autism. In J. Russell (ed.), *Autism as an Executive Disorder* (Oxford: Oxford University Press, pp. 57–100).

19. Rowe, A. D., Bullock, P. R., Polkey, C. E., and Morris, R. G. (2001) "Theory of mind" impairments and their relationship to executive functioning following frontal lobe excisions, *Brain*, 124, 600–16.

20. Fine, C., Lumsden, J., and Blair, R. J. R. (2001) Dissociation between "theory of mind" and executive functions in a patient with early left amygdala damage, *Brain*, 124, 287–98.

21. Perner, J., and Lang, B. (1999) Development of theory of mind and executive control, *Trends in Cognitive Sciences*, 3, 337–44.

Notes to chapter 11 Seeing the Brain Through a Scanner

1. Gillberg, C., and Coleman, M. (2000) *The Biology of the Autistic Syndromes* (London: MacKeith Press).

2. Green, D., Baird, G., Barnett, A. L., et al. (2002) The severity and nature of motor impairment in Asperger's syndrome: A comparison with specific developmental disorder of motor function, *Journal of Child Psychology and Psychiatry*, 43, 655–68.

3. Bauman, M. L., and Kemper, T. L. (1994) Neuroanatomic observations of the brain of autism. In M. L. Bauman and T. L. Kemper (eds.), *The Neurobiology of Autism* (Baltimore: Johns Hopkins University Press, pp.119–45).

4. Bailey, A., Luthert, P., Dean, A., et al. (1998) A clinicopathological study of autism, *Brain*, 121, 889–905.

5. Fombonne, E., Rogé, B., Claverie, J., Courty, S., Fremolle, J. (1999) Microcephaly and macrocephaly in autism, *Journal of Autism and Developmental Disorders*, 29, 113–19.

6. Lainhart, J. E., Piven, J., Wzorek, M., et al. (1997) Macrocephaly in children and adults with autism, *Journal of the American Academy of Child and Adolescent Psychiatry*, 36, 282–90; Courchesne, E., Karns, C. M., Davis, H. R., et al. (2001) Unusual brain growth patterns in early life in patients with autistic disorder: An MRI study, *Neurology*, 57, 245–54.

7. Huttenlocher, P. R. (1999) Dendritic synaptic development in human cerebral cortex: Time course and critical periods, *Developmental Neuropsychology*, 16, 347–9.

8. Huttenlocher, P. R., and Dabholkar, A. S. (1997) Regional differences in synaptogenesis in human cerebral cortex, *Journal of Comparative Neurology*, 387, 167–78.

9. Burkhalter, A. (1993) Development of forward and feedback connections between Areas V1 and V2 of human visual-cortex, *Cerebral Cortex*, 3, 476–87.

10. Casey, B. J., Giedd, J. N., and Thomas, K. M. (2000) Structural and functional brain development and its relation to cognitive development, *Biological Psychology*, 54, 241–57.

11. Griffith, E. M., Pennington, B. F., Wehner, E. A., and Rogers, S. J. (1999) Executive functions in young children with autism, *Child Development*, 70, 817–3.

12. Dawson, G., Munson, J., Estes, A., et al. (2002) Neurocognitive function and joint attention ability in young children with autism spectrum disorder versus developmental delay, *Child Development*, 73, 345–58.

13. Ashburner, J., and Friston, K. J. (2000) Voxel-based morphometry–the methods, *Neuroimage*, 11, 805–21.

14. Bauman and Kemper (1994).

15. Courchesne, E., Yeung-Courchesne, R., Press, G. A., Hesselink, J. R., and Jernigan, T. L. (1988) Hypoplasia of cerebellar vermal lobule-Vi and lobule-Vii in autism, *New England Journal of Medicine*, 318, 1349–54.

16. Courchesne, E., Saitoh, O., Townsend, J. P., et al. (1994) Cerebellar hypoplasia and hyperplasia in infantile-autism, *Lancet*, 343, 6–64.

17. Hardan, A. Y., Minshew, N. J., Mallikarjuhn, M., and Keshavan, M. S. (2001) Brain volume in autism, *Journal of Child Neurology*, 16, 421–4.

18. Abell, F., Krams, M., Ashburner, J., et al. (1999) The neuroanatomy of autism: A voxel based whole brain analysis of structural MRI scans in high functioning individuals, *Neuroreport*, 10, 1647–51; Salmond, C. H., Ashburner, J., Friston, K. J., Gadian, D. G., and Vargha-Khadem, F. (submitted) Convergent evidence for the neural basis of autism.

19. Townsend, J., Westerfield, M., Leaver, E., et al. (2001) Event-related brain response abnormalities in autism: Evidence for impaired cerebello-frontal spatial attention networks, *Cognitive Brain Research*, 11, 127–45.

20. Bolton, P. F., and Grifftiths, P. D. (1997) Association of tuberous sclerosis of temporal lobes with autism and atypical autism, *Lancet*, 349, 392–5.

21. Ohnishi, T., Matsuda, H., Hashimoto, T., et al. (2000) Abnormal regional cerebral blood flow in childhood autism, *Brain*, 123, 1838–44; Zilbovicius, M., Boddaert, N., Belin, P., et al. (2000) Temporal lobe dysfunction in childhood autism: A PET study, *American Journal of Psychiatry*, 157, 1988–93.

22. Brothers, L., and Ring, B. (1993) Mesial temporal neurons in the macaque monkey with responses selective for aspects of social stimuli, *Behavioural Brain Research*, 57(1), 53–61.

23. Baron-Cohen, S., Ring, H., Bullmore, E., Wheelwright, S., Ashwin, C., and Williams, S. (2000) The amygdala theory of autism, *Neuroscience and Biobehavioural Reviews*, 24, 355–64.

24. Bachevalier, J., Malkova, L., and Mishkin, M. (2001) Effects of selective neonatal temporal lobe lesions on socioemotional behavior in infant rhesus monkeys (Macaca mulatta), *Behavioural Neuroscience*, 115, 545–59.

25. Prather, M. D., Lavenex, P., Mauldin-Jourdain, M. L., et al. (2001) Increased social fear and decreased fear of objects in monkeys with neonatal amygdala lesions, *Neuroscience*, 106, 653–8.

26. Aylward, E. H., Minshew, N. J., Goldstein, G., et al. (1999) MRI volumes of amygdala and hippocampus in non-mentally retarded autistic adolescents and adults, *Neurology*, 53, 2145–50; Pierce, K., Müller, R. A., Ambrose, J., Allen, G., and Courchesne, E. (2001) Face processing occurs outside the fusiform "face area" in autism: Evidence from functional MRI, *Brain*, 124, 2059–73.

27. Haznedar, M. M., Buchsbaum, M. S., Wei, T. C., et al. (2000) Limbic circuitry in patients with autism spectrum disorders studied with positron emission tomography and magnetic resonance imaging, *American Journal of Psychiatry*, 157 (12), 1994–2001.

28. Howard, M. A., Cowell, P. E., Boucher, J., et al. (2000) Convergent neuro-anatomical and behavioural evidence of an amygdala hypothesis of autism, *Neuroreport*, 11, 2931–5.

29. Abell et al. (1999), Salmond et al.

30. Abell et al. (1999).

31. Fletcher, P. C., Happé, F., Frith, U., et al. (1995) Other minds in the brain: A functional imaging study of "theory of mind" in story comprehension, *Cognition*, 57, 109–28.

32. Happé, F. (1994) An advanced test of theory of mind: Understanding of story characters' thoughts and feelings by able autistic, mentally handicapped and normal children and adults, *Journal of Autism and Developmental Disorders*, 24, 129–54.

33. Happé, F., Ehlers, S., Fletcher, P., et al. (1996) "Theory of mind" in the brain. Evidence from a PET scan study of Asperger syndrome, *Neuroreport*, 8, 197–201.

34. Baron-Cohen, S., Ring, H. A., Wheelwright, S., et al. (1999) Social intelligence in the normal and autistic brain: An fMRI study, *European Journal of Neuroscience*, 11, 1891–8.

35. Castelli, F., Frith, C. D., Happé, F., and Frith, U. (2002) Autism, Asperger syndrome and brain mechanisms for the attribution of mental states to animated shapes, *Brain*, 125, 1–11.

36. Frith, U. (2001) Mind blindness and the brain in autism, *Neuron*, 32, 969–79.

37. Kampe, K., Frith, C. D., Dolan, R. J., and Frith, U. (2001) Attraction and gaze – the reward value of social stimuli, *Nature*, 413, 589.

38. Gusnard, D. A., Akbudak, E., Shulman, G. L., and Raichle, M. E. (2001) Medial prefrontal cortex and self-referential mental activity: Relation to a default mode of brain function, *Proceedings of the National Academy of Sciences*, 27, 4259–64.

39. Douglas, R. J., Koch, C., Mahowald, M., Martin, K. A. C., and Suarez, H. H. (1995) Recurrent excitation in neocortical circuits, *Science*, 269, 981–5.

40. Lamme, V. A. F., and Roelfsema, P. R. (2000) The distinct modes of vision offered by feedforward and recurrent processing, *Trends in Neurosciences*, 23, 571–9.

41. Friston, K. J., and Büchel, C. (2000) Attentional modulation of effective connectivity from V2 to V5/MT in humans, *Proceedings of the National Academy of Sciences of the United States of America*, 97, 7591–6.

42. Fink, G. R., Halligan, P. W., Marshall, J. C., Frith, C. D., Frackowiak, R. S. J., and Dolan, R. J. (1997) Neural mechanisms involved in the processing of global and local aspects of hierarchically organized visual stimuli, *Brain*, 120, 1779–91.

43. Ring, H., Baron-Cohen, S., Wheelwright, S., et al. (1999) Cerebral correlates of preserved cognitive skills in autism – A functional MRI study of Embedded Figures Task performance, *Brain*, 122, 1305–15.

44. Blair, R. J. R., Frith, U., Smith, N., Abell, F., and Cipolotti, L. (2002) Fractionation of visual memory: Agency detection and its impairment in autism, *Neuropsychologia*, 40, 108–18.

45. Puce, A., Allison, T., Asgari, M., Gore, J. C., and McCarthy, G. (1996) Differential sensitivity of human visual cortex to faces, letterstrings, and textures: A functional magnetic resonance imaging study, *Journal of Neuroscience*, 16, 5205–15; Kanwisher, N., McDermott, J., and Chun, M. M. (1997) The fusiform face area: A module in human extrastriate cortex specialized for face perception, *Journal of Neuroscience*, 17, 4302–11.

46. Morris, J. S., Frith, C. D., Perrett, D. I., et al. (1996) A differential neural response in the human amygdala to fearful and happy facial expressions, *Nature*, 383, 812–15.

47. Schultz, R. T., Gauthier, I., Klin, A., et al. (2000) Abnormal ventral temporal cortical activity during face discrimination among individuals with autism and Asperger's syndrome, *Archives of General Psychiatry*, 57, 331–40; Pierce et al. (2001).

48. Critchley, H., Daly, E., Bullmore, E., et al. (2000) The functional neuroanatomy of social behaviour: Changes in cerebral blood flow when people with autistic disorder process facial expressions, *Brain*, 124, 2203–12.

NOTES TO CHAPTER 12 A DIFFERENT BRAIN – A DIFFERENT MIND

1. Gallagher, S. (2000) Philosophical conceptions of the self. Implications for neuroscience, *Trends in Cognitive Science*, 4, 14–21.
2. Hoban, R. (1967) *The Mouse and his Child* (New York: Harper and Row; Harmondsworth: Puffin Books, 1981), p.30.
3. Frith, U., and Happé, F. (1999) Theory of mind and self-consciousness: What is it like to be autistic?, *Mind and Language*, 14, 23–31.
4. Sainsbury, C. (2000) *Martian in the Playground: Understanding the Schoolchild with Asperger's Syndrome* (Bristol, UK: Lucky Duck Publishing).
5. Lee, D., and Hobson, P. (1998) On developing self-concepts: A controlled study of children and adolescents with autism, *Journal of Child Psychology and Psychiatry*, 39, 1131–44.
6. Hurlburt, R., Happé, F., and Frith, U. (1994) Sampling the form of inner experience in three adults with Asperger syndrome, *Psychological Medicine*, 24, 385–95.
7. Perner, J. (1991) *Understanding the Representational Mind* (Cambridge, MA: MIT Press).
8. Perner, J., Frith, U., Leslie, A. M., and Leekam, S. R. (1989) Exploration of the autistic child's theory of mind: Knowledge, belief and communication, *Child Development*, 60, 688–700.
9. Sainsbury (2000), p.60.
10. Coleman, M., and Gillberg, C. (1985) *The Biology of the Autistic Syndromes* (New York: Praeger), p.20.
11. Sperber, D., and Wilson, D. (1995) *Relevance, Communication and Cognition*, 2nd edn. (Oxford: Blackwell), pp.15–16.
12. Rumsey, J., and Vitiello, B. (eds.) (2000) Treatments for people with autism and other pervasive developmental disorders. Research perspectives, *Journal of Autism and Developmental Disorders*, Special issue, 30 (5).
13. Howlin, P. (1998) Practitioner review: Psychological and educational treatments for autism, *Journal of Child Psychology and Psychiatry*, 39, 307–22; Lord, C. and McGee, J. P. (eds.) (2001) *Educating Children with Autism* (Washington, DC: National Academy Press).
14. Panerai, S., Ferrante, L., and Zingale, M. (2002) Benefits of the Treatment and Education of Autistic and Communication Handicapped Children (TEACCH) programme as compared with a non-specific approach, *Journal of Intellectual Disabilities Research*, 46, 318–27.

15. Rogers, S. J., Hall, T., Osaki, D., Reaven, J., Herbison, J. (2000) The Denver Model: A comprehensive, integrated educational approach to young children and their families. In S. Harris and J. Handleman (eds.), *Preschool Education Programs for Children with Autism*, 2nd edn. (Austin, TX: Pro-Ed, pp. 95–134).

16. Sheinkopf, S. J., and Siegel, B. (1998) Home-based behavioral treatment of young children with autism, *Journal of Autism and Developmental Disorders*, 28, 15–23.

17. Siegel, B. (1996) *The World of the Autistic Child: Understanding and Treating Autistic Spectrum Disorders* (New York: Oxford University Press).

Index